1994

What is critical theory, and to what extent can it claim to exist as a free-standing entity independent of the object of enquiry? Is the much discussed gulf between Anglo-Saxon empiricism and Continental post-structuralism more apparent than real? In *The myth of theory* William Righter explores the nature of thinking about literature, and the assumed polarities between the abstract reasonings of philosophy and the concrete manoeuvres of critical practice. He goes on to examine the role of theory in critical observation, through extended case studies of the work of critics including Barthes, Bloom, Poulet, Eliot, Empson, Kristeva and Derrida. His underlying argument is that criticism uses theory, but is never effectively directed or controlled by it: the inherent radicalism built into critical practice fragments and transforms general concepts in the act of applying them.

The myth of theory

# The myth of theory

William Righter

Published by the Press Syndicate of the University of Cambridge
The Pitt Building, Trumpington Street, Cambridge, CB2 1RP
40 West 20th Street, New York, NY 10011-4211, USA
10 Stamford Road, Oakleigh, Melbourne 3166, Australia

First published 1994

Printed in Great Britain at the University Press, Cambridge

*A catalogue record for this book is available from the British Library*

*Library of Congress cataloguing in publication data*

Righter, William.
The myth of theory / William Righter.
    p.   cm.
Includes bibliographical references and index.
ISBN 0 521 44544 2 (hardback)
1. Criticism.   2. Critical theory.   I. Title.
PN98.S6R54   1994
801′.95 – dc20   93-30388   CIP

ISBN 0 521 44544 2 hardback

# Contents

*Preface*                                                                    *page* ix

   I    From chaos to case                                                  1

  II   The bizarre territory                                              23

 III  The curve of the mirror                                          44

 IV  From 'so complex an irony' to 'such a textual logic'    68

  V  From 'wit' to 'astonishment'                                    86

 VI  'Fool' and '*pharmakon*'                                          99

 VII  'The monstrous clarity'                                        122

VIII  From 'ensemble' to 'exception'                              149

 IX  Pagan perspectives                                              170

  X  The Tao of criticism                                            190

*Notes*                                                                          217

*Index*                                                                          222

Crossing and doubling, many-fingered, bounded,
Those desperate stars, those worms dying in flower
Ashed paper holds, nose-sailing, search their bounded
Darkness for a last acre to devour.

William Empson 'Letter II'

# Preface

An essay on the theory of literary criticism that eschews theoretical commitments of its own – its ground or 'foundation' if you will – must be taking an unsuitable form of risk. But I hope that the further implications of the case studies that follow will justify the exploration. They describe the strange and pervasive power of critical practice: theoretical standpoints are necessarily evoked yet the grandest theoretical design becomes oddly evanescent and particular theories disintegrate in the circumstances of their use. Hence the myth of theory is also its life; its value lies not in what it claims but in what it does, and what it does is not what it is thought to do. We shall find that theory seldom operates as it would intend. But it creates at the cost of a necessary fiction that transforming energy which saves us from the entropy of established practice. Its evocation transcends its function, its myth, its literal claims. The rhetoric of criticism employs and transmutes – yet its structures fail the test of generalizability. It was as an illustration of this point that I had thought to title this book 'worms dying in flower'. But the allusion and its analogy might have been obscure to some, and have led to misunderstanding on the part of others. So I have contented myself with printing the appropriate lines.

Perhaps two presuppositions should be made clear. My case studies do not intend a coverage of modern critical theory, but an investigation, often comparative, of models of the uses to which concepts have been put. They begin in a familiar Anglo-Saxon mode and move into that elaboration of theoretical awareness which is our present inheritance and condition. The connections are in part analogic and should direct us more deeply into the implications of our recent past. One might, indeed, have chosen others, but I hope that the present models will touch the essential features of our critical thought.

Secondly, talk of the rhetoric of criticism is impossible without talk of its subject. Critical theorists from Aristotle to Bloom have devised a language to explore or explain literature which can only make sense through the examples they give. Examples from critics imply further examples. Ultimately these set the terms. Part of the story of this book is of the disappearance of theory into exemplarity, and the subversive effect of example on the conceptual structures critical theorists have sought to employ.

Yet I fear that the results may please no one. Apostles of the theoretical energies of recent years may find an unwelcome scepticism about theory in general, and traditionalists an analogous disenchantment with 'common sense'. My consolation must be that it is a book unlike others, for it claims the value of an inductive approach not much employed by current theorists, and a detailed analysis of critical language not much undertaken. It is through the dark glass of the example that the oblique working of theory is revealed. Therefore an essay on the necessity and folly of critical theory.

Of course I am indebted to the courtesy of friends and colleagues, mostly associates of the Centre for Research in Philosophy and Literature of the University of Warwick, who have read and commented on the manuscript or on particular chapters: Andrew Benjamin, Michael Edwards, Edward Larissy and Michael Wood. I am especially grateful to my longtime collaborator in Philosophy and Literature at Warwick, Martin Warner. I have profited from the comments of the two anonymous readers of Cambridge University Press and from the careful reading and comment of Rosemary Righter. Chapter VI was published in a slightly different version in *William Empson: The Critical Achievement*, edited by Christopher Norris and Nigel Mapp, also published by the Cambridge University Press (1993). For case studies involving French I originally used that language but here I have used the most accessible translations, or in the absence thereof have translated the necessary passages myself. Certain of the French terms are explained in the text, then retained in the original when it served the purpose of clarity or contextual shifts of meaning.

# I    From chaos to case

When I. A. Richards set out his account of the 'chaos of critical theories' as they appeared in 1924 it was deployed as a comic scherzo on the miscellaneous:

A few conjectures, a supply of admonitions, many acute isolated observations, some brilliant guesses, much oratory and applied poetry, inexhaustible confusion, a sufficiency of dogma, no small stock of prejudices, whimsies and crotchets, a profusion of mysticism, a little genuine speculation, sundry stray inspirations, pregnant hints and random *aperçus*; of such as these, it may be said without exaggeration, is extant critical theory composed.[1]

The collective wisdom that follows is a rag-bag of incongruities. But Richards's ironising does not assess the message that such a bizarre miscellany may contain. The mosaic of hints does not suggest a coherent subject, for the 'stray inspirations' and 'random *aperçus*' do not address the same kind of questions; nor does it suggest any kind of consensus as to what expectations of a critical theory there might be. Furthermore, the effect of so many different kinds of what might pass as critical theory blurred the identity of the word 'critical' itself. For the diverse kinds of explanation which were applied to the understanding of literary language and of its position in the world were not so redirected as to govern the working of commentary. Neither models, nor procedures, nor methods naturally arise. And Richards's own theory which was meant to provide a unifying ground for critical activity only reached the method of 'practical criticism' indirectly. The concept of mental organisation linked to the emotive theory of poetic language did not of itself produce a programme for the critic. What is essentially an analogy between mental and verbal structures might imply the notion of the poem as the isolated object of structural analysis. But the steps that led to this seem more devious: the experiment which showed the direction was at least partly based on historical and social curiosity as to what one's cultural moment brought to the poem. Only gradually did certain theoretical dispositions find their interesting form of use. And the use quite rapidly demonstrated how little it needed the theory.

1

For Paul de Man forty years later the conflicting claims of critical theory are those that shape a particular historical moment. The sketch in the opening pages of *Blindness and Insight* is the portrait of a moment of conflict.[2] And the confluence of many forms of theory suggests that rather than isolated hypotheses they are part of a whole whose elements must be understood in terms of each other. One's outlook is totally historicised. The turbulence of one's own critical perspective – the movement from phenomenological criticism through the impact of sociology, anthropology, a new psychoanalysis to structuralism and its successors – is both a process which has its history and a moment of crisis of which one might draw the portrait. This latter represents one's own self-awareness, the divided voice. Such a conflict as Richards would transcend, de Man embodies. One cannot with a clear scientific principle step out of history. But contemplation of it produces its own distancing and scepticism. And de Man's later work insists on the fragmentary nature of the critical enterprise, one which is not informed by any stable principle of unity: ' if some secret principle of summation is at work here, I do not feel qualified to articulate it ... '[3] The engagement with theory has been worked through so that whatever began in ideas ends in the particularity of the fragment.

Those compass bearings amidst the chaos, and adaptations of the critical metaphor to forms of crisis, will be examined in the cases that follow. But I wish to begin with a simple model of the relation of critical practice to theoretical presuppositions, one which paradoxically embodies a role for theory in the very assertion of the autonomy of critical practice.

It has often been argued that there is no critical activity without its theoretical grounds. However ruthlessly the critic cleaves to the particular case, turns his back on the falsifying generalities of more speculative modes, he is nevertheless an instance of a speculative stance. Tease out the implications of what he is saying and how he says it and there will be found in the most theory-resistant of Anglo-Saxons claims as general as those of the most theory-ridden of continentals. The notion of 'practice' itself has its theoretical cutting edge, which may be hidden for tactical purposes, or merely ignored, but awkwardly rediscovered as a range of implications.

Reasons for the pervasiveness of theory usually derive from two kinds of consideration. One lies in certain features of the language any critic employs. However matter-of-fact, however particularised, there is no way in which such a language can avoid concepts that carry a high degree of generality, and the implication of generality points to commitments which require larger expression in theoretical terms. Thus there is no critical language that is conceivably theory-free. We have only to take the smallest step backwards to see a configuration of presuppositions, or have the slightest touch of historical distancing to discover the attitudes, traits and mental dispositions of a given and identifiable time, as an Edmund Wilson may chart decade by decade the revisions of his mental landscape. What one sees in such configurations may be only theoretical in a weak sense, but nevertheless imply a passably coherent rationale.

The other reasons are more precisely related to the critic's overall sense of his discipline. The particular observations about any literary work are only intelligible in terms of some level of generality in the critic's purposes. Whatever light he proposes to shed on what, whatever area of understanding he proposes to create, is part of some programme or project, whose sense or direction is identifiable and expressible in terms of an outlook or general group of intentions or attitudes implicitly held. One cannot be involved in that sort of thing without intending to do something with it which is expressed in the character of the project itself.

Of course these two sorts of reasons are far from mutually exclusive, but are perhaps worth representing separately. For one expresses an intrinsic feature of critical terms, the other the general pattern of purposes built into the critical enterprise, an enterprise difficult to conceive in terms of totally neutral scientific description. In one sense the distinction may seem unclear, and in another obvious. But it may provide a useful setting for an old literary quarrel, an ancient chestnut, much discussed, and which still resurfaces, especially among those with a Cambridge connection. If its allure may seem somewhat dimmed through being perhaps a little overworked, it still suggests a useful paradigm, which may become more useful still in being extended beyond its original terms. And the correspondence between René Wellek and F. R. Leavis about 'the romantic view of the world' has come to provide a classic frame for the awkward relations between conceptual reasoning and critical discrimination.[4]

Even if the issue is put in terms of firmly deployed demarcations between 'philosophy' and 'criticism', these lines should not pick up the colouration of the old Platonic quarrel between the philosopher and the poet where inspiration and irrationalism have their place. One assumes that both philosophy and criticism are rational activities, and whatever their differences they are concerned with the giving of good reasons. Further, in the comparing of the two one is doing something else again, something harder to classify, but a necessary 'meta' activity. So Leavis in defending the claims of criticism steps outside of that 'discipline' to argue the kind of general case that the discipline itself would exclude. Or does this mean that Leavis is willy-nilly doing philosophy of a sort, in perhaps some weak or modified sense, but one necessary to even the most minimal statement of his case?

So to Wellek's request for an ideal or 'norm' which might govern the particular critical observation, or the wish that 'you had stated your assumptions more explicitly and defended them systematically' indeed 'abstractly' and with a fully stated consciousness that 'large ethical, philosophical and, of course, ultimately, also aesthetic choices are involved ... ' Leavis's marvellously articulated disclaimer is embarked on ambiguous ground:

I in my turn would ask Dr. Wellek to believe that if I omitted to undertake the defence he desiderates it was not from any lack of consciousness: I knew I was making assumptions (even if I didn't – and shouldn't now – state them to myself quite as he states them) and I was not less aware than I am now of what they involve. I am interested that he should be able to say that, for the most part, he shares them with me. But, he adds, he would 'have misgivings in pronouncing them without elaborating a specific defence or a theory in their defence.' – That, I suggest, is because Dr. Wellek is a philosopher; and my reply to him in the first place is that I myself am not a philosopher, and that I doubt whether in any case I could elaborate a theory that he would find satisfactory. I am not, however, relying upon modesty for my defence. If I profess myself so freely to be no philosopher it is because I feel that I can afford my modesty; it is because I have pretensions – pretensions to being a literary critic. (*S*, p. 61)

Several features of the language, tactics and rhetorical character of this will be brought out in the appropriate places. But one feature of this opening bears on the matter of becoming 'conscious'. Here Leavis takes on vividly and personally the total responsibility of consciousness for a wide area of assumptions that obviously trail their implications behind them. One is deeply and acutely conscious, but feels no need to spell out what one is conscious of. Yes, the assumptions exist, yes, they have implications, but Leavis claims to lack the appropriate language or forms of argument in which to propose a systematic explanation or defence. This is puzzling in several ways. At one level it seems to pose the question of how he explains these assumptions to himself. Does he mean that he holds them and is aware of them but cannot explain them because he lacks the necessary concepts to make them intelligible to himself? Unlikely as it seems this is one reading to which the passage lends itself. The other is that one has a perfectly adequate conceptual ground for working out and explaining one's assumptions, but will simply not do so as it would plunge one into a world of 'clumsy' and misleading generalities, an alien language which would obscure rather than illuminate the real character of critical observation. This suggests a fastidiousness in the face of quite inappropriate demands for explanation, a refusal to translate the world of 'feel into' or 'become' into the falsifying world of 'think about'. And it almost suggests that any attempt to make any more general remarks about literature would be necessarily confusing in the inappropriateness of its ground. And certainly one can see making this point, but with difficulty avoiding the implied reflexivity, for it would be difficult to say that one was conscious but did not understand, or that one understood but could not say, or that one could say but was simply determined not to.

Of course a simple paradox arises from any of these positions, and the problem is to decide whether it is trivial or whether it poses a serious obstacle to the intelligible statement of Leavis's critical stance. Can there be stance without statement? For we might find it difficult to approach and discuss the world of 'feel into' without some of the language of 'think about'. And certainly the language in which Leavis puts these matters is a recognisable form of 'think about', with distinctions and categories, in which the world of 'feel into' is being defended. Defended negatively to be sure. That is, no grandiose and overarching conceptual scheme with an evolved terminology connecting it with a larger map of human knowledge, or 'placing' the reader's act of 'feeling into' in the larger order of things. There is simply an invitation to 'think about' how different the world of 'feeling into' really is. To some extent this seems to hypothesise the opacity, at least the intellectual opacity, of 'feel into' (as a strange use of 'intelligent' sometimes seems to have in Leavis an opaque, iconic quality rather remote from its usual sense) which is almost set aside as some essential mystery, perhaps not unlike 'tactile value' in representing something which precisely escapes the language of conceptual relationships yet can nevertheless only be articulated through it. Perhaps there is also a distant analogy with Pascal's 'reasons of the heart', except that in Pascal such reasons are transitive and directed to further ends, while the critical 'feeling into' seems to exist largely for its own sake, as a part of the 'complete' response. Although one can probably 'feel into' the better to 'place' provided that the context of placement has been established by the same sort of feel.

The continental divide is the relationship between 'abstract' and 'concrete'. 'Philosophy, we say, is "abstract"... and poetry "concrete".' The 'we say' of this sentence seems to indicate general usage, and whatever qualifications might be proposed are either ignored or do not affect the logical consequences. Philosophy works by the rules that govern the logical form of abstract argument; poetry is an opening to a concrete experience; and criticism's aim is, 'first, to realise as sensitively and completely as possible this or that which claims his attention ... ' Natural as this may be made to seem there are at least two obscure areas here. One lies in the relation between this realisation and the presumed further intention of writing it down. Leavis seems to oscillate between a psychological language of consumption, in which the force of the poem is taken internally, as an experience which exists for its own sake, and a much vaguer sense that this experience might be communicated. And the latter might be given verbally, between friends, as table-talk, or in teaching, as well as possibly in writing. But the idea of 'completely' suggests a reference to internal states of mind. The notion that one should wish to give the complete, exhaustive account of a literary work in writing would be both odd and trying in several ways. Of course 'completeness' in this context is only the indication of an undescribably vague hypothesis, or of an ideal whose terms can hardly be spelt out – if only because tomorrow is another day and one's experience of any important work changes with a further moment of reflection. And completeness must stand in for something more cautionary: responses that are partial, quirky, fanciful or cranky do not measure up to an imaginary standard of what a full understanding of something would be. Nevertheless, with 'realise', 'sensitively', 'completely' what is being sketched is a phenomenology of critical response in which every term is mysterious – either because it refers to inaccessible mental states, or because criteria for its use cannot be given.

The other obscurity lies in an unexplored ambiguity of the relation of criticism to the literary work of which it must give an account. Leavis seems to assume that there is a clear division between abstract and concrete language, that poetry is 'concrete' and therefore the discussion, explanation, appreciation of it is automatically assimilated to the 'concrete'. There is no serious consideration of what the implications of this might be, or how this correspondence might bear on the intellectual limitations that such a critical practice might imply. Nor is it felt that the matter need be explained or justified; it is simply assumed.

Any characterisation of critical language itself is subordinated to a strong sense of the critic as a person and what he does. And this is put in terms of active verbs. The critic 'asks', 'places', 'enters into possession'; he articulates and illustrates 'in comparison and analysis' and argues 'by choice, arrangement and analysis'. The picture is of relentless and active quest in which nothing is taken for granted and nothing wholly at rest. Unless, as mysteriously as before, a term like 'place' might suggest that the fullest degree of engagement might achieve the perfect point of consummation. Might there be some ultimate point of completeness of response in which a 'placing' might be irrevocably right? I have given reasons why such a view, if held, might be difficult to explain clearly. Rather than the ideal end-picture the emphasis is so markedly on process, on the interchange which goes into the development of judgement, something reflecting the trial and error both of critical discriminations and of life's experiences.

This contrasts vividly with the mechanical sense of 'measure' which indeed shows Wellek at his weakest. But the process of attaining completeness of response combined with a 'peculiarly strict relevance' conveys a mixture of activity with precision which is perhaps difficult to describe further except in terms of the occasion. I shall return to this problem in several of its forms, in the multiple relations of describing and doing. For if it is clear that particular occasions multiply into 'constant preferences', 'relative permanencies' and structures which lead to 'utmost consistency and most conclusive coherence of response' the possible norms deriving from them would only be clumsy and misleading if stated in general terms. So indeed, the 'norms' remain, yes, they are there, but are only statable in a language that runs counter to their localised working. The theory may well be there but must remain offstage, although the curious suggestion is made that Leavis may have 'advanced theory' without having 'done the theorising'. The implication that a certain form of practice pushes forward its own theoretical grounds is posed, and, perhaps necessarily, abandoned.

So we have returned to the same dilemma. Now I think it would be facile to make too much of what seems in some ways a surface contradiction, yet the aim is conceived in terms of the general enterprise of establishing the primacy of the particular, with the attendant procedures of practical criticism. Hence the denial of general discourse affirms it and is conveyed through it. What is important lies beyond Leavis's immediate problem of how he may consistently state his case. If he theorises while denying doing so, and denying the utility of doing so, it must be because what he wants to defend cannot be defended or even discussed without slipping into an explanatory vein which is in effect a form of theory. And some such situation must arise if one even comes to grips with the possibility of having assumptions, as Leavis in his own way has clearly tried to do. So the reply to Wellek is, even while denying it, ultimately an acceptance of Wellek's rules of play. Yet the important issue lies beyond the immediate presentation: how can one escape the infiltration of general explanation into the most total devotion to the concrete case? And is it either necessary or desirable to legislate such a form of intellectual 'apartheid'? And beyond this, if the primacy of the concrete case is central to the whole notion of the critical enterprise, how can this be expressed without entering into contradictions that run deeper than the verbal terms of its formulation?

There is another aspect to the problem of conceiving the critical enterprise itself which relates to my second kind of reason, in which the assumptions in question are less methodological and more substantive. One could, as Wellek suggests, extend the notion of the effective working of normative language which runs through Leavis's work: the highly moralised vocabulary, the references to 'life', 'health', 'sincerity', etc.

This is thought to add up to some kind of 'philosophy'. But this points to one constant feature of this exchange, that several meanings of 'philosophy' are straining against each other: the formal sense of the pursuit of truth by means of deductive, or as Leavis would have it 'abstract', arguments; the holding of general attitudes towards the world which can be summed up or expressed, perhaps rather colloquially, as a 'philosophy' (the contrast between idealism and realism in the exchange could be formulated in both the stricter and the looser set of terms); and the weaker or more extended sense in which methodological commitments have general philosophical entailments. These meanings are partly confused by Wellek's relative openness in his use of the term, and Leavis's willingness to play one aspect against another for his own rhetorical purpose.

What arises most vividly if indirectly from this is two kinds of explanatory scheme: one works through systematic relation to an overall integration of the multiple features of understanding; the other moves contrastively through the playing of one particular against another to create islands of similarity and difference out of which an intelligible landscape may slowly emerge. Let me try to throw some oblique light on these differences by focusing through another explanatory scheme, or at least changing the language game and adapting a couple of terms from structuralism. The Saussurian distinction between 'paradigmatic' and 'syntagmatic' is a house of many mansions and I hope that the following use fits reasonably with variables of the previous game. Let us take the 'paradigmatic' to imply linkage in terms of general categories to the other systemic relationships in the structure of language in terms of a function and place in a class, and the 'syntagmatic' to be of particularised and sequential connections. Of course these are not separable: the syntagmatic chains become intelligible through the paradigmatic relations of their elements in a larger order. This is of course like the earlier argument that particular observations are not really separable from the more general terms that relate them, as the linguistic structure is seen vertically as part of an ordered system or horizontally as part of a sequence.

Now what it seems that Leavis is doing in terms of this analogy is two things simultaneously: one is the characterisation of criticism as a syntagmatic discourse that can exist without the paradigmatic structure, while at the same time proposing a critical paradigm based upon a series of established positional relations, the principal concepts of which are terms like 'placing' and 'centrality'. These words have a double character. They indicate the sort of scheme, map or general plan in which relational positioning is possible, yet they also have a powerful normative sense that seems to function as a value assertion. Leavis likes the idea of the map or chart of English poetry, with 'the essential order ... seen as a whole'. Yet 'centrality' does not exactly indicate the centre of the map. It is more like the indication of the size of a town or height of a mountain. And the cartographical image works on the notion of a complex area filled with multiple kinds of superimposed information, in which the critical activity can unfold the dual function of location and emphasis.

The connection of features through similarity is seeing a relation in sequence, rather like following the contour of a map and seeing where a continuing level catches a tissue of similar features. Yet there are also those other features of a complex topography where other kinds of relations appear to give either contrastive definition or odd mixes of partial affinity and nuanced difference, or of opposites which contain each other, where demarcations are themselves clumsy representations. Fit, and degree of affinity, may stretch the representational powers of the map. Here is the kind of area of complex relation that is continuously redrawn. For the critic is map-maker and necessarily revisionist in seeing the consequences of his rereadings. Some affinities must be more deeply marked, differences defined, features whose centrality has grown upon one more forcefully indicated. And undesirable elements suitably relegated: the faint black lines which indicate the motorway are barely visible beside the slag hills which, through a process of naturalisation, have joined the great mountain ranges of the mind, the canonical points of reference.

I once argued that the critic does what the landscape painter does, rather than what the topographical map-maker does. But I can see that this might allow a certain degree of illusionism into the critical representation – as the mountains in a Chinese landscape fade into the mist. And one can also see how, rather like the strategist's plan of battle, the topographical model gives more precise uses to the critic's exercise of his powers. (And indeed the touch of 'technico' has done without some of its other undesirable associations.) The power of making is present both in the altering of relations as one shifts one's sense of placement and power of magnification as the centrality of something grows, to diminish, and of course to exclude. I shall want to return to the problem of canonicity in a more comparative context. But as features of the map are darkened, and others fade, the normative use becomes more prominent, and never more than in the process of effacement. The 'centrality' of evaluation lies in this continuous revision of the canon and yet there is the prospect of the perfected canon in which all will be perfectly placed, with all process and relativity absorbed in the perfect, and one assumes immutable, model.

In the exchange with Wellek the predominance of process over end possibly produces an illusion of flexibility, a sense that the dialectic will go on and on, that there will never be an end to the rethinking process. No doubt this in fact is so and there were even changes in Leavis which indicated changes of mind on the canonical position, of say, certain works of Dickens. Yet some of the pressures of valuing had the effect of determining the shape that the canon would have, and that the fundamental terms of this were non-negotiable. Therefore the problem of stating them, on enquiring into their rationale, or seeing the further implications of adopting them, would reasonably have, as Wellek clearly saw, quite far-ranging implications for their use. In practice there are two distinctly visible effects of this refusal. One is the rather bland assumption that the bludgeon which is about to fall on some non-canonical work, or on some critic who has uttered concerning it, is in one's hand by infallible natural right and is being applied in the wholly impersonal spirit of duty. The other is more notable in the work of some of Leavis's epigones: a very cautious set of movements within the canon might lead to slight changes in the placement of this or that work, or some trifling adjustment of relative aspects of canonical figures. So it is quite dashing of Strickland to suggest in a footnote that 'Leavis, for all his breadth of imaginative understanding, tended, I believe, to under-rate Flaubert'.[5] Normally the principles of the canon are never raised, much less challenged. And indeed would need to be raised in order to be challenged. The very unrationalised nature of the canon is one guarantee of its unassailability.

However there remains the question of how the examination of concrete cases, the movement from particular to particular, following the connections or similarities as they declare themselves, is to be directed to any wider understanding at all. Why should they, without the active participation of some more general rationale, or some otherwise conceived set of intellectual controls, move in any one direction rather than another? Why should the case-by-case method lead any one way rather than another? The procedure might wander at random wherever the bent of the last case led it – perhaps thus creating the general form, if such a thing is conceivable of 'Empsonian irresponsibility'. Certainly there are essays in *Some Versions of Pastoral* or individual passages from the cases in *The Structure of Complex Words* which seem to move on lateral paths until the tension between the lateral movement and the presumed design is almost intolerable – as sometimes with Derrida the complication of argumentative lines through the play with unexpected linguistic elements seems to toy with and deflect the reader in some perverse joy by shifting the plane of awareness, or altering the rules of play, or both.

Such a centrifugal movement of mind in which particulars threaten to break away from any control by a central guiding purpose is of course wholly alien to anything in Leavis where the observation of 'a peculiarly strict relevance' seems inseparable from an intentional sense of the project in hand, with a degree of directedness reflected in every aspect of his language. I have already mentioned the active character of the verbs, but there is also the marked pronomial presence (more explicitly in this essay perhaps than most) suggesting a permeation by the will. Perhaps one word that reflects this will in a more than conventional way is 'discipline' and the talk of the separation of disciplines. Of course this has come to be the usual term for a suitably institutionalised slice of what is taught, although this meaning is a passably recent one. And it would be a mistake not to recognise the moral, even perhaps the military, force of the word's usage in the kind of colouration which Leavis gives it.

I have sometimes diluted the very notion of 'discipline' into the more neutral 'area of discourse' (I shall discuss the rationale in Chapter VIII) which would deprive one of the force of the notion that there is a critical discipline, even a discipline of letters, with established practices, skills, procedures, aims and dare one say, 'standards'. The notion involves a rich mixture of purpose and principle, principles which are internalised in aspects of character as well as existing externally in rules and controls, as the military colouration suggests coordinating these into directed action. And the conception implies that criticism is a form of action, not merely with respect to literary matters, but of social action, even perhaps of combat, against the amalgam of ignorance, laziness, frivolity, grossness, laxity, insincerity etc. which characterise the bad critic and corrupt the good reader, and by extension corrupt society as a whole. Critical action is social action, and as the stone of critical precision falls into the middle of the pool, the ripples indicate the circles of intellectual and social relevance which frame the act of critical intelligence.

It is not that the social dimension in itself acts as a concealed premise, for there are presumably the same values running through both literary and social considerations, but certainly the effect of this public dimension is to shift explanations into political and social terms, and whatever articulation there may be of value commitments will be expressed through such terms. It is not that the one underlies the other, but that common considerations are present to both of them. Yet there is also the uneasy assertion of the separability of criticism, that the distinctive thing, working by its own methods and being its own discipline, must not depend on philosophy, or one presumes any other alien discipline to establish its own values. One makes a paradoxical paradigm of the case-by-case method, by a de-limitation which may be illusory, yet is seen as a necessary condition of the critical activity itself. If one is arguing that criticism which involves the powerful presence of purpose and will directed, by way of the act of reading perhaps, towards our experience of life as a whole has a relevance in that whole, can the relevance be located in the character of the critical method itself?

Leavis is positive in the assurance that 'it is necessary to have a strict literary criticism somewhere and to vindicate literary criticism as a distinct and separate discipline' and has a strong sense of the either/or, that one is clearly talking about criticism or something else. And one effect of this precision of demarcation lines is to indicate or imply that it is a single sort of activity rather than a group of however closely related ones. Yet there is a double use of what is conceived of as a central method, something necessary to the realm of 'concreteness' in response to the challenge of saying what a case is like, the critic 'shows or demonstrates' rather than argues or proves. I shall later consider the resemblance this has to some of the possible methods of philosophy itself. But first I want to look at several features of the way in which the critic makes his point. In this context Leavis has a double task, first in showing what criticism is in itself, how it characteristically works, showing that criticism is distinctly different, fixing the demarcation; and secondly, showing how it works, justifying the demarcation in terms of the shown uniqueness of the configuration it involves, displaying it in action, and so making clear how different it is from other methods or disciplines.

So the critic shows differences, say between Blake and Shelley, and Leavis in justifying the special character of such an activity shows its difference as well. But surely the criteria for recognising differences are not the same in the two sorts of case? We may recognise that there are particular differences between certain poems of Blake and Shelley, and still be puzzled as to how to classify what seems like a more general argument about the nature of criticism itself. And even with the more strictly critical case the problem of seeing the difference between Blake's 'astonishingly original' technique's 'extraordinary precision' and Shelley's 'vaporous, monotonously self-regarding and often emotionally cheap' quality requires a recognition that is composed of many different moments of perception and assessment, where perhaps differing criteria were employed in differing contexts yet still added up to an overwhelming impression of difference. Yet however complex the interweaving may be Leavis has the conviction that there are certain simple and fundamental things that if pointed out are seen, like Hume's 'simple impressions', and which are the building blocks of critical epistemology, the basis of critical knowledge. If one could not see such elemental differences one would be critically blind. Adjustment might come through the resituating of particular perceived differences in contexts that might vary their force, in 'a process of relating and organising'.

How much may reasonably be inferred from the thumb-nail sketch of the process by which consistency and coherence grow out of the particular (*S*, p. 62) is of course made more conjectural by the limitations Leavis imposes on his own explanation. But, if it is not too fanciful, there seems an implied phenomenology of critical judgement, which sets the discrete particular on its path towards 'constant preferences', 'relative permanencies', and eventually a 'structure' or as we have seen, a map. And it looks as if the variables in this process lie in the relations between things shown, which must be incontrovertibly perceivable if duly and properly shown. Is a degree of certainty implied in the process? The shown difference in a comparison is never claimed to have a cognitive certainty. And much of 'it's like this, isn't it?' seems to point to the kind of aspect-seeing which is very remote from any form of certainty. But the confidence invested in the map must indicate a growing assurance of solidity that is based on something. Perhaps an ostensive version of truth has an ostensive development.

However, that further kind of showing, the almost 'meta-showing' of what the nature and function of criticism really are, requires another kind of description, a showing what they look like in the purposive terms that we have already seen. Do the hortatory tone and pervasive didacticism have shadows called 'norms' or 'ideals'? If one is being shown how to do something properly there must be some way of determining whether one is succeeding or not. Certainly it would be difficult to give general rules for comparison, to indicate what we should compare with what. Although normal classifications give us areas in which comparison is reasonable it is often the value of good criticism to see around the corners of those classes. Wider experience may give a sense of what is of interest, but be far from indicating rules. But is one on the right track, doing criticism properly? A different sense of what rules might be comes into play. We compare the small thing we are doing with the sense of the whole enterprise. The particular comparison might be perhaps simply seen: absurd or illuminating. But in the terms of the scope of the larger matter of seeing what one is doing and why, can one characterise adequately in the language of 'I did not say ... I illustrated concretely ... '?

Certainly in the case of Blake and Shelley it would be difficult to see this sort of prescription being carried out in the terms which are claimed for it. Leavis handles the comparison with a superb sense of rhetorical and polemical force. Take the charge that Shelley's poetry is 'repetitive, vaporous, monotonously self-regarding' and often 'emotionally cheap, and so in no very long run, boring ... ' Here is surely an extravagance of normative force, but it would seem odd to take it as a model of 'completeness of response'. (Although here Shelley may have become merely a counter in a rhetorical attack whose real target is Wellek.) Or, consider the reasoning which dismisses Blake's 'symbolical philosophy' for the independent life his symbols have when they 'function poetically'

and 'Earth', 'starry pole', 'dewy grass' and 'wat'ry shore' are seen 'to
have a direct evocative power'. This is simply asserted without explaining
why this is so when presumably the references to 'earth', 'sky', 'flowers
and grass' or 'crystal stream' of Shelley (these and many more are to be
found in 'Ode to a Skylark') have no direct appeal and are vaporous, etc
... So it is not a concreteness in terms of direct evocation that is in question
but rather concreteness as an abstract concept or general idea which is
gestured towards almost as an ideal or a norm might be.

Of course here the language becomes saturated with value terms both
explicit and implicit: the best of Blake contains symbolism, although it
almost seems to be 'best' in spite of this, and 'his symbolical philosophy is
one thing, his poetry another'. Perhaps this is merely the problem that
afflicts so many readers of Blake, that they wish to be able to read the *Songs
of Experience* without involving themselves in the elaboration of thought
that leads to the *Prophetic Books*. One sympathises, but if the symbolism
is part of the best poetry is it not necessary to understanding it? What is
impressive in the vocabulary, the manner, the sense of the whole project is
the predominance of valuing over understanding. And if we do not really
begin to understand Blake fully (have anything like 'completeness of
response') without a substantial awareness of the great mythopoeic
movement of mind which will end in the *Prophetic Books*, how adequate a
description is a critical account that simply dismisses it all?

Something similar happens both with Wordsworth and with Shelley's
'Mont Blanc'. Wordsworth as philosopher is dismissed: 'it is as a poet that
he matters'. It is difficult to imagine that anyone, including Wellek, ever
thought otherwise. It is one thing to argue that Wordsworth is a
philosopher of consequence, and quite another to argue that whatever the
source or value of Wordsworth's philosophical ideas an understanding of
them contributes substantially to the understanding of his poetry.
Similarly, do we have to choose between 'an epistemological proposition'
and 'a state of excited bewilderment and wonder' in the opening of
Shelley's 'Mont Blanc'? They are hardly incompatible. Now, all of this is
frightfully obvious, and no doubt Wellek's hooking of the Blake poem into
a systematic explanation is a touch literal-minded. Not really 'critical'
might one say? 'Critical' has become a value word with respect to its own
rough area of discourse which might simply be 'talk about literature'.

Equally simplistic no doubt is any such expression as 'the romantic view
of the world', which is perhaps a rather flimsy specimen of historian's
shorthand. (Perhaps here one should note that Wellek is rather oddly
described as 'a philosopher'. He is rather an historian of ideas whose
methods and interests are quite different from those who 'do philosophy'.)
Whether or not we need this kind of shorthand for interpreting particular

poems it can certainly be expanded to a more serious account of pervasive patterns of thought, as Burckhardt or Pater did with the ideas of the Renaissance. And the feeling might linger that something is lost when the reading is closed off at the edge of the poem, as if views of poetry can only be founded in the immediate experience of the particular poem.

Yet attempts to contain the reading at this level not only are seen to be impossible, but are quite openly accepted as such, and the argument radiates out in the most far-reaching ways. From particular poems of Shelley to 'certain Shelleyan habits' which 'carry with them a tendency to certain vices' and in the diagnosis of such vices 'the literary critic finds himself becoming explicitly a moralist'. Again two familiar problems appear. Does the requirement of the moralist admit of being contained within the prescribed terms 'of particular analysis' or does it force an extension to more general – and hence more philosophical – modes of argument, with their concomitant claims about human conduct and social 'norms'? And again, does this moralised role arise within the activity of criticism itself, in terms of particular critical analysis, or does it require some further principle established in some other way? I cannot see that Leavis makes any serious attempt to deal with this.

Further, one might ask if these vices point directly on to 'the romantic view of the world' in all its slipshod glory, or even on to the idealism which acquires an 'unfavourable presumption' through the fact of Shelley's espousal. We are close to the argument that the very existence of Shelley's poetic 'vapour' is evidence which points to the general falseness of idealism itself. Where can 'particular analysis' have led us here, if not outward in widening circles again? And what can 'particular analysis' mean in this steadily widening context? It is a curious term in itself, conjoining particularity with the word which indicates a form of logical procedure at the highest level of abstraction. Perhaps it is a term with its own heavy value-loading which seeks to persuade us of the existence of a special separate, identifiable discipline whose opaqueness may nevertheless dissolve before our eyes into plural vocabularies and multiple levels of claim. What is such analysis beyond the seeing of those discrete and individual perceptions of similarity and difference with which we began? Yet they have led us to the boundless sea.

So do we have an inclusive or an exclusive model of critical activity, or have we seen an exclusive model which nevertheless manages to violate its own terms and reach beyond itself in ways which it would exclude from the core activity of the critic's special form of reasoning? The more the latter is represented in its pure form the more it appears mysterious and opaque, but instantly when seen in use becomes many things rather than one. Perhaps there is a sense in which these questions do not matter. Whether we choose to call the whole range of kinds of discourse that may bear upon literature, its nature, its forms, its genesis and its contexts – psychological, social, economic, etc. – criticism, or take criticism to be a restricted and discretely observable activity separate from this larger family, may be only a matter of the natural elasticity of a term which may be used strictly or otherwise according to need. But such an easy latitude would be fatal to the Leavis project of establishing the identifiable core of a practice. And if we have seen that core look so dependent on contiguous and related concerns, so penetrated by and interfused with the further intellectual moves that it has tried to exclude, does not the notion of the paradigmatic activity become a fictional centre, like the hole at the heart of the nebula?

Certainly in its very claim to a cultural centrality (and as a corollary its institutional centrality) there lies the simple move from recognising the importance of literature to one's cultural tradition, to the necessity of a form of intellectual enquiry consonant with that importance. Increasingly distanced from its elevated neo-classical past, in which, in its Aristotelian ancestry at least, it was a sub-sub branch of philosophy, criticism was in Leavis's view threatened both by a form of university teaching in which literary study was conventionally historical, and the corrupting demands of Grub Street. Hence the invention of an intellectual centre in the independence of criticism is substantially characterised by negative moves. The rhetoric of Leavis is rich in gestures that fend off the potential usurper and define identity by saying what it is not. And this corresponds in a larger way to the powerful element of resistance that criticism is meant to offer to cultural chaos, thinness and cheapness in its defensive gesture, its policing activity as Eagleton puts it, with the essential centre, the essence of it all found in the guardian stance. 'Périssons en résistant' said Arnold, and the evolution of literature as our new body of sacred texts gives that resistance a dimension of the sublime. Even if the negative procedures of its reductivism may put its own nature and indeed, very existence in doubt. 'For, as Wittgenstein remarked, 'we are under the illusion that what is sublime, what is essential, about our investigation consists in its grasping one comprehensive essence'.[6]

In following the vocabulary in which Leavis has attempted to establish the identity of 'one comprehensive essence' I have focused primarily on three areas of difficulty, where it has seemed as if the realisation of such a project became impossible: first the impossibility of formulating and describing the nature of the critical enterprise in terms which are proper and exclusive to it. Second, the impossibility of isolating the critical activity from the historical, social, psychological, indeed, alas philosophical and for Leavis, especially, moral vocabularies with which they are so deeply enmeshed. And finally, most pervasively and importantly, the impossibility of using the language of the particular case, the specific concrete language of critical comparison, without the use of general concepts and categories which relate concrete observations to a larger sphere of intelligibility.

It is this third area of difficulty that I wish to consider in somewhat more depth, because I think there are far-reaching implications for the way in which one describes critical language, and especially for the ways in which that language relates to certain forms of philosophical reasoning. One can of course claim in Leavis's own case that the sharp and vivid contrasts that he presents between two languages, two methods, two wholly separate enterprises, is done for the purpose of dramatic contrast rather than meaning exactly what it says. And certainly it contains that aspect of directing our attention, pushing us towards a distinctive quality of mind, something closer to a recording of responses which are at least partially affective, and which would be felt in terms of relation and responsibility. Much indeed of the language has appealed less to anything precisely cognitive, than to the realisation of feeling (shades perhaps of Richards's emotivism) to which the appropriate response is expressed in congeries of attitudes. Much of this is expressed in the language of reaction, of immediacy of response. Also one must remember the institutional attachment to 'practical criticism' which may well have suggested the functional isolatability of a particular language game. This is perhaps rather as we might try to isolate the skills of connoisseurship among the many aspects of art criticism or art history. In this way the notion of 'criticism' might exist within multiple parentheses, as a more narrowly conceived game played according to distinguishable if not entirely specifiable rules.

Is it between the dissolution of any notion of the critical paradigm and such a bracketing off that the intelligibility of the notion of criticism is forced to choose? Or might it be possible that the critical paradigm is sustained through the activity of criticism alone, and need not be made intelligible in other terms? Leavis might well claim that his essay's ostensible purpose (aside from that, no doubt, of crushing Wellek) was at best quite secondary, and his own quasi-theoretical remarks are merely *obiter dicta* of a persuasive kind, indicating the true path which can only be followed in practice. But this returns us to the difficulty with which we began about the contradictory nature of acting without presuppositions or the dubious one of refusing to state them. Suppose we follow the difficulty by asking about alternative statuses for the characteristic moves, whether the language game is played out in parenthesis or not.

Of course there is an extraordinary open-endedness to the characteristic moves: 'this is so' and 'yes, but' imply no particular form of argument, but are so context-related as to take their sense and function almost entirely from that. The conditions which govern the 'so' are indeterminately variable: 'so' as matter of fact, 'so' as recognisable resemblance, 'so' as interesting analogy, and so on. The manner of the dialectical play adapts to many strategies, and the application may be as descriptive as it is in some of the Socratic dialogues where one wonders (perhaps especially in the *Protagoras*) if the transparent speciousness is intended as ironical comment. Practice converts the manner into mere device, by which the controversialist draws his antagonist – real, hypothetical or straw – in order to traverse a set of prepared positions while manoeuvring to a fairly predictable conclusion. And it can be frozen into one or another of the pedagogical procedures in which such games may be exercised, like the rather mechanical dating puzzles into which Cambridge practical criticism was sometimes capable of degenerating.

But if these moves can be applied in many ways and at many levels, in whatever rhetorical, tactical, pedagogical or cosmetic ways, is there a sufficient characterisation given of the basic moves themselves to say that there really is a method which can be described and used? If one were to say that the description is the use it would not help us much on the particular occasion because much in the reply to Wellek follows no such procedure, but works by direct and positive assertion.

General accounts which attempt a further description of the way in which the logic of the concrete can be characterised are suggestive but tentative. The procedure of Leavis is compared by Renford Bambrough to John Wisdom's characterisation of philosophy itself 'as a process of comparison, of setting one thing beside another. "This is so, isn't it?" and "Yes, but … " are reminiscent of Wisdom's three fundamental operators: "You might as well say … ", "Exactly so" and "But this is different"'.[7] But the comparison is not worked out, and the resemblance seems largely in the mixture of conversational manner and the concentration on the notion of comparison, the setting of cases side by side. It is related to the more general claim of Wisdom's that all reflection, including its most abstract forms such as deduction, comes in the end to case-by-case procedure. But the application to philosophy requires the same contextualisation and without it the description of the possibility of making comparative moves would be like describing a tennis game in terms of 'Toss, hit, bounce, hit … etc.' Its truth would be qualified by its weakness as description. Even if we could then recognise such an account when watching a game. 'My abstractions have been designed to defend the concrete' says Bambrough. But the case in its concreteness has been hard to present. It is perhaps because of this recognition of what he has been doing in trying to make sense of the case-by-case method that Bambrough makes important concessions to the role of abstraction and generalisation in order to 'set out what in particular stands where and in what relation to this and that and the other thing'. And he criticises Leavis for not making 'strong enough and wide enough claims for this technique of comparison on which all reasoning and not just all critical reasoning is founded ... '

Now how are critical claims to be made which are both strong and generally intelligible? We have seen that one of the necessary features of 'placing' or of 'setting instance by instance ... the concrete and intricate task of the critic' is that no general criteria for the success of these placements can be given. And words like 'relevance' only beg the question. We may grant that the procedure may be recognised in action, and to some degree learned or imitated as a form of practice. But if the conditions of success cannot be given the fact of success can only be shown through pointing to a vague feeling of the appropriate, and the fact of the success or failure merely indicated as pure assertion. Sketchy terms like 're-semblance' and 'difference' may be given more precise senses in controlled contexts, as in the minute discriminations of colours and shapes applied to natural objects and which provide for Lévi-Strauss's 'savages' an elaborate and 'systematic' picture of the natural world. It suits a variety of practical and social purposes perfectly well, but is without general models and hypotheses, if rich in particular deductions or inferences, which form a 'science of the concrete'. There is a 'logic' in these classification systems, as there is in totemism or kinship systems, but even the formal repetitions and combinations in relational patterns of knowledge do not call upon our normal forms of generality. Although of course names exist for large groupings and relations, as well as an accounting for causality. Such patterns of relationship may be elaborated and extensively described.

Does the procedure described in *The Savage Mind* resemble the Leavis map of relations? In a sense a 'logical' series of distinctions has been evolved on a principle of antinomies and explanatory systems are evolved from this. And the structures of mythical thought find their own level of abstraction. The analogy with the map might have its use, if the whole of Leavis's thought could be compartmentalised effectively. In mythical explanation, one myth competes with another, not with an alternative mode of thought, and competing mythical narratives may coexist. The mythical explanation does limit itself to particular occasions, sequences of narrative events and their consequences. What is in question is how the jaguar invented fire, not the place of animals in the natural order. A tissue of relations may evolve in which causality is immediate and localised rather than a matter of general law. The jaguar's Promethean act of inventing fire is in no way connected with some other important service that the pangolin may have rendered mankind. Out of affinity and difference the mythical map may take shape.

I do not wish to push what may seem a fanciful analogy, but the mythical map may correspond roughly to one of the uses I wish to suggest of criticism as a model of practical reason. This model is systematically self-limiting. On this view it is impossible to see the effect of the particular beyond the immediate context in which it is made, because an attempt to do so would outrun the possibilities of one's method. For criticism it would be to step beyond criticism. And therefore to direct one's attention towards, say, such a language of historical generalisation as that of 'the romantic view of the world', or the supposed philosophy or whatever diffuse general ideas about themselves and their world imaginative writers may have been thought to hold. To think like that is to lose the force of the critical discrimination in what is at best dilute and at worst empty. There must be no flight from the immediacy of the concrete case and no value beyond it. Which means also that there is no way of saying why it should be so. The case-by-case procedure simply leads to more cases; particular examples propose further similarities and differences but nothing beyond them. The denial of the use of generality becomes a legislative device for justifying the pursuit of a self-limiting language game in its own terms.

At some moments Leavis seems to follow such a course, perhaps largely to dramatise the setting apart of the critic's special role. Elsewhere as we have seen he seems closer to Bambrough's version of the Wisdom programme in which the particular comparison is more like the basis for seeing further patterns, where the patterns of resemblance take us further into the nucleus of which they are a part and where the particular steps reveal new perspectives and relations. Here the single observation is treated as part of the cultural continuum, as moment of awareness, of insight, as instrument for seeing more. The reasons critics give are thus situated and full of resonance. Each point on the map relocates all of the others.

But how is the force of this relocation to be seen, its effectiveness to be measured? For if what constitutes the criterion for a good description cannot be given why is not the map in a continual state of transformation before our eyes, rather than growing steadily in clarity of outline and solidity of relief? The intelligible patterns should grow clearer. And our experience of the working of case law should tell us how the pattern has been evolved. But we do not recognise where we have been, or may find the marks on the map misleading. Rather than recognising and accepting we are startled and alarmed. Pascal says of *l'esprit de finesse* that its principles are in common usage and one has barely to turn one's head. But our understanding of the case method has not helped us. We have grasped 'relevance', 'placing' and 'centrality', and common practice does not help us to use them. We may be taught to use them in a certain manner, but wonder why it should be so. Any cultural shock or change of perspective may put the picture in question. Or we may wish to accept the terms in which the map has evolved, but be unable to do so?

How will he persuade us? It is sometimes as if Leavis takes the cultural determinants as powerful and overriding, fits the case to them, then justifies the original determinates in terms of the rightness of fit. But how else is the cumulative, developed process to be described? Such things tend to be figurative, like strands of a rope, or Wisdom's contrast of the legs of a chair to the links of a chain. Conviction arises out of seeing the pattern emerge and cohere: if too many of the strands are not contested, and the legs are quite obviously for that particular chair. And certainly here, perhaps in Wisdom as well, the general features of the method are invoked but by their nature resist description. What remains are the figures: the map, or the chair.

For one thing the map suggests the known world, as if literature were there to be understood and ordered. The map and its maker exist for each other. Any mark is part of a continuity. Erasures are in effect marks. The force of persuasion is to point to more and more features, to enlarge the map or enrich the details. Leavis suggests an almost mystically global sense of the whole man's involvement with the whole culture, whether characterised in the methodological terms of the 'complete reader' or in more substantively Lawrentian terms. As a disciple puts it with admirable clarity:

Leavis's understanding of what we mean by criticism is that it entails a wholeness of response: our judgment of what we read is a judgment of all that is implied or revealed by a writer's use of words as well as of its place in the world as we know it. To confine the role of the critic to mere exegesis or to consider historical or ethical considerations as if they were separate is to attempt the impossible. There is no such thing as 'pure literary analysis ... '[8]

So the enterprise envisaged by Leavis is built upon a contradiction, and the most narrowly conceived critical remark points outward to the whole of one's cultural and social life. We have seen the working of this in whatever level of critical explanation. It has been impossible to establish the 'strict literary criticism ... and to vindicate literary criticism as a distinct and separate discipline'. Hence it is impossible to say that there is a language of criticism as such, a method or procedure that is proper to it. And to seek the equivalent of any 'ground' in the working of a method is to find one's sense of 'place' in movement through multiple kinds of description and multiple relational systems. That these systems should be in some respects theory-ridden and in others value-laden would imply that freedom from either theory or value is an illusion.

But the contradiction does not amount to bad faith. It is rather commitment to a necessary fiction, and the emergence of a notion like 'criticism' out of these multiple and overlapping activities is given its contingent identity through Leavis's rhetorical force. In this one recognises that all culture is contingent, and that the place of criticism on what constitutes a larger map is part of the palimpsest of markings and erasures. The notion that awareness of cultural crisis should both compel and transform the idea of criticism will be seen in other contexts, which draw upon a nature both persistent and transitory. If out of miscellany an identity is shaped, that shaping lies through the powers of adaptation, not in the specific contours of the golden nugget at the heart of it all.

# II    The bizarre territory

> In our time, the claims of common sense, must evoke not Descartes, but
> M Homais.
>
> Picard[1]

> The territory allocated to criticism is however bizarre: particular ... it is
> nevertheless promoted to the dignity of a universal language.
>
> Barthes[2]

Two ironies, one of despair, one of contempt. Picard expresses a moment
of self-recognition which poses the dilemma of those who wish to find in
critical language the common ground, shared with an educated but not
specialist public, and dedicated to the notion of 'making sense'. If there are
puzzles, opacities, uncertainties in the reading of a literary work (or even,
alas, a text) why not clear them up, make sense of them in such a way that
they enter into a common understanding? And why have we reached the
point that the most reasonable of procedures is also the most ridiculous?
Over the making of sense the image of Homais looms like a bank of fog.
It is indeed this common sense which provides for Barthes's polemic the
foreground of the 'bizarre ... territory'. For the identified area is one both
of the quotidian and the remarkable, where the most ordinary language is
involved with the most extraordinary claims. And if there is more to this
than the easy play of paradox – in which the most conventional practices
of academic tradition are radically 'defamiliarised' – one must assess the
shaping of a curious historical effect. How has the project of the common
understanding come to seem so utterly beneath the intellectual dignity of
serious thought about literature? It is the bizarre territory of banality,
stripped like a lunar landscape of the intellectual activity which would give
it life. The particularity which would there exercise its universal claims
would define itself through the exclusion of alien and inappropriate
disciplines, develop and preserve the purity of its tradition by institutional
means – features which suggest Leavis's strategy in the establishment of an
independent discipline. And to Barthes the bizarre territory is ruthlessly
defended by refusals, reductivism, purifications, insistence on assumptions
carrying the force and validity of tradition. It is the normative world of a

23

literary and academic establishment, which in turn of course sees the true bizarrerie in him, in the new interests and methods 'hazardous and grotesque' as Picard called them, of 'la nouvelle critique'. So two bizarre territories are juxtaposed: one which Picard sees as imposture, bringing its panoply of diverse linguistic, sociological, and above all psychoanalytic 'jargons' to complicate and unsettle an established form of discourse; the other which Barthes sees as exclusive to the point of emptiness, which achieves its purity by lying back among comfortable assumptions in the self-consuming bizarrerie of common sense.

Although the two polemical pamphlets of the mid-sixties, *New Criticism or New Imposture* of Raymond Picard, and Barthes's reply *Criticism and Truth*, raise far-reaching substantive, methodological, and institutional issues, the quarrel over 'la nouvelle critique' which centred on Barthes's study of Racine was strangely transitory. When one thinks of the decades required to establish the 'new criticism' in America, the many stages of adaptation involved, the struggle against marginalisation within the universities, the apparition of 'la nouvelle critique' was sudden and dramatic, in what seemed an intense and highly ideologised controversy. Yet it swiftly faded and the very concept rapidly vanished into the rich cross-current of theoretical argument for which it had briefly seemed a vehicle. It will be worth considering whether the very idea of 'criticism' was too fragile a principle of unity, literary study too narrow a field of operation, for the variety of theoretical energies it brought into play. This raises in turn the question of what distinctive limits we might wish to give to the notion of 'criticism', or of critical thought in circumstances where the introduction of new methods, or the energies derived from other related fields, are brought to bear on an established understanding of the nature of the subject.

While it would undoubtedly be deceptive to see close analogies in the development of the two new criticisms, both originally defined themselves as a revolt against a tradition of historical scholarship that saw literary understanding in terms of the historical and biographical circumstances of a work's creation. The Anglo-Saxon new criticism derived from the desire to get directly to the poetic text whose features can be examined like primary data in an unmediated state. The simple 'practical criticism' exercise of looking at a poem in isolation from its context almost fatalistically creates the fiction of a naked text, a pure and isolated verbal construct waiting for the appropriate analytic approach. That this was merely an operational fiction was of course understood. Richards, its inventor, had a wide range of social and historical interests, and *Practical Criticism* itself was partly designed as an enquiry into the cultural presuppositions of critical reading. One has already seen in Leavis the tension between the idea of criticism and the claims of his moral and social commitments.

These early developments, in the twenties, were hardly conceived of as a movement, and what became in America the 'new criticism' was a suitably Anglo-Saxon accumulation of practices. In spite of Ransom's book of that name, and the enormous influence of a pedagogical handbook in Brooks's and Warren's *Understanding Poetry*, the 'new criticism' had no prophet, nor programme, and only *post facto* any rudimentary attempts to create an ideology or movement. It might in practice, in a spirit similar to that described by Picard, have presented itself in the form of an opposition, but it did so gradually, and piece-meal. In England Richards clearly thought of practical criticism as an experiment. And if I have represented Leavis as a prophet of a critical paradigm, an independent discipline and activity of criticism, he would not have thought of this in terms of the 'new' but rather those of his continuity with Dr Johnson. If one adapted the methods of practical criticism, a term with which he was uneasy, it was merely as a useful means to a wide and traditional literary understanding. The shortcomings of his colleagues and the established methods of literary teaching lay in the routinisation of the relations of literature with historical context, where the vitality of criticism was compromised by the lack of disciplined and active attention. But this presupposed not the importation of the intellectual energies of other disciplines – indeed, as we have seen, the very opposite – but a refinement and intensification of what was residually there. The quarrel with his predecessors and colleagues was not Barthes's quarrel with the Sorbonne.

What marks Barthes and 'la nouvelle critique', both no doubt in fact and in Picard's polemic, is the importation of non-literary interests and methods: 'recourse to new methods: psychoanalysis or psychocriticism, Marxism analysis, structural analysis, existential or phenomenological description, original combination of these methods, etc.' (*NC*, p. 9). The 'etc.' is perhaps the most powerful term, for this miscellany has only an additive shape, and certainly no coherent and distinctive character. Indeed Picard asks, does this constitute a movement worthy of its proper label, and what constitutes the claim to such a label? The 'new methods' are themselves of such diverse origins, with such substantive commitments in psychological, economic or social studies, that a common denominator is hardly obvious. Yet a variety of things may be brought together by a common aim.

'This criticism arises through opposition' (*NC*, p. 10n.). Its very existence is created by the act of opposition, and its nature therefore defined negatively insofar as it has any unity at all. Picard's title suggests that the choice is between something which is authentically new and something which is an imposture, which claims a false reality through claiming a unity that is not there. But then, he knows as well that movements may have diverse elements and take shape through opposition. The deeper sense of imposture has to do with 'criticism' itself, with whether or not the 'new' procedures are effective and accurate means to understanding the works to which they are applied. In the case of Barthes's *Sur Racine* one must judge by the works of Racine. I shall look at this case only, and not consider Picard's other target, the *Genèse de l'œuvre poétique* of Jean-Paul Weber, which makes some of the targeting look a little too easy. And I shall not be concerned with whether or not there were distinct and identifiable intellectual contours to something we can call 'la nouvelle critique', except to say that by pillorying such a fictional entity Picard gave it more life than it previously possessed, and that Barthes's reply gave to it, if for a passing moment, a further touch of shadowy substance.

It is also worth mentioning two historical considerations that bear indirectly on this exchange. I have alluded to the institutional aspect of the quarrel, and there is an oddity in envisaging open war between a (largely fictional) 'nouvelle critique' and a (perhaps somewhat fictional) Sorbonne. The most creative figures in what might be reasonably called 'la nouvelle critique' – Poulet, Richard, Starobinski and others – had careers largely outside the mainstream of the French teaching establishment. Any conflict between tradition and innovation may have been fortuitous and circumstantial, but there was at least some inner/outer on which polemic could possibly play, even if these distinguished 'outsiders' took little part in this. Within a decade, however, the position was reversed, and the following generation, of structuralists and post-structuralists, quickly became the academic establishment, holding the most prestigious chairs at the Collège de France, the 'grandes écoles' and in the universities. Simultaneously the topicality of phenomenological criticism, or of the thematic criticism to some extent connected with it, receded or became the subject of comment by way of still newer fashions. We shall see some uses of Richard in the work of Kristeva and Derrida. And for Barthes, the course of development that would take him through structuralism and beyond was not very clearly foreshadowed in his prefaces to Racine. But Barthes's work at any one time contained many possibilities within it, and Picard was wise to say he would judge by the work of Racine 'and not in appealing to an ideological concept which remains to be defined'.

This judgement by way of Racine is simply that of putting Barthes's method to the test by examining some crucial readings, both for their accuracy and for whatever value or otherwise the method might give. I shall look at three or four examples in which Picard argues that the understanding is wholly mistaken through 'dialectical caprice' which blinds Barthes to the sense which the context requires him to see. Such caprices in fact take three general forms: the substitution of dialectic for contextual sense, of rampant subjectivity for scholarly objectivity, and of following the requirements of some general argument rather than paying attention to the particular case. These terms are not very seriously examined, and the assumption that there is something simple and natural which is the opposite of subjective is directly and uncritically made. The three rough categories of accusation surface, regularly and uncertainly, as themselves general explanations of why particular readings have gone wrong, and why certain patterns among those readings have been perversely established in defiance of 'good sense'. This level of the argument is too loosely pursued. The real force of Picard's argument lies in the particular case.

These are not always easily separable from the thematic reading of figurative language in general. And much of the argument is directed at the notion of thematic interpretation itself as representing some unconscious current in what the author said rather than the conscious version of what he thought he was saying. So misreadings are substitutions of some significant patterns of sub-text for a more publicly understood meaning. Picard's method is partly to show that the attribution of thematic character to interpretation is not clearly or consistently done. 'Solarity' means something quite different when attributed to Nero, Alexander and Phaedra. With Nero there is some connection with his incendiary role, and hence with matters of fact; with Alexander it is a moral attribute that the image reveals; and with Phaedra 'a special characteristic of Greek mythology – whose assimilation to the character remains to be interpreted'. Hence the solar figure is not a coherent link through the variety of its uses but a different sort of thing in different cases. The effect is to diffuse the metaphorical force and break the chain of association, for the connections are so loose that the figure seems less than coherent. The analysis of context dismantles and destroys the thematic overview. And the dramatic contrasts he has drawn from Barthes – light and dark, freedom and captivity, power and vulnerability – rather than forming overarching patterns that link thematically the many aspects of the oeuvre, become the individual features of particular, if many-sided, dramatic actions. This action in turn is governed by inherited conventions – rhetorical, social and theatrical – and the grasp of these conventions and the historical circumstances that have created them are necessary to any understanding.

Yet if one supposes that these two antithetical ways of reading tell us things of different kinds, what principle of comparability will be of help to us? The difficulty here is at least partly that, in what looks as if it is an issue of understanding the particular case, any attempt to decide between alternative readings is directed away from that case towards the methods, loyalties and principles involved in justification. The very pointing to the error in the particular involves a larger framework in one's sense of the appropriate. Take the straightforward case of Barthes's assertion that Britannicus is fascinated by Nero in a way that reflects an 'erotic rapport' authenticated by Tacitus and that the line 'He forsees my plans, he hears my every word' refers to some such fascination with Nero's omniscience.[3] Picard's point that this merely refers to the fact of being surrounded by spies and agents may indeed represent the substance of the action correctly (*NC*, p. 34n). But selection from Barthes's own context simplifies his argument and exaggerates the difference. And indeed, Picard's understanding of the action may be correct without fatally compromising the notion that the complex psychological relations between the two figures suggest further explanation. It is certainly the character of that further explanation that is of central importance to Picard. The turning of Racine's 'violent but modest theatre' into one of 'unleashed sexuality' explores a pervasive eroticism against which particular attributions of misreading constitute a form of damage limitation. In this circumstance one reading may be clearly necessary without absolutely excluding others, and the effort to peg one's wider rejection of a style of reading to this sort of particularised difference in understanding is only partially effective through pitching the notion of understanding too narrowly. A large part of his own argument 'arises through opposition'.

Does Picard go so far as to claim that if there were a distinctly visible pattern of repeated images these would have no relevance to the understanding of Racine? The issue is never formulated in this sort of way. It is simply argued that there are cases where certain expressions and images cannot mean what they are said to mean, and further that the pattern of them could not add up to a reasonably drawn picture of Racine's work. The attack on this second level is on Barthes's manner of generalisation. In the case of 'solarity' the general claim does not fit all of the examples in the same way. In others of Barthes's larger claims there are too few examples. Barthes's evocation of '"The perfect condition of Racinian *tenebroso*"' (*NC*, p. 41) is only found in a single example, even if it is 'at the heart of Racinian imagining'.[4] In the identification of the plays as 'tragedies of aphasia' Barthes gives no more than a passing reference to the several cases. Beyond the attribution of qualities in highly generalised and hardly substantiated ways lies the creation of such fictions as 'Racinian man' whose character and conduct can be described in terms of general laws.

Most of this is argued at the level of what would be the reasonable criteria for establishing a substantial critical point, or some general understanding, usually of Racine seen in some kind of totality. Again this leads us away from the close consideration of the particular cases to concern with what sense can be given to the notion of thematic criticism, and, above all, what are the proper uses, if there are any, of psychoanalytic terminology and explanation. In his treatment of this controversy Geoffrey Strickland remarks that 'What is disappointing about the debate is that the conflict of interpretation took second place to the disagreement over principle ... '[5] This is almost akin to wishing that you were in another country listening to different protagonists. It expresses a natural wish to translate the terms of the argument into Anglo-Saxon practice, where the Leavisite query, 'This is so, isn't it', would be met with the appropriate mixture of assent, qualification and counter-example. But the way in which the claims of one reading or another could be supported is, in his quite sensible analysis, rather prudently couched as 'the reader may still prefer' or 'in terms of their relative plausibility', and Strickland himself is rapidly drawn into the meta-critical arguments about 'objectivity' and 'poly-valence' which both of the two antagonists have most at heart.

I say both because it should be clear that however much Picard may have thought that his standard involved judging by way of looking at the text of Racine, the most important object of his polemic is a kind of argument, a way of doing criticism: the misleading use of imagery to suggest a hidden dimension to the text. It is this hypothesis of the hidden dimension, with the coded language of depth psychology revealing truths that are profound and strange, that confronts the belief that one is pursuing realistic critical ends in an objective and rational way. The intrusion of psychoanalysis in this pervasive way puts in question a traditional sense of what character is and of how human beings are to be understood and described. A narrower use of such concepts to describe abnormal mental states might have its place in its specialised context. An extended aside criticises the work of Charles Mauron without significantly distinguishing it from that of Barthes except to suggest that by inventing a term for his method, 'psychocritique', he at least sets apart the nature of what he is doing: searching out the unconscious forces in poetry through patterns of imagery. What makes Barthes more subversive is the adaptability of his psychoanalytic approach to every aspect of literary language. Barthes dismisses all of these remarks as belonging to an outmoded psychoanalysis.

Beyond this the subversion extends to the normal assumptions about the nature of literature itself. Picard sees quite clearly that Barthes undermines the established institutional separation of literature from other forms of language, and therefore its cultural pre-eminence, partly by treating literary language like any other aspect of language, but above all by seeing it as a repository of some deep irrational stratum of human feeling and consciousness, rather than the controlled and disciplined world in which all of human nature is shaped through artistic form, a rational system of decisions and values. So what is at stake in the choice between readings is not one's sense of the accuracy of fit, what makes sense, but one's whole understanding of what literature is about. What understanding 'one may prefer' here or there in the oeuvre is as nothing to the dethroning of the literary artefact and tradition. For the method of reading which produces an amalgam of obsessions in 'Racinian man' defies the duly dignified picture of both Racine and human nature. Picard argues against this with a passion that suggests a defence of civilisation against barbarity and crassness, against a perverse and irrational refusal to see the institution of literature as a sacred part of mankind's values.

If this perversity and barbarism are the products of generality, dialectic and system, it is nevertheless a system of a different kind that Picard invokes against them, a system built on the cumulative principle which has established the proper grounds of canonicity, both with respect to literature, its character and scope, and to critical procedures embodied in accumulated skills and transmitted practices. It is a 'system' of habits and attitudes. And its defence requires a different method from the kind of systematic conceptual argument that it rejects. As it is not constructed on a conceptually rationalised plan it is not entirely expressible in such a way without accepting criteria and methods it would wish to exclude. So Picard is pushing for a generalised truth claim to the validity of certain methods without employing abstract arguments that would force him to adopt a systematic approach of the very kind that he rejects. Therefore the force of his arguments is in ostensive gestures towards the way in which the traditional codes have been violated, complemented by a *reductio ad absurdum* directed at the applications of the general claims of Barthes: '*Always, never*: the truths of which criticism makes itself the prophet are absolute, universal and definitive' (*NC*, p. 35). On the other hand, as a believer in rationalism it is not clear how the appropriate logic of literary discussion could altogether exclude general claims. This is probably not intended, but the further implications of the non-systematic system are hardly considered.

The analogy with Leavis presents itself: is Picard's defence against 'system' another version of Leavis's strictures about 'philosophy'? Certainly both turn on the same pivot, the rejection of abstraction – Picard also speaks of Barthes's 'labour of abstraction' – and the presentation of claims for an activity which can be pursued rationally in terms of the concrete. The problem may be exacerbated in Picard's case by the unresolved relation between professed rationalism and the rejection of the consequences of abstract ratiocination. And no doubt the relation of literary history and 'criticism' would have had a different institutional mix from that of Leavis's Cambridge, with personal attitudes towards the academic establishment shaped by different historical circumstances. The conceptual stance seems to a large extent held in common. But implications in one's own circumstances and tradition are different. Picard is the conscious defender of something analogous to what Gilbert Murray called the 'inherited conglomerate' of Greek belief – that accumulation of pieties, practices and attitudes which fell apart in the late fifth century in the face of the sceptical, relativistic, but above all logical, arguments of the Sophists. Perhaps it would be a mistake to call such a conglomerate a system in even the sense that I have spoken of Picard's 'system' of skills and practices, habits and attitudes. But there is a resemblance in another form of traditional configuration which could not withstand the putting in question which came from a conceptual reformulation and rationalisation. It is one of the implications of Barthes's own critique that the rationalism of Picard has become a cultural object, ossified into a totemic Cartesianism whose true inheritor is, alas, M Homais. 'Rationality' like Leavis's 'intelligence' has become a cultural emblem to which the commitment is essentially moral.

Part of the difficulty with this lies in the assumption that whatever is concerned with any depth within the text is automatically an apology for and indulgence in irrationalism. Something which fires Picard's eloquence:

It is permitted to say it? Some of us are tired of shadows and undergrounds. We've had enough of standing about, doubled up in the catacombes of literature. The dubious and pathetic discoveries that one makes are truly not worth the aching they require. To believe that the *profundity* of a work is in its lower depths and its cellars is to be – as is so often 'la nouvelle critique' – the dupe of metaphor. The depth of a thought is in an intelligibility which reveals itself to an effort of the intellect and not what is hidden. The depth of an expression is in what it says, and in the implications of what it says, and not necessarily in what it dissimulates and reveals at the same time. Why is the profound linked to the obscure and the invisible? To go deeply into an idea is not to sink oneself into the darkness of its abyss, it is to measure in full light its significance. One of the paradoxes of 'la nouvelle critique' is precisely to devalue conscious thought while having, at least in principle, recourse to a logical and articulate language. (*NC*, pp. 133–4)

This is largely an attack on Richard's *Poésie et profondeur*. The affront is the very notion that there is somehow a surface level of rational activity on the part of an author, but under it another level, full of imperfectly controlled associations and areas of meaning beyond the author's rational control. Such meanings are revealed through patterns of imagery and other clues appearing pervasively through the writer's language. It is hard to see why a notion so banal should create such profound offence, when a theory of artistic creativity based on pure rationality would itself seem a curiosity. Nor can one imagine that Richard, or Barthes for that matter, would have wished to abolish any place in literature for the working of rational processes. In fact, Picard seems to have exaggerated the difficulty by conceiving the creative process and its understanding in a Manichean way: rational, surface, conscious, etc., opposed to irrational, depth, unconscious. The surrealisation of literary thought is seen as commitment to destructive values, and the moustache as more important than the Mona Lisa. In the end he substitutes a moral fervour for the rationality he intends to establish. And the rhetoric of this fervour obscures the unresolved issues.

Neither the test by way of reference to the text of Racine, nor the systematic analysis of the general implications of the use of psychoanalytic language, has been seriously undertaken. The test of the particular case has elicited largely the symptoms of shock, and the general issue stated but not explored.

It is partly his moral tonality, which gives to Picard's essay its decisive character of relentless indignation, that makes it an easy target for mockery. If the defence of the value of literature rests upon such moral feeling, the strong expression of that feeling has exposed Picard to characterisation as a crotchety Sganarelle, or indeed an Homais mouthing platitudes and tautologies (perhaps the 'liberal humanist' of Eagleton's fancy). Barthes attacks the comfort of assumptions which lie behind the irritation and taking of offence to create a parodic portrait of flummoxed complacency. With respect to the nature of literature itself it is supposedly defended by pure tautology: 'The final imperative of critical versimilitude is ... *on the subject of literature, say that it is literature*' (*CT*, pp. 54–5). This use of caricature articulates the contrast in styles: ponderous and furious; ludic and furious. But the use of parody infiltrates the argument of the antagonist allowing Barthes to play a double language game, combining a straight rhetoric with a mock rhetoric. The mock rhetoric reinvents Picard according to the critical *bondieuserie* of a mythical 'critical verisimilitude'. It would be hard not to feel that there is a touch of childishness in all of this. The cuteness and overkill are sometimes close to embarrassing, and there is evidence that Barthes later felt rather uneasy about it. It lacks the natural and direct savagery of Leavis, who was surely a great controversialist: 'I am sorry that Mr. Bateson has been ill' is a masterpiece of dead-pan irony, and it comes from a depth of passion wholly alien to Barthes.

It is no doubt a distortion of any larger and fairer picture of what is after all a many-sided and changing critical oeuvre to work so narrowly in terms of the controversy that Barthes himself called 'this rather artificial duel'.[6]

But as well as crystallising the conflicts of a particular historical moment, a moment of profound transformation in French critical thought, *Criticism and Truth* is Barthes's most extended essay on the claims of differing ways of talking about literature and the relations between them. Much of it is polemical and dismissive. The debris of established values includes most of the concepts associated with neo-classicism, including 'taste' and 'clarity'. The notion that the concept of taste could have any vitality, or indeed any use but a restrictive one, is held unthinkable. And clarity is a self-flattering illusion. The derision of clarity as having no uses that are not impoverishing may seem an oddity. But the attack seems largely directed at the implication that clarity reflects a kind of transparent ease which can be turned into a cultural icon. Some of the best polemical shots are against the fatuous notion that clarity is a special feature of the French language and that the French critical tradition is thus privileged by some innate gift of the gods. We shall see again in Bloom a contempt for clarity, and it would be interesting to have the grounds for assessing Barthes's view of the notion more fully. But there is not a great deal beyond identifying one of the standard components of the professorial bag of clichés.

This is to some extent aligned with another pervasive assumption that the literature that involves us most deeply is that which involves us in real difficulties of reading. This has seemed to some to make a value paradigm out of difficulty and a fetish of 'unreadability'. But this can be put in a less portentous way by saying that if a text is too transparent its interest somehow vanishes. Intellectual vitality and critical imagination both flourish in conditions of resistance, and the most rewarding involvements of modern criticism have been with the complexities of figurative language. The reaction against the cultural ideal of clarity has the common-sense aspect that difficult things cannot be put without difficulty and through the use of a language which reflects that difficulty, sometimes in the adventurous nature of its descriptions. They may violate not only the neo-classical proprieties of much French tradition, but the equally traditional English belief that all profound and important ideas are simple and clear. The 'Racinian *tenebroso*' would appeal neither to Descartes, nor M Homais, nor to Hume, nor to J. L. Austin. But it has a certain power as a description of that world of conflict generated in the interstices of a rationalist language and a turbulent heart.

The inventive power of description does not automatically fit comfortably to the schematism Barthes's essay evolves. Essentially there is a double movement in *Criticism and Truth*. The attack on 'critical verisimilitude' intends to demolish the established separation of orders of language. This is followed by a rather fragmentary sketch of the relation of criticism to a science of literature. The analysis of the orders of language partly shifts institutional commitments: 'separation, hierarchy and stability...' are not merely the desiderata of those who wish to see clear patterns of order in literary studies, but in society and the world as a whole. The universities and 'critical verisimilitude' are treated as the last gasp of a fossilised world. Every form of living intellectual energy is naturally ranged against them for it will both affect and then be the product of the break-up of that hierarchical and restrictive system. One of the many results of such a break-up in the early modern period will be the dismantling of that body of restrictions and separations, so that literature will no longer be seen as a thing apart.

The many consequences of this are followed up in an attempt to erase many of the distinctions between literature and other languages. The dispassionate study of language has many levelling effects and the special cultural apartness of literature cannot be maintained. It will among other things bring literature closer to other languages related to it, including those that comment on it. The notion of 'writing' swallows both, and 'the writer and the critic come together, working on the same difficult tasks and faced with the same object: language' (*CT*, p. 64). How literally this is meant to be taken or how much can reasonably done with it is open to doubt. Because Barthes certainly goes on acting as if literature had distinguishing characteristics, and as if in talking about it one knew what one was talking about. Either categories are so deeply embedded in one's culture that it is impossible to shake off their spell, or one's revolt against them is in many ways tactical. One effect is to create what he calls a 'crisis of commentary'.

So much of the weight of Barthes's undertaking lies in the sense of this crisis that it is astonishing how little he says about the nature of 'commentary'. An equalising and levelling effect is certainly sought bringing together the language of the creator and commentator, the 'journey through writing' drawn from Sollers which is fused into a 'total intellectual discourse'. Rather than separating out the various kinds of discourse for which one might think that different approaches, methods, etc. might be appropriate, the effect of fusing is not merely to remove literature from its cultural pedestal, but to remove the idea of appropriate correspondences by which the right investigative language, the right sort of 'commentary', can be directed to the right object. This might seem to fit a little oddly with what is said in a different context that 'true "criticism" of institutions and languages does not consist in "judging" them, but in *perceiving*, in *separating*, in *dividing*' (*CT*, p. 33). But this may seem to be a different aspect of the weapons system devised against the Sorbonne, and both are consonant with the general intention which reallocates the roles of author and commentator and in doing so attacks the 'linguistic order'. It would seem that 'commentary' can either be part of the established order or part of its undoing, and that its crisis at least partly consists in its movement from one to the other.

The old critic, 'the critic of resemblance', is a creature of his own marketplace, mouthing his *idées reçues* in a way which conforms to expectation, which 'leads to silence or its substitute, idle talk' (*CT*, p. 55). He quotes a remark of Jakobson from 1921, speaking of an 'amiable chat' (*CT*, p. 55) which is lacking in awareness of its principles or methods; it rests upon such unanalysed assumptions as 'objectivity'. We might in some of these remarks hear the voice of Leavis on the Sunday papers. But we hear also something quite alien to Leavis, for it is the very lack of concern with theory, the lack of the true Cartesianism which is the method of doubt, of self-consciousness about method, which abort the possibility of serious thought about what we are doing, and sink us into 'idle talk' and 'chatter'.

'Concreteness' would thus be the hallmark of a certain incuriosity, lacking the intellectual energies derived from more abstract modes of thought. Yet the uneasy relationship of the particular perception to other forms of understanding will exercise Barthes's imagination in attempting a 'transformation of discursive speech'. There is a curious suggestion from Lacan, a substitution 'for the traditional abstraction of concepts a total expansion of the image in the field of discourse, so that it no longer separates the particular case from the idea, and is itself truth' (*CT*, p. 66). In some devious way the interest in the concrete case of the old criticism resurfaces, through this meeting of particular and general in the psycho-analytic. It is not worked out, and the notion of the identity of the case with what arises from it is unrationalised and unexplained. But the 'image' does combine this duality of visual concreteness and representative power.

Neither this fusion nor that of the 'total intellectual discourse' can wholly shed their dualism, and the demands of an account of literature that accommodates both localised awareness of the figurative richness of the image, and the general claims of larger contexts of understanding, is met by another dualism and another fusion. One is the division of criticism from a science of literature, and the other is the installing, through linguistics, within that science the fullest account of the nature of literary language. 'What poets have long known by the name of *suggestion* or *evocation* the linguist is beginning to approach, thus giving a scientific status to floating meanings' (*CT*, p. 70). In effect, the most elusive elements of language become the subject of scientific analysis. Jakobson's constitutive ambiguity of literary language becomes a dependency of a general science of language. But this ambiguity is not further thought out or given the operational terms that Empson gives in *Seven Types*. The relation of something as profoundly important as such a constitutive feature seems not to have required for Barthes any working out of how it might be critically used. Nor does it seem to have occurred to him that this might be of interest. Perhaps this results directly from the assumption that whatever methodological interest literary study may have will be derived from linguistics, psychoanalysis, or whatever passes for 'scientific'.

Hence, a dual approach is wildly one-sided, with a serious ground indicated for scientific study, a vast new and rich opening that is a vehicle for systematic thought, while criticism occupies a marginal, indistinct and mysterious 'bizarre territory'. This is the sort of doubleness parodied by Eagleton: 'Literary criticism is rather like a laboratory in which some of the staff are seated in white coats at control panels, while others are throwing sticks in the air or spinning coins. Genteel amateurs jostle with hard-nosed professionals, and after a century or so of "English" they still have not decided to which camp the subject really belongs.'[7] What these two sets of figures might represent in practice is difficult to say, and certainly the irony, whether so intended or not, cuts more than one way. What happens behind the whizzing dials, and who in the end are the real children of Laputa?

Barthes's sense of this dualism is in fact quite modest and leaves most things to our imagination: 'une certaine science' which may possibly come to exist is devoted to the conditions and forms, both created and creatable, of works of literature, but does not concern itself with content. The linguistic model is alluded to as the source of a 'hypothetical model of description', but the nature and operation of description in literary study comes through only in fragmentary suggestions. Again conditions and linguistic features seem to be in question, but not meaning. Most of this is too vague and haphazard to give any indications how one is to follow up the crucial 'linguistic rules concerning symbols' (*CT*, p. 74), or how such a science, loosely formulated as it is, would apply to literature. It is not very clear what the men in the white coats would be doing. One suggestion of interest is an analogy between Chomsky's notion of linguistic competence and something which seems to be equally innate, a 'literary competence'. But nothing has been done with this. (The notion of 'literary competence' has since been followed up by Jonathan Culler.) How the presence of such a faculty could be scientifically explored is again left to our imagination.

The other feature of such a science rather oddly derives from his interest in myth. Clearly impressed by the formal studies of the transformations of myth of Lévi-Strauss, he seems drawn by two things: one is the notion that a large body of narrative could be formally studied in what is purported to be a scientific manner; the other that the collective source of myth means that such studies could progress without the involvement of the insufferable genius or the tiresome intentions of individual authors. 'The science of literature can only link the literary work to myth, although the literary work is signed and myth is not' (*CT*, p. 59). A series of analogies seems to be at work leading from science through ethnology through the study of myth to that of a depersonalised study of the written word: 'it is a mythodology of writing which awaits us ... ' It is hard to see much more than gesture in this, although one direction such studies may have taken led towards *S/Z*, and indeed the structural analysis of narrative in Todorov, Genette, Bremond, etc. The extent to which these carry out a scientific enterprise is open to question. Certainly the taxonomy of plot structures, and the relation of such structures to character types, goes back at least to Propp who might be said to be doing both ethnology and a sort of literary study. To what extent Barthes foresees its development at this point may not be worth pursuing, but the hints about myth do not exactly build on his own work on myth.

I do not mean to make heavy weather of unexplored possibilities, but there are two points of interest in this shadowy science. One has to do with the force of the linguistic model. Is, say, Todorov's account of plot structures in the *Decameron* more scientific because of his use of the notion of a generative grammar of plot structures than R. S. Crane's analysis of the plot of *Tom Jones*? This may simply be a matter of using the word 'science' in different ways. But you could argue that Todorov's notion of 'grammar' was sometimes figuratively applied, and that the schematic treatment of plot structures may account for similarity and difference in useful ways, but that the schematism is largely a way of making an orderly pattern in description. Of course Crane is concerned with a single plot rather than the comparative features of many, but if descriptive adequacy has any connection with scientific criteria, Crane is vastly richer in both scope and precise observation. As for the hypothetical method, one cannot see that it bears closely on either case. The empirical tradition, with, in Crane's case at least, an Aristotelian ancestry, could claim in terms of descriptive accuracy, causality, and even the conceptual use of its relational terminology, to be as close to a scientific model as a narrative analysis derived from Lévi-Strauss.

Without a closer attention to how a scientific method could be evolved, or how the hypothetical method could be adapted to literary uses, what the criteria would be for adequacy of description and how description enters into a larger sense of science, talk of 'the general logic of signifiers' sounds like a whistle dying upon the breeze. Barthes has not seriously considered any of these matters, and is using his concept of science partly as an almost visionary speculation, and partly as a tactical device. The only rough picture of what seems to be projected is a sequence of extended descriptive systems, employing interlinked technical vocabularies, depending not on the use of hypothesis or deductive methods but on seeing the potential interrelation of the terminologies one wishes to employ. We shall see an elaboration of such a method in Julia Kristeva's *The Revolution in Poetic Language*.

If a certain tentativeness and vagueness condition the scientific enterprise, the portrait of 'la critique' does not thereby gain in precision. What distinguishes the critic has nothing to do with anything that may be said about his methods, but simply his own nature as a writer. The primary responsibility of the critic is to his own sense conveyed in his own language: 'what controls the critic is not the meaning of the work, it is the meaning of what he says about it' (*CT*, p. 81). One is tempted to accept a straightforward implication of this: critical language is not referential. It does not derive whatever sense or validity it may have from any correspondence with its supposed subject, but strictly from considerations internal to itself. So critical truth, if there is such a thing, cannot be a version of a correspondence theory to be judged in terms of its accuracy or power of enlightenment with respect to a 'literary' text. It is to be understood as a verbal structure in its own right. But insofar as this is so, what kind of critical use can we make of it? What is the point of the 'on' in *On Racine*? For what seems to be a version of a coherence theory of critical truth can only make sense at some cost to the status of the subject, of what such a truth is supposedly *about*. Perhaps one should not take this too literally. This indicates a high pressure area in the conflict between a notion of criticism which requires no method but the deepest fidelity to its text, and one which is concerned with the independent intellectual development of literary thought. Can such an independence be intelligibly stated without loss of the very coherence it claims? For the disappearance of its subject would put in question its *raison d'être*, while the tyranny of that subject would destroy its independence.

The dozen, rather impressionistic, pages that Barthes devotes to 'la critique' skirt around this problem in a series of formulas that are vague, open-ended and more suggestive than programmatic. 'The relationship of criticism to the work is that of a meaning to form' (*CT*, p. 80). And 'the "meaning" which it is fully entitled to attribute to the work is finally nothing but a new flowering of the symbols which constitute the work' (*CT*, p. 87). One language represents another, but not in a form that is alien: literal-minded explanation. The critic cannot claim to 'translate' the work, and particularly not to make it clearer, for nothing is clearer than the work. What the critic can do is to 'engender a certain meaning by deriving it from the form which is the work' (*CT*, p. 80).

Again,

every metaphor is a sign without a substance, and it is this far-off quality of the signified that the symbolic process, in its profusion, designates: the critic can only continue the metaphors of the work, not reduce them: once again, if there is in the work a 'buried' and 'objective' signified, the symbol is nothing but euphemism, literature is nothing but disguising and criticism is nothing but philology. It is sterile to bring the work down to pure explicitness ... (*CT*, p. 87).

Therefore criticism is not explanatory, or 'commentary' in the crass sense of turning a difficult language into one that is transparent and easily accessible. Nor does it capture the meaning of something else which is simply there, but it creates a meaning which is a new flourishing, symbolic as the work itself was symbolic. One works with an ambiguous border country of affinity and otherness: ' *The symbol must go and seek the symbol*, a language must fully speak another language: it is in this way finally that the letter of the work is respected' (*CT*, p. 89). It is of course not the intention to specify how this is to be done. And the force of certain words is unclear: how 'other' is the language of criticism, and what is a reasonable criterion for 'fully'?

It is difficult to tell from this little sketch how far Barthes has considered the difficulties, or how far he thinks explanations can be extended. Insofar as there is a description by hints and suggestions, there are three crucial terms that point directions that I would like to follow: 'anamorphosis', 'the logic of the symbol' and 'irony'.

Anamorphosis is one of the few strongly descriptive terms that is directed to the characterisation of critical language itself. It seems to help define the coherence of signs within the second language which is criticism:

The critic separates meanings, he causes a second language – that is to say, a coherence of signs – to float above the first language of the work. In brief, we are concerned with a kind of anamorphosis, given of course that on the one hand the work never lends itself to a pure reflection (it is not a specular object like an apple or a box), and on the other hand that the anamorphosis itself is a *guided* transformation, subject to optical constraints: out of what it reflects, it must transform *everything*; transform only according to certain laws; transform always in the same direction. Those are the three constraints which limit criticism. (*CT*, p. 80)

The playing of an optical image on to a linguistic one shifts the model of explanation. Is this something which is appropriate to criticism, while the linguistic model is more appropriate to the science of literature? Barthes says nothing about the connection. The notion of an anamorphic picture combines illusion with coherence, and distortion with relevance. It does not resemble, and yet it does, if through a glass darkly. It is tied to the original work, indeed cannot get away from it. Multiple anamorphisms are possible, in a way which may resemble aspect-seeing. And from this one is potentially launched into a series of optical figures which include point of view and perspective. But the very brief discussion focuses more on the controls that operate through the anamorphic connection than on whatever liberties are possible to the second language. Even if 'float' suggests the indistinctness of an imaginative hovering, yet 'separates' still suggests a strict immediacy of presence. And the anamorphic responsibility has a necessary connection defined in optical terms: one cannot somehow help seeing the whole and being accountable for the whole. The relation of the seeing and the seen will be governed by certain determinants, 'certain laws' of visual transformation. Again, one cannot cut loose, or reconstruct, an image that is disconnected from its source – even if there is little that can be said about the nature of these laws. Except that one sees the same form from the same direction; both subject and commentary have through their positional relation to each other their determinate character. There is no kaleidoscope or scrambler by which multiple shapes can be jumbled, and selected fragments juxtaposed for effect. This seems to exclude a literary version of Malraux's museum in which selected fragments could be isolated for the sake of the startling and revealing comparison. Perhaps this stretches the case to another use of criticism. Barthes has rather strictly conceived his image to combine the integrity of the critic's project in its own terms with its responsibility to its subject. He has projected a necessary relation between two implications of image.

How would this apply to the quarrel over Racine? Is psychoanalysis a convincing form of anamorphism? You might argue that characters of Racine seen through this particular lens and according to the consequent optic law might be consistently and clearly represented. And we should be able to distinguish between haphazard and inconsistent use of the psychoanalytic optic and its more disciplined and effective use. But the judgement as to whether or not it is a critically effective anamorphosis, as opposed, say, to an optic derived from some cranky form of allegory, must be made in some other way. How are we to choose an optic, or decide about the efficacy of one that derives from such a far-reaching view of the mind as psychoanalysis? If the latter were an established scientific view of the mind it might matter in a quite different way than if it were simply a coherent body of signs. The 'always' and 'everywhere' that so offend Picard might have different kinds of force. And this also raises the problem of whether or not such an anamorphosis would apply evenly through the work, whether or not its own symbolic structure added up to a satisfactory whole. Satisfactory no doubt depends again on some further criterion concerning signs and symbols. But one thing that such a view is required to do is see the anamorphic projection as a version of Racine. And if Picard (or perhaps Hume's 'disinterested spectator') cannot recognise Racine in this version some further form of conviction is required.

The 'logic of the symbol' is more mysterious in dealing with the way in which chains of symbols relate in a series of transformations that are 'controlled, not random', yet are stretched through the very imaginative process employed by poetry itself. The forms of transformation indicated by psychoanalysis and by rhetoric are linked in a brief list that gives a table of equivalents: substitution and metaphor, displacement and metonymy, etc. The patterns in which unconscious processes transform our dreams can also be described in the rhetorical terminology which we give to figurative language. Whether this table of equivalents could be put to serious critical use or not would require study of the particular application, and I shall come to the detailed working out of such a correlation in the next chapter. Barthes merely gestures towards the linked associations that Richard has found in Mallarmé 'permit distant but legitimate connections', in which the nature of such liaisons is justified by their existence within poetry itself. A series of correspondences is evoked: mental processes, many of them unconscious; creative processes involving symbolic transformation; and critical processes which are a symbolic reworking of the latter. 'Controlled' and 'legitimate' though these processes be, it looks as if the critic does not state their general form (nor indeed does Barthes) but the creative and interesting critic is working in such terms, rather than those of a stale mimeticism which ignores the symbolic processes of transformation.

Two kinds of description would be required for this. One is a description of the symbolic process itself; it is totally omitted, but one assumes that it would come from a fusion of psychoanalytic and linguistic terms. (And in their very presence one sees the difficulty of separating the science of literature from criticism proper.) The other is the actual language of critical description. Any account of how the latter works is presumably the link between these levels, a pointing out of how the enactment of a symbolic process relates to the general laws. This might in these circumstances be a detailed accounting for the language of *Sur Racine*.

Here, as elsewhere in Barthes's account, there is a slippage away from the immediate problem and its claims, towards more general forms of understanding. Even having turned away from the science of literature to sketch the function of criticism, one finds the terms of the argument fixed once again in the nature of linguistic and psychological laws. It must function by way of them. He seems aware that this narrowing of the bizarre territory is an impoverishment of our power of talking about literature. But he can find no other consolation for the role of criticism than that distance which consists in irony. And the ground of this irony is that criticism is placed in the dilemma we have seen in others, beginning with Richards, in that difficulty which is intrinsic to a language commenting on language. But this dilemma poses an entrapment that Barthes does not stay to consider, and the irony is more profound than he knows. Unless it is one that he enacts in the fabrication of a science to point his way to a non-ironical distancing.

No doubt for Barthes himself, and perhaps for that moment which our quarrel over 'la nouvelle critique' has represented, *S/Z* would have appeared as the example of a new science of literature, while for us it seems rather a sublimely inventive and eccentric work of criticism. Does this mean that Barthes's creativity has worked against the grain of his own intention? If so the 'crisis of commentary' may truly arise from a lack of reflexivity in critical irony. Such a failure of reflexivity may have undermined the possibility of self-knowledge.   I suggest this not of Barthes's work as a whole where a wry capacity to outflank himself is a pervasive quality of mind, but of an historical moment in it, a moment in which it was felt necessary to give shape to 'la nouvelle critique' and which succeeded in doing so only by disintegrating the notion of criticism itself. The very effort to say what it is and how it works is the process of eroding it. Historically the defence of a movement was its ultimate phase, and logically the object of enquiry receded as the argument towards spelling it out advanced.

Perhaps, in a way which we will follow further, of the making of sense there is no bottom. Even when the making of sense is itself despised. Barthes, imaginative, generous, humane, indeed, full of good sense, has tacitly accepted the contradictory nature of his project. In setting out a field of imaginative action, he has felt the necessity of showing that this action is 'controlled', but has found the nature and operation of such rules impossible to describe. Indeed, it is often said that we cannot conceive of a language game without rules – another issue to which we will return. Can we conceive of one where the rules exist, but are unstable, for they will apply only to the next set of moves, and the conditions these are to meet have not yet evolved? It is always the next move that counts, and those of the past are approximate pointers at best and restrictive clauses at worst. How could a rational description of such a field show the employment of stable rules, and give criteria for their successful application?

Of course I am making the matter difficult by acting as if criticism composes a single language game rather than a miscellaneous hodgepodge of them, but one has been tempted to do so by Barthes's own separation of the way of science from the way of criticism, and the subsequent descriptive attempt on a non-existent essence, whose very non-existence is the boundary-stone of its field of action. If in literature there is something to describe or explain, the process of doing so is a continuation of the metaphors of the work which is itself a 'sign without content' which both has and has not an identity of its own. Any identity might be simply positional, in the fact of continuation, in that 'it occupies ... a place ... ' as if spatial representation were more distinctive than characteristic of function, of how one plays what game. If one does not get to the bottom there is rather a movement outward which in finding its own symbols must continually reinvent its own rules of play. If those rules are unstable it is by nature of the conditions in which they would operate, and if the description of those conditions is necessarily radically incomplete the reinvention must satisfy us in terms of its all too dangerous allure rather than the fulfilment of stable criteria. Which is effectively to change the desideratum of this field of imaginative action from one of safety to one of danger. And if in this version of bizarre territories no one explanation is better than any other, that may be a matter of indifference to the 'truth of writing' subsumed into a 'love for the truth of myths'. (*CT*, p. 78)

# III    The curve of the mirror

A critical argument often arises from a felt lack of understanding, a puzzle, a feeling that not enough has been said about a work that poses interest and difficulty, or merely from exasperation at the failures of one's predecessors and colleagues when one is convinced that all of the wrong things have been said. But it seldom arises out of the desire to fulfil a general plan in order to show how the principles of that plan are the true model of critical practice. Practical criticism has its subject directly in view, and so often the theoretical project quite naturally develops a life of its own. The large literature of the last two decades devoted to the exploitation of theory is often thin on examples, and modest in its claims about the ways in which theoretical reasoning connects directly with practice. Classification systems, such as that of Frye with its typology of myths and genres, suggest themselves as natural meeting points of theory and practice, as do those that explain fundamental features of the working of genres or aspects of poetic language through tropological or rhetorical categories. But the systematic application to the study of a particular text of a theory and its methodology is sufficiently uncommon as to suggest something slightly unnatural in the whole enterprise.

It would seem like a cautionary element in Harold Bloom's 'The Breaking of Form' that precisely this 'how it works' aspect of the handling of critical theory is also seen in terms of a high level of generality, in a distinction between 'theory of poetry' and 'poetics' that he draws from Curtius. So the recognition that the relations between theory and practice are in his essay set out in uncommon detail, is joined to theoretical claims of a more far-reaching kind than one which would merely offer the justification of a technical vocabulary:

By 'theory of poetry' I mean the concept of the nature and function of the poet and of poetry, in distinction from poetics, which has to do with the technique of poetical composition. This distinction between the concepts 'theory of poetry' and 'poetics' is a fruitful one for knowledge. That *de facto* the two have contacts and often pass into each other is no objection. The history of the theory of poetry coincides neither with the history of poetics nor with the history of literary criticism. The poet's conception of himself, or the tension between poetry and science ... are major themes of a history of the theory of poetry, not of a history of poetics.[1]

Curtius actually implies a triple distinction rather than a double one: theory of poetry, poetics and literary criticism, moving from the most general to the most concrete. And the interest in Bloom's essay lies in his intention to approach the most general issues with respect to the nature of poetry in order to apply them to the close reading of what he considers a great poem of our time, John Ashbery's 'Self-Portrait in a Convex Mirror'. In such a reading the middle ground between the most general theoretical interest might well be seen in the rhetorical distinctions which could correspond to what Curtius calls poetics, although no more than Curtius does Bloom work in terms of a strict separation of levels. That such levels do indeed 'pass into each other' seems an accepted condition of the enterprise.

There is a further, perhaps more far-reaching, ambiguity which, however it may relate to the original intention, arises when one tries to grasp the precise nature of the relations between theory and practice that the essay proposes. Is Bloom's general theory and methodology a pre-existent systematic approach, whose assumptions can be stated quite independently of their use, a coherent set of speculative instruments prepared and ready for the practitioner's hand? Or is there some sense in which it is substantially modified by the circumstances in which it operates, and in important ways is re-created through its engagement with 'the poet of our moment and our climate'? Of course it seems simplistic to ask whether the method exists for the sake of the understanding of the poem, or the poem largely as illustration of the system and its method. There is certainly a complex series of adaptations at work. But it does matter whether or not there is a generalisable system whose validity lies not only in any of its possible adaptations, but in some general truth that it exemplifies. I shall take it from the form of Bloom's presentation that the former is the case, that claims about the nature of poetry in general, about how things work in poetry, and how they work in Ashbery's poem, are interlinked in such a way that our ultimate point of reference is something not unlike a natural law which operates through the history of poetry. But certain qualifications may appear in their appropriate place.

This means of course that the truth claim of the method about itself is different from whatever it may claim about the poem. It is akin to saying that the justification of a method lies in the general principles which animate it rather than in the felt satisfaction in the reading which follows from them. The point of this essay is in establishing that link: the *a priori* validity implicit in the method will have its *a posteriori* demonstration.

Perhaps it is fair to mention here one of the first of the qualifications, that historical context sets certain limitations on the validity of the method: it is not wholly universalisable, and its generality is limited to those historical periods for which it is devised. The dramatic form of the poets' struggle that unfolds in English poetry on our side of a Miltonic watershed is not attributed to the Elizabethans or to other earlier poetry. Whether or not it would apply to the classical world does not seem to matter although our critical models owe their source to ancient rhetoricians. A selective pair of analogies from French and German poetry are rather *pro forma*, except for the crucial figure of Hölderlin, who is important to us as a belated Pindar in a sense that Pindar could never be. I mention this at this stage because the opening remarks that set out what looks to be a universalisable theory of poetry, very distinctly state its historical limitations, and hence see it in a historicised manner. It follows that those remarks are themselves historicised, and this historical self-consciousness is essential to the explanation of the rationale of his critical procedures.

So the very dense pages of the first half of Bloom's account that are devoted to theory are to a considerable extent concerned with giving an appropriate context for that theory. In order to explain the theoretical elements one must give them a kind of circumstantial identity: to reach Ashbery one must first of all find oneself, and the theoretical pages are among other things a placing of himself. This placing has many dimensions. Barthes speaks of the paradox that Racine, supposedly the model of neo-classical propriety, is the author who has brought about a convergence of 'all the new languages of the century'. Here too there is a convergence of 'new languages', but the use and assessment of them has its inward-looking aspect. These pages are a mixture of sorting and of display. As such, both are a résumé of a group of arguments that Bloom has used in other circumstances, and consequently something of a personal anthology of themes from his own work, which here have been drawn together and rearranged to be brought to bear on a particular poem which is their appropriate focal point. Looking outward there is an exercise of choice, examining the various languages of our multi-languaged time, to determine which aspects of which of them provide the more useful fragments of ground and directing clues. Otherwise the reflection on the frame of reference that elucidates Ashbery's poem is simultaneously on one's own work, in focusing and defining oneself, in deciding which of the many facets of it are relevant to the revised self-portrait which is the form of a critical essay.

Nowadays we all assume that the critic is responsible to a number of strains in the complicated climate which surrounds any serious thought about literature. Could one possibly write as if certain widely purveyed views of literature were not in one's view? Can one do other than regard the activity of criticism as somehow a nexus, a congested crossing point where all of the streams of thought that have come to play on literature awkwardly co-exist? Suppose we believe that one can reach through and beyond those elaborations, and dismiss the clumsy and barren pseudo-scientific jargon of linguistics, the hazy pretentiousness of Lacanians, the drear schematising of structuralists, the reductive banalities of Marxists and the comic gyrations of deconstructionists, would we be the happier for a fictional innocence and clarity? To attempt such a dismissal would of course require its own justification, and no doubt its own meta-critical rationalisation. And such a rationale would incorporate the ground of those negative choices. The judicious method of Bloom is a mixture of listing, weighing and ticking-off in which the multiple claims of the moment's paraphernalia are assembled, used, criticised, rejected or transformed with well-calibrated degrees of engagement and distance. The various coordinates must be recognised and arranged in an acceptable set of working relationships which point the way to the essentials of Bloom's purpose, without cluttering or deflecting from his design. There is so much to be accounted for by way of using it, or tersely dropping it into the interstices of a polemical turn. So in three pages one moves by way of Burke, Curtius and Freud into coordinates which are formal, historical and psychological. The Curtius passage is of special importance because it gives so straightforwardly (without arguing the matter through in any way) the character of what the theorist of poetry is, and suggests the mysterious dynamics of the internal working of the 'poet's conception of himself'.

I realise that in attempting my 'further description' I am bound to fail to do justice to the richness of the manipulation by which the many intellectual angles of vision and points of reference are brought into play, often in the most tangentially allusive way, first brought forward then somehow left to find a relational place in the thickening (and sometimes thinning) palimpsest. The trace remains, and the accumulation of trace elements is part of the method. The glancingly allusive flow of references is a process of constant relocation of the traces with respect to each other, touchstones caressed in passing which suggest affinities without necessarily achieving a precise integration into a structured argument. So on pages 3–4 the steps move from the poet's conception of self to the Freudian notion of the child's fantasy-making powers in a 'changeling fiction ... one of the stances of freedom' because of its basis in disjunction. Hence a criterion of freedom, the poet's special form of it, 'the freedom to have a meaning of one's own', which evokes in turn the versions of tradition and of poetic language against which the poet may achieve it. Alternating views of language produce a dramatic confrontation between the magical and the nihilistic – again with the explanatory force carried through allusion, by way of Benjamin, the Kabbalists, deconstruction in general and de Man in particular, Coleridge and various others.

Two propositions are intended to follow from this kaleidoscopic presentation. One is that the two opposing views of language turn into each other at their outer limits. The other asserts that it does not really matter what view of language you adopt as long as it is extreme enough. For the extreme is necessary to the poet's agon and it is the agon that matters and not the terms in which it is worked out. So any possible consideration of the character of poetic language is subordinated to the conflicts and dynamics of creativity, and any feature of what poets do with language is an internal indicator of the form that such a conflict is taking. Would it be a mistaken inference to say that Bloom values that language for the conflict it reveals, rather than for its own character as product of that conflict? At this point it is premature to put such a question, and in any case, inference would hardly be the right word. For this is a tissue of ideas, figures, commitments, which are meant to be seen in a single sweeping movement, as background to the critical agon which is seen by way of them. The bits of the mosaic must be carefully fitted to the critical awareness: Burckhardt, Schopenhauer, Curtius, Freud and Emerson are fluttered past as apostles of the agonic sublime. It seems unnecessary to set out exactly in what ways they are so, or how in their own ways they would relate to each other, or which aspects of their work make the strongest claim to such a role. They are there as emblematic figures in a larger landscape, their revelation, as with Proustian places, so largely contained in the name.

I have given a rather flattened and 'impoverished' account of these opening pages, wanting to avoid for the moment some more colourful and visionary aspects, the contrast of dearth and plenitude, or the somewhat muscular and militant rhetoric which establishes the tone. And these constitute only a selective representation, which take me through approximately the first nine of the eighty-seven moves into which I have divided the opening twenty-two pages, the theoretical section of Bloom's essay. It will not be useful to continue in detail, but to point to certain patterns in the elaborate design. The variety is such that these opening pages can at least serve as a miniaturised model of the whole, even if at the cost of a quite limited justice. And here, as with what follows, the rapidity with which connection, comparison and association move, may create a synoptic panorama, yet one in which the connections are of a quite variable order. Should we wish to work out more fully the relations between the 'Kabbalistic magical absolute' and 'Coleridge's version of the magical view' steps would be necessary to construct the meeting point from more fully articulated contexts. Not impossible of course, but something involving a variety of steps that would have not only contestable features, but involve contestability of different kinds. The single comparison involves many arguments.

However this would be a subsidiary point if I were to list my eighty-seven theoretical moves like an analytic table of contents. I certainly should not have meant that any of them were therefore complete in themselves, and discretely separable. The eighty-seven moves in effect contain others implied within them, and the best that I can offer in this kind of commentary is an indication of the complexity, feeling that the attempt at a full *catalogue raisonné* would push beyond the limits of normal tolerance. I must be content with a sketch of a sketch, with selective highlighting on the grand design, trying to touch those aspects that give an understanding of the way in which the theory of poetry is constructed, and the force it ultimately has.

I have already raised the question of how the parts fit, and suggested that they fit in oblique and variable manners. Explanation itself has its own capacity to 'swerve' in the face of the demands that might be made on it. Take the way in which form is related to trope, the breaking of form 'explained' by an erotic analogy, with the discovery of love in the moment of its irreparable loss, or elsewhere as the meaning constructed through the shattering of vessels. I put this somewhat cryptically to emphasise that the working of explanation is largely analogic, and that often in a somewhat unexpected way. There is no intention to clarify in any conventional sense, and indeed there are some hard words for 'clarity', made in the context of what it is to clarify one's own meaning:

By 'clarify' I partly mean 'extend', because I think I have been clear enough for some, and I don't believe that I ever could be clear enough for others, since for them 'clarity' is mainly a trope for philosophical reductiveness, or for a dreary literal-mindedness that belies any deep concern for poetry or criticism. But I also seem to have had generous readers who believe in fuller explanations than I have given. (*DC*, p. 2)

These 'fuller explanations' seem themselves to have an indeterminate character for which 'clarity' might not be the acceptable guideline. If philosophy provides models of clarity, so much the worse. Bloom like Leavis has his reservations about philosophy: 'Many critics flee to philosophy or linguistics, but the result is that they learn to interpret poems as philosophy or as linguistics. Philosophy may flaunt its rigors but its agon with poetry is an ancient one and will never end' (*DC*, p. 9). But how does 'theory' stand in relation to such general explanations, for the concern with theory is expressed as such, with the specific aim of 'insight into the theory of poetry'? The characterisation of this language will take us in several different directions. And Bloom's claim for the scope of the teacher of literature would make criticism only a small part of the undertaking which makes up the 'Scene of Instruction'. Rorty has wished to show the growing place of 'culture criticism' in modern intellectual life, in the wake of the retreat of other traditional disciplines. But for him this has little more than an ostensive identity, and if Bloom is his example, the further description of what Bloom is doing remains an empty space.

One point of departure takes us back to the remark of Curtius that situates the theory of poetry in the poet's conception of himself. Both psychological and historical dimensions spill out of this. The poet's awareness of himself is paramount, and the grounds of self-understanding pose the inner dimensions of our reading, which inevitably is expressed in psychological language. We must describe what is happening in some inner recess where poetic language is shaped, which requires as its descriptive vocabulary a language adapted to the creative process. This is conceived by Bloom in terms of the conflict with one's own poetic tradition. Through such conflict the creative moment is achieved. Yet to speak this way is to speak historically. One moves from the inner dimension largely framed in Freudian terms, into the historical dimension in which the inner conflict is worked out, the psychological stances entering into poetry, and hence into poetic history, largely through shifts in the poet's language which can be tropologically described. The fusion is complete, although the difference between historical and psychological dimensions can be described. Indeed, we cannot conceive of a poet without seeing his place in a succession of poets and recognising his awareness of that place. Nor can we express that awareness without a model for the relationships which this implies, relationships which involve personal, inner dimensions.

The Freudian model is a constant, but its use is largely taken for granted rather than explained, and the degree of presence is highly variable, from the casually allusive to a concerted attempt to give solid application to the notion of 'defense'. But it is essentially a point of reference rather than a conceptual scheme within which the possibilities of critical method evolve. The evocation of a conjoining of methods derived from psychoanalysis and rhetoric suggests an approach close to Lacan's grounding of linguistic figures and devices in psychic conflict. But this is not directly considered, and the psychoanalytic reference is to an orthodox Freud or at least his tradition. And the reason must be that Bloom is concerned with poets as persons, with the real and palpable conflict found through the play of figure. We should want to come to an assessment of the central dramatic action represented in poetry, where Anna Freud's study of the ego and mechanisms of defence is put to direct use. Here he allows what is almost a caveat to the effect that these mechanisms cannot be directly observed, and hence are only understood in retrospect. And 'As I apply Anna Freud, in a poem the ego is the poetic self and the id is the precursor, idealized and frequently composite, hence fantasized, but still traceable to a historical author or authors' (*DC*, p. 14). In effect the psychological dynamic of the inner conflict of the poetic self can only be seen through the historical imagination. But this is not immediately translated into critical reading.

Its elaboration comes from a letter of Hölderlin to Schiller which models the 'anxiety of influence' – so central to Bloom's work – which distances in the very moment of acknowledging the master's power, and which Bloom turns into the dramatic action of overmastering the master: 'Hölderlin actually undoes and isolates Schiller, who is made to ebb ... ' (*DC*, p. 18). This points to the late Freudian notion of the primacy of anxiety even in the denial of it. Hence the poet reveals that primacy in the transcendence of it, revealing its presence in the heart of the sublime, a revelation of the failure of that further transcendence of the human condition itself. Of course, this point is not made through the examination of poetic language, but through biography, and through the rather heightened interpretation of a letter of which other readings are possible. The strongly interpreted biographical point calls for the generality of the Freudian notion, used more as an insight about the human condition, rather than an explanation of 'Hölderlin's sublime strength'. One must turn to language to find more direct and less speculative ways of seeing the universal psychic pattern in the work itself. Yet here too the connection rests on an assertion to be ostensively demonstrated that 'in language itself defense is compelled to be manifested as trope' (*DC*, p. 19). That trope is of course figure perhaps follows another aspect of 'defense', that against literal expectation which is essential to the poet's strength, and for which the only vehicle is the unexplored possibility of the figurative, that 'swerve' from normal patterns of usage which make possible the poet's deviant means of creation.

In effect, the placement of the notion of 'defense' in poetic theory is made through a simple and massive assertion: 'Defense therefore is the natural language of Hölderlin's poetic imagination and of every post-Enlightenment imagination that can aspire convincingly to something like Hölderlin's Sublime strength' (*DC*, p. 19). In this context the ground remains biographical, asserting that the poet knows that the figuration for Sublime poetry is found in the 'anxiety of influence'.

So three basic tracks lead to the model of poetic theory: psychological, historical and linguistic. The psychological bases the poet's break with his predecessors in the psychic individuation by which sons break from their fathers. The historical argues that this underlies the way in which the poetic sublime can be achieved from roughly Wordsworth to Ashbery. The linguistic holds that this movement of psyche and of poetic language is incarnated in the variety of trope the examination of which is no doubt the major task of critical language. While these are obviously closely interlinked, they require a substantially independent form of establishment. In the case of the psychological ground it seems largely taken for granted that the notion of defence touches psychic bed-rock. In moving it to a literary case the assumption is made that it applies *mutatis mutandis*, but the concept is in fact vague enough for it to be used descriptively in a variety of ways. This is probably its real merit. But degrees of connection between the psychic underlay and the poetic achievement could have any force from strict causality to simply that of an interesting analogy. In practice this seems to cause no worry, and any deeper theoretical obscurity goes past in the night.

When the notion is historicised the oddity appears that by implication the psychological role of defence must not have applied until after the Enlightenment. Was the relationship of fathers and sons so fundamentally different? Or was it simply not transferred for some reason to the field of poetry? Or did the concept of the sublime not apply before the poetic role of defence declared itself? One hopes too that the relation of the sublime and defence in this historical epoch does not enter into a pattern of circularity that would weaken their meaning. Bloom's general assertion about this relation would have to be established through seeing the psychological/poetic equation in a substantial number of convincing cases. But I suppose that he might reasonably assume that in the prolix and somewhat repetitive works that have developed his own canon he has made such an extensive use of these terms that their descriptive use is at least persuasively present and here requires no further explanation.

As for the variety of trope as the vehicle of defence, the effect of the legislative gesture that underwrites it is best seen in the working of the psychological analysis that is applied to Ashbery's poem.

Certainly this separating out of three major components of poetic theory involves considerable simplification. There are other keys and many touchstones. We have seen at least part of the cast list of prophets of the sublime. The flow of names suggests that every angle of approach must be explored through multiple disciplines, the agonistic sublime found in the most diverse aspects of our culture. It is as if a Leavisite passion for centrality were super-imposed on a vast jumble of cultural icons, all turned in the same direction by the 'inevitable', 'inescapable' lodestone. A galaxy is embraced, drawn together, if its components are only mentioned in passing. I have already noted that this style of presentation is more allusive than substantive, depends more on the aura of names than on giving those names a differentiated role. What is largely shorthand is swallowed up in the hortatory tone: go by way of Schopenhauer, go by way of Freud, etc., and you will find all roads lead ineluctably, inevitably, towards the one great thing ... And all things weak will be forgotten. The sequence in all of this has no discernible principle; there is no reason why the cases should not have come in whatever order, or why other cases might not be given instead. The effect is cumulative and unstructured.

In filling out the general frame for the case that will justify and employ all of its elements the method is almost the opposite of that employed by Barthes in *S/Z* where the relations between lexic elements, codes and commentaries are correlated through the controlling presence of the narrative itself, which makes the division and classification system follow the order of the narrative. The formal identification of the codes might pre-exist or be applicable to any narrative. But their development flows directly from 'Sarrasine' – although in fact the commentaries are wildly centrifugal and enormously varied in substance. They simply pick up an aspect of a lexic fragment and follow the implications as far as they are of interest. Yet there are no steps beyond the narrative steps. There are no reasons why the codes should succeed each other according to any particular pattern, nor any schematism that governs the sequence of the commentaries. This is another form of controlled disorder, with the control within the narrative and the disorder in the relation between the various features of the meta-sequence. There is no meta-story 'so far': only the story. And the codes at least are restricted to features intrinsic to the text even if the commentaries find directions of their own.

Of course the fact that Barthes follows the narrative is not itself a determinate of the nature of the theoretical grounds of his project, but simply of its linear development. And the circling movement of Bloom sorting through the relevant coordinates is simply not intended to have an exposition of such a kind. Neither argument nor narrative exercises control, but rather a loosely related system of allusions and analogies. Yet the aim is to uncover general laws of the operations of the poetic sublime. Perhaps the notion of law must be understood somewhat generously. In the primary conflict between fathers and sons there are many way-stations, and in the poetic version of this conflict the mixture of belonging and breaking away can involve multiple degrees and forms. There is not a mode of the breaking of form, but only an inventory. To characterise confrontation and evasion in a general way would be as bizarre and useless as a quantificational system for measuring poetic strength. This problem so runs through Bloom's work that the terms themselves seem to call for a kind of explanation that it would be unintelligible to give.

Certainly the implicit attack on Eliot's version of tradition which would seem to lay the dead hand on any 'breaking of form' for the sake of continuity seems reasonable enough a position to state. Yet Eliot's own commitment to tradition and its continuity is also 'broken' by his own startling originality. Bloom's more active picture of the poet's relation to his past may emphasise the breaks as opposed to the continuities and the revolt against the past more than its assimilation. But as a romantic riposte to Eliot's classicism it is not clear that one gives a more accurate description of the poet's relation to his predecessors by evoking the operation of some general psychological law – following from that 'anxiety of influence' developed in so much of Bloom's work. It is simply a way of describing some cases by attributing a cause. If those cases should be identical with all those of which one used the terms 'strong' or 'sublime' one would have to consider that the notions themselves lost their force through circularity. And that they should operate clearly within an individual poetic oeuvre might be complicated by the thought that any poet has many predecessors who are the springboard of many reactions, and any complex work will be composed of multiple assimilations and tearings apart. Even in the case of the one great predecessor who evokes the most profound urgency of defence, one would wish to see the forms of such defence revealing itself through the language of the work, rather than, as in the case of Hölderlin, simply alluding to the way in which the poet may possibly himself have thought about it, on at least one occasion. And here the evidence might be mixed, with traces of assimilation and revolt in many forms and in differing degrees. So even if we could accept that such over-riding general psychological laws operate in poetic history there may be a radical indeterminacy in their application.

Before looking at the extended application that Bloom proposes of his theory and its methods to Ashbery's poem, I think three further comments would be useful about the language through which that theory operates. One follows from the problem of how the Freudian law of defence would operate as an explanatory principle. It is intended to be precise and determinate, almost mechanistically so. I have already given some reasons as to why such terms cannot be used in this way, and I shall give further when we see them in practice.

Secondly, another class of important concepts such as 'insight' into poetic theory suggest the opposite of 'defence' in their built-in ambiguity. The connection of insight with theory has a certain attraction because it shifts a word usually applied to particular cases to a more general ground, and seems to give its use an expanded dimension. But should it do so would it alter something in the character of poetic theory itself? We often claim insight into those things that have a primary obscurity or uncertainty, or which are lodged in such traditionally elusive retreats as the human heart. We sometimes speak of critical insight as the unaccountable property of a rather special kind of person who sees into what has density and resistance, or perhaps equally into the kind of difficulty which is impalpable or diffuse. Theory as the object of insight changes its role from general form of understanding to the object of understanding, and the explanatory force of any theoretical scheme might relate oddly to the excitement generated by such an object. There is no effort to give this any further sense, or to explain the standing of one's explanations. On the surface, the effect of it seems radically libertarian. Theory as the object and vehicle of insight is the more subject to our variable pleasure. If insight of this sort is the means of determining which are the predominant, rather than say secondary or vestigial, theoretical considerations that govern literary study it is difficult to see how such decisions would be reached or justified. The radical open-endedness in the vocabulary makes good reasons impossible to give.

Thirdly, there is the effect of the historicised contexting on many of the terms. They are mediated through an historical sense. Take the famous 'ratios' on which so much of the argument depends. They seem largely rhetorical categories within which to carry out the description of mental states, and above all the shifting and changing of mental states. The notion of course implies relation, and certainly their figurative derivation from mathematical and even mechanical models almost purifies that sense of movement, of 'betweenness'. 'Defense', tropes, figures, images, are all relational terms, if not quite in the same pure sense as 'ratio'. One reads 'through ratios and not into them' as if they have no substantive identity at all but express the shifting connections seen and reseen, and indeed revalued. But this relational language finds its ground in the historical affinities that constitute the tradition. So the moment of focus on Ashbery himself, the moment of identifying and naming, is like the historical investment of those rhetorical categories. 'The poet of our moment and of our climate, our Whitman and our Stevens...', both suggests an assimilation to a tradition and an analogy which destabilises it. On the notion of tradition a word like 'our' exerts a massive pressure. Is Ashbery an inheritor in ways we might reasonably see, or has there been not only that defensive and self-creative 'swerve' on the part of the poet, but a swerve in ourselves as well, in some uncharted path where the tradition meets an individual talent in a quite unexpected way? This doubleness does not easily resolve itself. And the fleeting nature of 'moment' has its further destabilising force.

It is not, of course, in looking directly at the Ashbery poem that one wants fully articulated coordinates firmly ordered in a Leavisite 'placing'. But the parallel track which might suggest such a thing seems to create continuity more than analogy, yet expresses that connection in a puzzling way. It is a claim to some kind of deep correspondence that holds: 'Ashbery, like Stevens is a profoundly Whitmanian poet, frequently despite appearances' (*DC*, p. 22). Appearances are of course so traditionally superficial that it is well to mistrust them, and the deeper affinities between a writer and his predecessors, his true ancestors, may not always be striking at surface level. But Bloom hardly bothers to make the case for the deeper affinity beyond mentioning a string of titles, perhaps because it is too obvious to require more than allusion. But 'despite appearances' seems to mean that resemblance is no real evidence of affinity. Pushing the paradoxical might suggest that for truly strong reading the very lack of resemblance indicates depth of relation – so deeply has defence obscured the nature of the blood lines. Of course one can argue in a rather global way that all 'strong' American poetry derives however indirectly from the 'Song of Myself'. But this seems too loose for any serious critical purpose. Is any poem of introspection by an American writer, any consequent concern with the self and its identity to be seen as Whitmanesque?

There is certainly a straightforwardly Leavisite project here of creating the central terms of a canon and assimilating the highly valued works of the tradition to it. I suppose, if suitably pushed, one could see 'Prufrock' as a Whitmanian poem, its rhetoric inverted and demonstrating that independence of 'swerve' characteristic of strength in the pursuit of an antithetical self. If difference is clearer than resemblance, the latter might be seen in some aspects at least of 'East Coker' and 'Dry Salvages' – although these might also be the same aspects of which it could be argued that Eliot's originality and authenticity weaken, where he has reached for a conventional version of that tradition of American concern with identity. The references to Stevens suggest more the affinity of a highly generalised poetic project than of any particular inheritance of poetic language. And one of the difficulties for Bloom lies in failing to articulate the characteristics of the language, transmitted through the central works of his canon, with that more impalpable spirit which he calls 'the central or Emersonian tradition of our poetry'. However extensively the terms of rhetorical analysis are elaborated, the method which excludes any close concern with resemblance and difference means that certain connectives in terms of poetic language cannot be expressed. The heart of the tradition seems to be evoked in terms of some vision of psychic depth, and looking too closely at what features of poetic language are shared and what are not might run the danger of suggesting that the tradition was composed of things that did not resemble each other very much.

No more than in his language does any more general feature of poetic stance link Ashbery to Whitman. Wry, ironic, intensely observant, turning a casual, downbeat diction into the stuff of an intensely metaphysical post-symbolist poetry, Ashbery in no way resembles the grandiose and self-assertive Whitman. Of course there are ways in which a markedly diffident stance may indeed be an aggressive one, and understatement may become a powerful form of self-assertion. Evasion may be an oblique form of confrontation, and the Boyg's path round about may well lead to the heart of the matter. In life as well as in poetry our 'belatedness' with respect to linguistic forms may be felt in our reluctance to take on easily the mannerisms we have inherited, or the postures that were natural to our grandparents and embarrassing to ourselves. This awkwardness pervades Eliot's attitude to Romantic and Victorian poetry. And Barthes's *A Lover's Discourse* is a sublime example of the comedy of indirection into which our 'moment' has forced the language of love.

But what constitutes an ancestry that shows the determinant features in the creation of a poet's distinctive voice, or which opens towards his most important accomplishment? I shall, to try the terms of the game, consider an alternative which I have no intention whatsoever of proposing as my own reading of Ashbery, but simply a way of looking at the problem of ancestry, resemblance, and what can be learned from them about the tradition. It is possible to argue that the most important influence in the 'Self-Portrait' lies not in American poetry at all, but in French symbolism, particularly in the negative exploration of the self in Mallarmé – the dissolution of the self through the fragmentation of moments of consciousness. One might begin with mirrors, a rich motif in French literature, and without going back to the Renaissance (although Parmigianino too had his contexts) or plunging too deeply into the pool of Narcissus. It has numerous incarnations in the work of Valéry and Gide as well as Mallarmé. One might take as a primary model of the artist's relating of consciousness to the poetic persona the dark mirror in Mallarmé's 'Hérodiade' in which the powers of reflection and self-knowledge are concentrated in a fusion of awareness and absence. Hérodiade is seated:

> Oh mirror!
> Cold water frozen by boredom in your frame,
> How many times and for hours, grieved
> by dreams and seeking my memories which are
> like leaves beneath your ice and its deep gulf,
> I appeared to myself in you like a far-off shadow,
> but, horror, on some evenings in your severe fountain
> I have known the nakedness of my scattered dream.[2]

Like Ashbery's poem this is a meditation, if only a fragment of one, perhaps somewhat distanced through a minimal dramatic context. We need find no difficulty in seeing a consciousness analogous to the poet's own. And the mirror which should reflect the self reflects the nothingness at the centre of the self, which in turn sees its beauty in the total revelation of this emptiness. We can easily prepare a Bloomian analysis which authenticates Ashbery's ancestry in this Hérodiade far more convincingly than in any Whitmanian 'Myself'. Take the preliminary *clinamen*, perhaps too unsubtly obvious. Ashbery swerves away from the submission to the total darkness, the self-obliterating abyss which lies beyond the mirror. There is clarity and relief in the visual image. The hands' formidable presence with their assertion of the artist's power, with a vivid presentational immediacy rather than absence, yet with that sense of fragility or elusiveness, are poised also perhaps for flight as the curve of the mirror both pushes them towards us, yet suggests the power of the distance pulling beyond the mirror's edge. It is the reverse of normal perspective, where the eye, rather than drawn in to a central focal point, is pushed over the edge of the intelligible into the outer space where nothing lies. The inversion of Mallarmé is his ruthless exploitation. And the metaphysical assertion of presence through absence is revised through replacing the artist's isolating vision with the acceptance of the quotidian and phenomenal. It is in the very matter-of-factness and low key with which randomness and unintelligibility become the familiar and humdrum, and the imagination's down-beat rejection of the arbitrary shaping power that asserts its mixture of metaphysical realism and the acceptance of essential absurdity that the randomness of the world is what poetry can establish as its underlying truth and form of order. And so on.

Further allusions are possible with other Mallarméan overtones. And of course the sixth section that Bloom values so highly with the 'breeze whose simile is a page's turning' is a direct allusion to the conclusion of Valéry's 'Le cimetière marin' with the action of breeze and page reversed. Perhaps I should repeat that I am not concerned with giving an alternative reading of Ashbery's poem, nor with establishing an alternative genealogy for it. As far as that goes I suspect it is more complex and many-sided than Bloom would have it. Certainly there are shades of Eliot (some clear echoes of 'Burnt Norton'), verbal mannerisms that remind one of Auden, and insofar as Stevens is present it is as much the Stevens of symbolist origins as the Stevens of any decisively native tradition. So if my interest here is entirely in how genealogies are constructed, in Bloom's case it looks like a combination of assertion and omission. It may well be that the fate of the modern poet is that he has inherited too much, that putting together his poetic identity is a daunting task of selection, that the resulting eclecticism hardly points to a simple direct line that is the 'tradition'. Of course it is a quite reasonable notion that by winnowing the elements of this complex inheritance one can separate the less and tangentially relevant factors and draw into the foreground those more central elements which make a crucial difference to a poet's work. And in hoping to draw the outlines of what may be a 'great tradition' or a 'strong tradition' the observed continuities and affinities may move through a series of focuses and shifted perspectives and emphases, of moving from particular to general and back again – a procedure largely followed by Eliot and Leavis, as, for that matter, Arnold.

Bloom does not bother with any of this. He assumes the existence of the true line of descent and merely asserts. Perhaps the design is meant to seem so obvious and so fully prepared by his other works. And is there a strong evaluative sense built into this, that if it were not this tradition and this particular swerve in the face of it, the whole thing would hardly be worth talking about? It is possible that the centrality of the tradition for Bloom is almost mystically defined and held, so that transplanting Ashbery to another tradition would somehow deprive him of that 'placing' that gives a grandeur and importance to his work. The context is given: ancestors, tradition, climate, moment (almost like Taine revisited – but selectively). The effect of altering these contextual elements to establish my alternative tradition would be to change the features drawn from the past, but leave the image of the present largely unaltered. Ashbery remains the poet of our moment, but in a vision of poetic history in which an American poet is part of a European context. There is a case to be made, although I have merely pointed towards it. But on the face of it there is as much sense in such a model as there is in Bloom's.

Suppose, however, that we have treated whatever context in terms of the primary movement of evasion, the swerve before the gravity-pull of tradition which is the primary assertion of the poet's independence. We are still on the threshold of the sequence of 'ratios' of which this is only the first. I do not however see from what is said of the 'ratios' that there is a fixed and limited number of them or that they operate in any particular order. Some logical links may be necessary features of some of them, in that those that involve 'reversal' could hardly have their effect without something to reverse. Unless what has been described in terms of reversal could also have been put as 'swerve', the primary move which rejects a pre-existing state of things. This is one of the general issues I wish to raise about the ratios: not merely whether or not what they describe is best done through this kind of terminology, but whether or not the terms are sufficiently distinctive to carry out with any clarity the moves that Bloom assigns to them. Which is to ask whether the terms of the ratios are effectively applicable. They have a connection with traditional rhetoric, but their dynamic of movement through 'thresholds' implies that the movements attain their identity from what they are moving through rather than having a distinctive character in themselves.

The only way of evaluating this is of course in context, and in observing the relation between the ratios. For Bloom's own strategy of adaptation of vocabulary to subject perhaps the key term after *clinamen* is *kenosis*, partly because it seems a dramatic vehicle for the kind of psychological force that Bloom requires, but also because 'Kenosis is Ashbery's prevalent ratio, and his whole poetics is one of "giving up / Its shape is a gesture which expresses that shape."' Such uses are straightforwardly descriptive and the question of the adequacy of the ratios as a descriptive vocabulary must be tested in terms of the contexts to which they are applied. Beyond this one must ask whether or not the ratios work as a system, and whether or not such a system is a desirable enlargement of our critical language. Does it provide a usable critical method which both extends our understanding and is repeatable in its use?

Interestingly, for the analysis of this poem he supplements the vocabulary of the ratios with 'the new rhetoric of thresholds' derived from Angus Fletcher, especially in the 'notion of the topoi of "crossings" as images of voice', and in Fletcher's account of *metalepsis*. It is as if there is the doubling of rhetorical systems to increase the descriptive power, or at least that the total rhetorical project has a doubling of notations. The better perhaps to push at the edges of descriptive possibility. And such expressions as 'images of voice' look deliberately paradoxical, designed to push against such possibility, as if tonalities could be captured in visual form. The very mention of images suggests another form of ratio 'between what is uttered and what, somehow, is intended'. He quotes Burke on the effect of images as plunging one into 'textures of relationships' which may prompt the query: 'Cannot those relationships be charted?'

In this Bloom comes to the heart of the problem of rhetoric. The most fully elaborated rhetorics have so developed in order to deal with the most elusive features of language. But then, new rhetorics must build upon old, even if by way of breaking with them. Sometimes the process of refinement and complication is cut by the necessary rejection and reach for the radical alternative. But the process is necessarily one of mapping patterns of relationships which modify or try to break out of increasingly static systems. And to move beyond the classifications of traditional rhetoric or those of formal linguistic structures to a language which can chart 'the permanent truths of desire' is a rhetorician's dream, even perhaps, a self-contradictory dream. For the standard criticisms of rhetoric lie in the rigidity with which terms and categories fit, and the ease with which poetic language so often eludes what looks like the clumsy and literal-minded reduction of figure in attributing to rhetorical terms their fixed explanatory value. Bloom is more imaginative and ambitious and seeks the understanding of poetry and prophecy in the very indeterminacy of figure which both naturally extends the power of description and blurs the features of any imaginable chart of relations.

Perhaps this pervasive problem frames the gap between Bloom's meditations on rhetoric and his attempts to apply his own rhetorical/ psychological descriptive terms. I have suggested that the central problem in assessing the ratios is that of determining their adequacy as descriptive language. And the supplement by way of Fletcher indicates the need for another operative vocabulary which might catch other dimensions of exactly what eludes a previous rhetoric – as fishermen may use nets of different fineness and shape of mesh. The relations of the cut of mesh may be difficult to give, but multiplication seems to add through what is implied by thresholds and crossings – before, across, after – a relational connective tissue not present in the ratios themselves. One keeps needing to describe or account for something in further and further ways, and the language of analysis must be continuously recharacterised and the scope of one's rhetorical terminology continually extended and revised.

In large-scale terms the ratios provide markers for the developmental stages of Ashbery's poem, which characterise the most important poetic features of the movements of mind of which Bloom sees it to be composed. In turn, the sequence of ratios sketches the progress of the poem and reveals its character as a total structure. Bloom assumes, perhaps correctly, that the six verse paragraphs contain separately definable moments of meditation, moments which he sees as embodying the ratios and which have their principal characterisation through them. Before looking at one or two of the uses of this it is perhaps worth noting that there is a way in which the identification of the ratio as the centre of such a movement has a solidly determinate effect which is uncharacteristic of Ashbery. It is not the sort of poem that so crisply makes out the discrete identity of movements of mind. Its very diffidence before the image in the mirror has the effect of making random moments of feeling and observation into an honest exercise of form.

Perhaps the rhetorical markers would be more clearly effective if the analysis were carried out with the detail and rigour which are announced. In fact, the use of the rhetorical structure of interlinked ratios is intermittent and much that is professed as the working out of a particular ratio moves quickly into another, more diverse, language which does not require the 'ratio' for its force. In some cases the ratio in question may be more consistently pressed upon us, but in others the obliquity is startling. Take *tessera*, the 'poetic transformation of such turning against the self' which he derives from 'A peculiar slant / Of memory that intrudes on the dreaming model / In the silence of the studio as he considers / Lifting the pencil to the self-portrait' (*DC*, p. 28). The movement of Bloom's own analysis is sketchy and analogic. By way of Dickinson's slant of light that imaged death, Coleridge's wounding sense of symbol, Anna Freud's defence mechanism turning against the self, we are supposed to reach the understanding that 'Ashbery, *as poet*, is compelled to present himself as being only a mutilated part of a whole already mutilated' (*DC*, p. 28). Now the issue in question is not whether all of this is far-fetched, but whether or not the notion of *tessera* both holds the various allusions together and creates a link between them and the passage.

It is not clear that it does either. In the passage the 'slant of memory' certainly qualifies the lifting of the pencil, and equally the way in which the voices of others infiltrate ourselves and subvert our identity or recompose it. The threat in the slant of light, the literalising of the Coleridgean wound are drawn from too far to illuminate or embody the poetic transformation of turning against the self. It is hard to see how *tessera* has any controlling force, or is even a useful string upon which to thread these diverse situations. And Ashbery's carefully wrought moves between yesterday, the self as it is today, the projection of self and its shadow into thoughts of tomorrow seems rather lost. And so indeed does *tessera*, for while Bloom picks it up again, it is after the argument has moved on, as if the mind still clung to the unassimilated example as the ratios shifted and the point of the examples became lost.

Of course one way of finding interest and value in much of this might easily come through the wide range of other ways of talking which subversively suggest themselves and are pervasively employed. The rhetorical concept is immersed in a context that does not arise from its own conceptual scheme. We may speak in many critical idioms of the evasion, uneasiness, repression, etc., which produce what Bloom charmingly calls a 'spooky Sublime'. And in practice the ratios are intermittently evoked, dropped, recovered and recast through the shift of examples which suggests that they are not entirely the unwobbling pivots. They are rather a tentative series of indications of what the psychological ground of a generalised poetics might look like if we were so rash as to try to characterise and use it. The theory-laden rhetoric is better at indicating its hypothetical intentions than at carrying them out. Its interest lies in a penumbral correlation between psychic process and forms of language, rather than its use as a critical instrument.

Yet the generalised poetic may distantly evoke what we can only discover through the poem. Or is it rather an extrapolated and abstracted idea of poetry, seen through an idealised and mystified poetics? In the mysterious depths behind the poem rather than the poem itself, in the presence of the poet as poet, not the mere John Ashbery, the implications of such depths and presences push the requirements of understanding beyond the interpretable structures of language with which an all too palpable rhetoric might be expected to concern itself. What is said about sublimation and desire brings us closest to this underlying 'evasion' of one's own project of charting the varied forms of figuration. In a sense, Bloom oscillates between the mysterious country of desire which lies behind the possibility of poetry, and the world of figures which is the vehicle for its expression. Which country can be mapped, and how fully? The language touches the buried 'depth in this demonic verse paragraph' of 'mysterious urgency', of the 'sublimation of unfulfillable poetic desires'. Perhaps it is in this reach for the impalpable that the self-contradictory character of this meta-rhetorical project displays itself. It is the reach beyond what can be described which is both quixotic and puts in question the more ordinary senses in which we may seek to describe.

A formula may lie behind this. The closer we come to a descriptive language that 'makes sense' the further we stray from the more general understanding that our quixotism requires, when the illusion of talking through the medium of an evolved rhetoric and psychology dissolves before the transcendent notion of the sublime. The push towards larger understanding that the full scope of 'theory' would involve us in might therefore imply the abandonment of the rhetorical categories as an interpretative language – indeed, to abandon interpretation insofar as it brings the poet into the humdrum world of ordinary speech where literal-minded questions such as 'what does it mean?' seem to require pedestrian and low-key explanations that are directly accessible and intelligible.

Both the new criticism and structuralism share the implied notion that there is some language into which the understanding of the poem can be translated that responds to our curiosity and informs our understanding, which is somehow intelligible – perhaps even clear – in a way in which the poem is mysterious and opaque. For the one perhaps it is a loosely conceived language of common sense, understood as part of the shared world of cultivated men, in which the difficulty and resistance of the metaphoric structures of poetry could find a recognisable place. And this was connected closely with the institutionalised academic teaching of criticism, with the pedagogical practice – or even sometimes art – of making the difficult accessible. For structuralism there was a technical, or quasi-scientific, framework of understanding, for which a developed descriptive vocabulary derived from structural linguistics posed clearly the type of understanding that could be attained. Whatever affective limitations it might have there is a direct appeal to a public language of explanation and a claim to the generality of a scientific model.

On the contrary, Bloom deepens the mystery and sinks the poem in its own depths. The rhetoric fashions not an interpreted world, but a series of nominal frameworks. Cultural crises, models of the mind, tropological features of the working of language, all create contexts and possible languages of explanation, but are not in fact used as such, and do not provide the frame in which the poems become intelligible in anything so quotidian as an interpreted world. They exist rather as features of the order of things, like the circles of the medieval heavens. And through these circles the poem passes like an eccentric meteor, seeking uncertainly for a borrowed light.

But in the view of this necessity the intellectual frames that are constitutive of theory, which might provide the ground of critical explanation, cut in two different ways. They both suggest the possibility of an explanatory system, and yet refuse it. Although the reasons seem different in the case of the two most important of these frames, the rhetorical and the psychological, or in effect the Freudian.

It is clear that the 'ratios' even when supplemented by the secondary rhetoric of crossings and thresholds can give no useful account of the sublime. Their very conception as relational descriptive devices precisely excludes them from any capacity to touch upon the transcendent character of the sublime. While Bloom has not said this, his actual use of them, or perhaps his failure to use them, has made this clear. Even if they were more fully and consistently applied they would simply be irrelevant. The failure lies not in their application, but in the conception itself, although the patchy and haphazard touches of application are evidence of the problem. And one cannot help but feel that behind this tortuous elaboration the rhetorical project and its theoretical implications have been tacitly abandoned.

The Freudian presence seems to Bloom the necessary condition of any discussion of language or art, but the meaning and the use of any precise aspect of Freudian theory is hardly considered. Freud is the 'condition of our time' whatever the value of anything in particular that he might have had to say, and the uncertainty as to what he might have said is accepted with an easy candour: 'Freud, who is indescribable as he is now inescapable'. In a literal sense it is probably true that Freud is part of our climate in a pervasive and indeterminate way. Yet it would seem that Bloom wants to do more than such a general evocation, that a direct use is envisaged for the Freudian 'sublime'. The central notion is certainly that of defence, treated partly as a variant of the Freudian notion of drives, and he quotes Freud that '"the theory of drives is so to say our mythology. Drives are mythical entities, magnificent in their indefiniteness."' And for drives Bloom simply substitutes defences. The indistinctness seems more valuable than any place fixed on the Freudian map of the mind. Certainly the notion of defence becomes gesturally sublime, in its mixture of rejection and fending off, like the wonderful description of Moses grasping the tablets of the law. And there is the 'priority of anxiety' which lies beyond the pleasure principle, no doubt a spur to the sublime gesture.

Of course Bloom is not responsible for Freud, and there is no reason that any dimension of his work should come into question except insofar as it informs our critical understanding. In this the Freudian sublime seems to be a figure in its own right, but one sufficiently indistinct as to operate beyond its own gesture of fending off – fending off among other things any possible reduction to whatever it might be that the interpreted dream was interpreted into. Rather than a series of keys to a hermeneutic code this Freud dramatises the resistance to mundane understanding, underwriting the psychic grounds of the poet's gestures of refusal. This at the same time universalises, yet points distinctly to the heroic unapproachable heights.

Ashbery is assimilated to Freudian man through the narcissicism of the mirror image, and by exemplifying through negation the Freudian sublime of the uncanny. Are we looking here at the mechanisms by which repression works, the negative gesture turning into self-effacing trope? Freudian negation is drawn into the ratio of *kenosis*, the poetics of giving up and discovery through absence. There are many astute remarks in all of this, say in the way that Ashbery's sublime, if such it is, is projected through uneasiness rather than transcendence. And it is perhaps the intrusion of the Freudian uncanny that assimilates the uneasy to what had been the transcendent. The Freudian uncanny or sublime points beyond the possibilities of interpretation.

In all of this Bloom reaches continually for the language of the unsayable, of what lies beyond our mediating prose, towards what might ideally turn critical language into visionary utterance. To this no commonplace criteria for the correspondence of text and commentary could be relevant, nor even the internal requirements of coherence or appropriateness of comparison. For every move would be consummated beyond the possibility of its saying. Those relational and even parasitical connectives to the original object of interest would be subsumed into the larger dimension of the critical sublime. And the ground of this, if such there need be, would be the interpretation of figure by figure. Here something at least distantly analogous to a deconstructive infinite regress begins to suggest itself, but one in which the refiguration finds a continual renewal, and the flow of descriptive vocabularies and explanatory systems is devoured in unlimited reshaping and reseeing. As in infinite regress there is no end to this process, and no limits beyond those of interest. And for Bloom this interest would be found in the agonistic sublime of the critic's struggle to deal with what lies beyond the limits of his own language.

This has its attractions, as well as its touch of absurdity, and, in the end, its *ennuis*. But what has it done to the theory that it has proposed? Is there a project for the refiguration of theory itself? Or does it somehow find its ultimate justification outside the area of its application, where meta-rhetorics can be re-created to add further accounts for the ever-increasing gaps between the language of poetry and our understanding? Perhaps beyond the critical sublime lies the theoretical sublime, where to the comedy of strong poems receiving strong readings, the strength of theory will also be measured by its intransigence in the face of those larger philosophical commitments which it might well assimilate. For if the 'breaking of form' is to be understood ultimately in a relational and systematisable way, surely the voices of both poetry and prophecy will have lost their force, the breaking will be absorbed in some smooth rationalisation, caught up in the entropic production of language games and systems which is as much part of our moment as any other form of crisis. Theorist and critic will need the authority of creation itself, and it is perhaps part of our own 'climate' that it will not be taken as insolence to equate the reading of Ashbery with Ashbery's 'reading of his tradition of utterance' as 'gestures of restitution' (*DC*, p. 37). Indeed, as for poetry, 'There is no reading worthy of being communicated with another unless it deviates to break form, twists the lines to form a shelter, and so makes meaning through that shattering of belated vessels'. But the equation is no more than indicated; we are at the threshold of the 'antithetical critic' if we have not yet wholly reached him.

Yet the grandeur of presumption has its own beauty. The antithetical critic has a central place in the cultural maelstrom. In this case the narrower task is to confront the self-eroding poverty of deconstruction – that infinite regress of negations. On the triviality of the ironising of irony Bloom is superb. But to find the antithetical critic in his act of restitution seems to draw much of its colouration from the equivalent of a cinematic montage where the faces of Parmigianino, Ashbery and Bloom are superimposed and fused together. Of course, the sense of the antithetical that I see most vividly is precisely what pushes these mingling figures apart – especially in the 'overdetermination' of Bloom and those elements of the indeterminate I see in Ashbery: between the rhetorical labelling systems and the psychological occult, the *force majeur* with which poem is fitted to category, fixing it like a gigantic fly in amber, and the mysterious moment of evasion and diffidence through which Ashbery indicates the depths that lie beyond the poem itself. And insofar as the antithetical critic is theory centred, and poetic theory places the imaginative work in its culturally antithetical role, the charm lies in the paradox that the greater the generality of this function the more fully illuminated the text – at least of any suitably belated poet of the uncanny sublime. Meanwhile, if Ashbery has eluded us, slipping away with the mirror's curve, what we have lost we could no doubt never have found, and the necessary public stance for our 'moment' will have been given a free-standing anamorphic life of its own.

# IV From 'so complex an irony' to 'such a textual logic'

The notion of a complex irony itself suggests a multiplicity of relations, and Empson's treatment of Shakespeare's sonnet number 94, 'They that have power to hurt and will do none', makes of the elaboration of irony its most powerful exploratory device, as well as using 'irony' as its central explanatory term. The multiple relations could, of course, be of many kinds, could involve concepts drawn from the most varied intellectual sources, with 'irony' itself expressing the subversive relationships that these might reflect upon each other. Yet it seems a difficult term to use in any schematised way – we are not tempted to 'seven types of irony', perhaps because something simply conceived becomes pervasively reflexive and extends itself through the kind of complication that eludes typology. This finds its first step in a recognition of the startlingly indeterminate: 'you can work through all of the notes in the Variorum without finding out whether flower, lily "owner", and person addressed are alike or opposed'. The scope of the task and the innate impossibility are faced directly: 'One would like to say that the poem has all possible such meanings, digested into some order, and then try to show how this is done, but the mere number of possible interpretations is amusingly too great'. The permutations of like and unlike yield '4096 possible movements of thought, with other possibilities'. I shall look in a later chapter at what such a ringing of changes might open up for us. Here I wish to stick within the terms of Empson's own line of thought, of 'honestly' considering 'what seems important'.[1]

Persuasion as to importance takes the form of a construction, which has the form and manner of paraphrase, but is really a caricature which distils a moral formula:

The best people are indifferent to temptation and detached from the world; nor is this state selfish, because they do good by unconscious influence, like the flower. You must be like them; you are quite like them already. But even the best people must be continually on their guard, because they become the worst, once they fall from their perfection ... (*VP*, p. 89)

Caveats and qualifications follow. But this little sketch will stand as the nucleus of something which is necessary to further explanation, a ground for the exploration of the play of ironies to come. I think he is trying to catch a balance here between something which seems simple until one's apprehension of possibilities takes over, and the vertiginous affect of these possibilities qualifying each other. The sketch for all its simplicity, and the rather disarming way of saying, in effect 'yes, there are people like this', provides a pivotal point for trying out the way the figures work, of putting to the test the ways in which 'the summer's flower is to the summer sweet'. The metaphor calls for its point of reference, a perhaps imaginary touchstone for the working of language.

Again, the 'root of the ambivalence' turns upon the variety and uncertainty of human character, on the presumed fascination which 'gives its immediate point to the profound ambivalence about the selfishness of the flower ... in its beauty, vulnerability, tendency to excite thoughts about the shortness of life, self-centredness, and power in spite of it to give pleasure ... ' (*VP*, p. 91). A series of correspondences is evolving in which the natural associations of the flower, a reflexive set of associations in which man and nature draw upon each other, are fitted to the invention of a person. And with this hypothetical character, which aspect of a comparison explains which? The 'uses of biography' here operate through a fictional Shakespeare and W. H. (and certainly, Southampton) which draw not on any knowledge we may have of them – far too fragmentary and unsatisfactory in any case – but simply on the assumption that persons must have existed in whom such ambivalence is instanced. Even if we knew more of author and circumstances we should need to reinvent them in the poem's terms, in terms even of 'the summer's flower'. Which is perhaps both to abandon intentionalism and to retain it.

The impression is of an extraordinary variety of styles of language and movements of mind brought together with an uncanny concentration, as if the magnetic force of the poem reassembled and reordered many dimensions of thought in a field created by it. Implications of terms might reach further but are hardly allowed to do so. The play upon the sexual ambiguities of the lilies that fester might find its Freudian placement, but nothing is said about it. The 'philosophical critic' as Eliot once called him seems deeply reticent about the use of any concept or abstraction that might qualify him for such a role. The development is rather by way of a descriptive language which turns into an extended alternative version of the inner life of the poem. The stages follow the patterns of the possibilities of implied relationship, tension, conflict, and the implications of the verbal manipulation by which these are brought into a strange equilibrium or even, uneasy resolution. Such turning of one's back on any acknowledgement of intellectual preconceptions may be puzzling and ultimately somewhat deceptive. Certainly its dramatic effect is that of an immediacy of participation, a mixture in the first instance, at least of the direct and almost unmediated presence of the text with a reassuring diffidence and tentativeness in the face of 'the vague and generalised language of the descriptions, which might be talking about so many sorts of people as well as feeling so many things about them, [and which] somehow makes a unity like a crossroads, which analysis does not deal with by exploring down the roads ... ' (*VP*, p. 90)

I have already mentioned how difficult it is to give any precise sense to the use of 'analysis' in Leavis, and the notion of 'analysis' here hangs in the air uncertainly with a hint that it itself might be different if it had taken the paths not followed. Insofar as it is a breaking down of the verbal – largely figurative – complexity of the poem in order to find a way to its meaning and force, Empson's own path is indirect. There is an uncertain feeling of one's way into the inner conflict of the poem, a reaching for 'what seems important' by way of a reconstruction, which does not really seem like an analysis at all, but the working out of an alternative picture. It is rather a building up process than a breaking down, the creation of a complex image of how that conflict might be seen. There may be a way in which it resembles and paraphrases, but as before, it does so quite unusually because what it carries out is almost the opposite of what paraphrase usually does: the reduction of the complex and puzzling to the simplified and easily assimilated. A summary might suggest such a reduction yet function otherwise:

I must try to sum up the effect of so complex an irony half by trying to follow it through a gradation. 'I am praising to you the contemptible things you admire, you little plotter; this is how the others try to betray you through flattery; yet it is your little generosity though it shows only as lewdness, which will betray you; for it is wise to be cold, both because you are too inflammable and because I have been so much hurt by you who are heartless; yet I can the better forgive you through that argument from our common isolation; I must praise to you your very faults, especially your selfishness, because you can only now be safe by cultivating them further; yet this is the most dangerous of necessities; people are greedy for your fall as for that of the great; indeed no one can rise above common life, as you have done so fully, without in the same degree sinking below it; you have made this advice real to me, because I cannot despise it for your sake; I am only sure that you are valuable and in danger.' (*VP*, pp. 100–101)

Within the narrative fragment which so poses as summary there is the hint of a variety of other forms: a letter, a confession or fragment of autobiography, a case-history, and of course a drama, a more grandly scaled realisation of conflict. The very 'gradation' of 'so complex an irony' implies an ascending curve in which the heightening of feeling pushes outwards from the constraints of form. Why indeed not convert an aspect of a Shakespearean sonnet into such a full-scale drama as the internal dramatic structure in such a work leaves open to one? Only quite separately and by analogy is any opening of this kind made. In the second part of the essay the outward movement is at least touched upon, in the expanding of dramatic contexts. One moves outwards from a situation to the possibilities of the 'cold person' as a dramatic type, through Angelo and Prince Hal. But does this do anything to turn these dramatic extensions back upon the sonnet, or bring them to bear directly in an interpretative way? We may follow up the further possibilities of the type into what becomes an extended Shakespearean thematics by a process of exploring analogies, which stretch progressively further from the original case. (And we may regret the absence of further stretches still that would take us into *Troilus*, those suggestions about Troilus himself, or the collectivity of the Greek army.) Where do the stretches stop? How far do they take us, with increasing or diminishing value, from the original case?

Certainly there is some unease in the possibilities of outward stretch (a passing qualm about the vertigo of 'Empsonian irresponsibility'?) which qualifies the dramatic extension. 'It is only partly true that this untidy process, if successful, might tell one more about the original situation; discoveries of language and feeling made from a personal situation may develop themselves so that they can be applied to quite different dramatic situations; but to know about these might tell one more about the original discoveries.' (*VP*, p. 102). This implies a movement outward from the personal to the dramatic which becomes doubly reflexive as the two sorts of case are used to illuminate each other. But such a double process implies both conviction carried in the moments of stretch, and in the characterisation of the original nucleus. For the latter seems to act as ground, but only one which is stable through the working out of one's exploratory fiction, or through the more explicit public drama. So in effect two stories reflect upon each other: the inner, invented tale of the 'little plotter', and a dramatic action containing Prince Hal or Angelo, which may itself be reinvented further.

The openness of the procedure allows extensions of a variety of kinds to play back upon the original 'situation'. The analogy with Hal could lead to the exploration of the notion of power. And the evocation of the plot provides another dimension to the sonnet's mood of bitter complaisance; the young man must still be praised and loved, however he betrays his intimates. ... 'So I shall now fancy Falstaff as Shakespeare ... and Henry as the patron who has really betrayed him' (*VP*, p. 104). But the sonnets here are mentioned in the plural and Empson does seem to assume a situation of the sonnets. This gives him some freedom to juxtapose imagery of clouds and sun, although these may be too much of a rhetorical commonplace to take us very far. If the case of Prince Hal works it is untidily, and depends on something more inferential than the direct correspondence of imagery. That of Angelo seems a stretch of a different kind, where the hypocrisy has a different function, and the notion of power seems compromised, perhaps fatally, by its own dramatic context.

Is the resemblance too distant to give the point any substantial interest? The criteria here are as difficult to state as the path of our intellectual curiosity is to predict. However the problem of the criteria for acceptable resemblance is less important here than judging the effect of narrative substitution. If one narrative in effect stands in for another, what kind of explanation is achieved? Do we have some interaction between these extended sketches which is analogous to the 'process of interaction between metaphors, which acts like a generalisation ... '? One has the suggestion of these concrete and vivid elements of language generating a general understanding and perhaps a general truth. Is it simply a working out of 'The summer's flower is to the summer sweet'? One can see how far such a figure can take us as it complicates through the poem's multiple contexts. Could something similar come from these sketches that imply a substantial narrative, containing a chain of conclusions about kinds of people? Perhaps Empson need not be directly answerable for this latter, but the pictures drawn may make of description something which functions as an extended metaphor with larger claims.

It might look as if interaction of this kind also plays into the hands of irony, as it has no very specifiable limit, no built-in direction indicated by the interaction itself, as if the process itself had no limits. In this it seems to strain against the concept of genre, or in this case of the genre in question, of pastoral, which derives its character from limitation. 'In pastoral you take a limited life and pretend it is a full and normal one, and a suggestion that one must do this with all life, because the normal is itself limited ... ' (*VP*, pp. 114–15). So Empson seems to be working with a double set of guidelines, one of which moves off, in an indeterminate way, towards the unpredictable or incalculable interactions of the working of figurative language, and the other that seeks the outlines of a controlling and limiting idea, derived, not entirely clearly, from the way in which genre suggests a shape, a built-in set of limitations. The literary whole in turn reflects a form of life, or at least the sense of the necessary limitations of life which are shaped through the genre. And the dynamic of *Some Versions of Pastoral* lies in the play of the incalculable possibilities of language against the limitation the idea imposes – a continuous trying and pressuring, although sometimes expressed with a startling casualness.

The effect of irony itself lies in such a continuing and destabilising pressure. And part of the richness of this effect can be shown in the variable turns in which irony itself can be seen. It is by turns, 'grave', 'subtle' and 'complex'. 'Grave' conveys a sense of depth, of the importance with which one's awareness of ironic implication permeates the poem and carries its force; 'subtle' suggests something of the way in which ironies double back on each other, so that one effect of irony in fact conceals another, that what one thought cut in one way cuts in others as well; and 'complex', as one has seen, implies directly the multiplicity of relationships. These latter two seem to represent that 'process of interaction', or at least aspects of it, which push against the possibility of limit, seeing the possibilities of irony in an open-ended way, accumulating more dimensions as the interplay of its possibilities is more fully seen. 'Grave' represents irony in the fullness of its measure, of irony seen through to the end, with its force going to the heart of things.

I will return to further problems in the critical use of irony, but here there is a triple aspect which Empson has fully employed without attempting to define, or indeed to schematise. There is no attempt to follow or qualify the established divisions, say between verbal and dramatic irony, perhaps partly because the former would involve verbal effects only intelligible in context, and the latter a series of stock devices (such as peripeteia) in dramatic situations which could be classified in terms of the mechanics of their action, but not in terms of subtlety or depth. In any case the equation of verbal and situational elements works through a mixture of fusion and differentiation, as the mind moves from the summer's flower to the 'little plotter' and back again.

It is the image of the crossing point which returns as the focus of moments of fusion or interaction, but also in which metaphor shows how 'the contradictory elements in the relation are brought out and opposed absolutely, so that we cannot know their proportions in real life' (*VP*, p. 102). The fact that the roads lead to analogous situations in the plays both sends us to them, yet pulls us up, returning us to the ironic nexus. The temptation to follow certain roads, to turn back, point to another without taking it, to continually redress the balance of directions in which one might move while allowing for one's own freedom of choice in the face of all of them, is represented as a mixture of temptation and assessment, of following with reservations, of 'possible movements of thought' which give to criticism the continuous sense of trying – and projecting a state of restless activity. (More exploratory perhaps, and less doggedly purposive than the sense of activity in Leavis.)

This in a sense is an implied portrait of a mental process, of the mind forced into complex movement by the need of understanding, in the shifting of focal lengths, alteration of degrees of involvement, rather than following the single road to 'get one plain meaning'. An activity is underway in which no fixed pathway can be confidently assigned, beyond feeling one's way among possible movements of mind towards what 'seems important'. Like 'relevance' in Leavis there are no specifiable grounds and importance is defined if at all through the shaping of first the preliminary, then the summary, fictions. Perhaps 'relevance' invokes a group of pre-selected aspects of contexts in such social and moral terms as to suggest the concealed premise, while 'importance' combines the criteria for a successful, coherent fiction with a judgement about its heuristic force.

Irony as a speculative instrument conceals its speculative dimension, and finds its effect through the power of continuous variation where reinvention could be extended, substituting adjustments or alternative versions of the invented figure. The process is one of finding in persons, in the subtle but distinct features of human character, one's illuminating metaphor, one's created figure which is a key to the figurative language of the poem. But the possibility is always there that plotters of other kinds could be evoked in spinning out the alternative narratives, that there is always an aspect of character which is hidden, which eludes us and which if suitably revealed and articulated would qualify or falsify what was understood before. And the irony consists in the capacity to see the one through the other, to understand that to every surface the language presents to us something other may lie adjacent or behind. It is the acceptance of open-endedness, not simply in contemplating 4096 possible movements of mind, but in contemplating the culled and important few in the light of qualifying possibility.

It is perhaps through this awareness of the rich uncertainty of human nature, while using the reference to persons in what becomes as near as one can possibly come to an ultimate term of explanation, that some doubt is cast on the authority of any determinates in trying to come to a satisfactory explanation of a poem like 'They that have power ... This resembles what Norris identifies as 'the sceptical and self-qualifying habit of Empson's mind. He seems constantly on the verge of defining the complex implications, verbal or generic, which might satisfy, by somehow pinning down, his sense of the poem's richness. Yet he constantly relegates this purpose, detecting behind these provisional structures a series of ironies and "placing" attitudes which prevent their treatment as an integrating function of form.'[2] But why is 'defining' or 'pinning down' so alien to the entire enterprise? I think it is partly through a recognition of a radical incompleteness with which the language of the poem presents its world; it is not merely lack of knowledge, or whatever deficiencies our distant perspective may involve, but something intrinsically unstable at the heart of the poem, before which we recognise again and again the tentative and partial nature of whatever attempts at understanding we may make. And this is mirrored in the language of criticism itself where approximation is accepted in the closest reading, discontinuity in the tightest sequence, the mixture of necessity and contingency in the fragile analogues by which we construct a picture of relative and partial intelligibility. We can force an oblique light into a depth that will always recede before us.

It is for reasons like this that irony has its greatest power as a critical instrument through that constant shifting of movements of mind; the implement which reveals critical uncertainty is also the best vehicle of explanation for this set of intersecting points where metaphor and the possible aspects of possible persons – 'so many sorts', as there are of purity and its corruption, desire, affection, dependence, deception and fascination – join in a descriptive enterprise where the figure of the text and the invented model exist reciprocally. In such an enterprise it may not matter if the conjunction of image and person strains our credibility. If the summary 'gradation' stretches the bounds of easy recognition, we can accept the figurative as pure instrument, imaginative if not speculative. It too, of course, is radically incomplete, and the sense of unfinished business hangs over the whole project. Are we not only at about 'movement' three, and feeling that we may have in some sense been victims of our own extravagance and gone somewhat too far? But in its incompleteness the essay itself incarnates the unstable mixture of possibility and limit which Empson has found in pastoral. If in imitating this the critical voice finds any characteristic sense of itself it is in the relation between the multiple possibilities and seeing how far one might reasonably go, in finding through one's own form a working equilibrium – seeing the centrifugal effect of the movements of mind, yet gathering them up and holding them, for a moment at least, in the mind's eye.

If we were to seek to construct such a procedure into something resembling what Julia Kristeva has called a 'textual logic' it would find its logical centre in the mapping of those relations through which the centrifugal forces were contained, in finding a more explicit and conceptual language for those tentative and perhaps arbitrary steps along the roadways that lead from the complex irony to its understanding and which one may perhaps master by refusing to follow. I do not pretend that either 'logic' or 'textual' would have precisely the same meaning in the context from which I have drawn them in Kristeva's work, although relating language, procedures and critical understanding will be at least sufficiently analogous that the alternative senses will be enabled to show something further about what such terms could possibly do for us, how such a conception of a 'textual logic' can be transformed from an aspect of the internal workings of poetic language to an indication about the critical procedures that explore them.

In doing this I shall draw only narrowly and partially on the vast matter and elaborate structures of *The Revolution in Poetic Language*, and try to capture the operational manner in which the 'textual logic' is unfolded about one or two aspects of 'the "mystery" of Mallarmé'. This selectivity will in a sense go against the spirit of the work for its concern lies not in any separable Empsonian moment of contemplation and puzzlement before the interest and difficulty a poem has posed, but in giving a totalised account of a pervasive change in poetic language which must be seen – irony and ambivalence included – in the total 'mystery' which that language contains. And yet, in a further movement, that 'mystery' is only part of the complex transformation of human consciousness represented in the poetic revolution in question. It is largely conceived as a focal point in a more general scheme, yet a point which can at least be tentatively isolated as described, and in doing so be seen as revealing the heart of the transformation of poetic language. Yet this heart can only be captured through the range of its outward reach, its appeal to and implication in the whole of the human situation in its social, economic, sexual, psychological, symbolic etc. dimensions. Here is a simple outrunner in the process of trying to focus this mystery through the centrality of the feminine, in which the mystery can pivot on a corresponding enigma:

We have already indicated that the 'mystery' of Mallarmé is in the semiotic function underlying language, this *chora* whose rhythm tears the syntactical guarantee of meaning and introduces beneath the text a 'music'. But Mallarmé himself, 'playing the game, freely albeit as a minor pastime', has made clear what is the meaning and the sense (that is to say, the denotation and the place of utterance) that produce this 'mysterious' musicality. It is about woman, about the castration that she represents, and about the power that this confers on her to release, through a trauma, in a subject, the semiotic process, and with it, an ecstatic climax. Mallarmé formulates this *Bedeutung* [meaning] of his poetic activity like this: ' ... revealing our Lady and Patron to show her unfolding or her emptiness, in the light of a few dreams, as the measure to which everything is reduced'.

One will not exaggerate in saying that the whole meaning of the Mallarméan texts, insofar as one can unify it, comes down to this 'unfolding and emptiness' represented by woman, intrinsic to the sexual climax ... [3]

And therefore:

One will be able to read each text of Mallarmé as the dramatic representation of the feminine enigma ....We will only mention a few of the aspects taken by this substitutive effect of the woman-metaphor of ecstatic climax. It will permit us to bring together Mallarméan texts with signifying practices of antiquity – the mysteries – in order to bring out, in turn, the subjective and social functions of such a textual logic. (*RLP*, p. 474)

Without attempting a total unpacking, perhaps a simplified list of the kinds of elements of the analysis would be useful to the steps that follow, indicating some features of what she says are themselves 'only some of the aspects' of the enigma, and try to bring together the inner and outer functions of the textual logic.

Here are some simplified, and perhaps rather short-circuited, steps:

(1) In the language of poetry there is an underlying semiotic process, working in a space where the rhythm tears at the syntactic guarantee of meaning and introduces the subversive music of the sub-text.

(2) This tearing which lies at the centre of Mallarmé's 'mysterious musicality' is represented by him through 'the feminine enigma' and 'woman' enters into this process through the castration she incarnates. The consequence of this trauma opens our consciousness in terms of semiotic activity and leads ultimately to a form of ecstasy which mingles the sexual and transcendental, the ultimate force possible to the poem.

(3) Hence the feminine in its role of vehicle for this representation of opening up, of emptiness and absence ('dehiscence et lacune'), is the supreme power, 'Lady and Patron' of the art of poetry.

(4) Hence all Mallarméan texts can be seen in terms of this central representation.

(5) And the metaphorical extension of this matrix leads to the linking of inner and outer in a combination which moves from language to psyche to society, and conveys the logic of the text – 'such textual logic' – as a series of such relations.

This is of course a transposition into my own language, if necessary from my point of view, and a transposition to be recast when I look later at another version of the problem of poetry's use of absence and emptiness in Derrida's treatment of the blank spaces on Mallarmé's page. Perhaps it will sound even more alien if one describes the Mallarméan project as one of self-consciously capturing that impalpable inner world which ordinary language does not touch, with the essence of poetry the reaching out to what cannot be said. The indirect paths through which the language of poetry both says and does not say may use the notion of the feminine as the ground of a kind of drama (of which each text is the dramatic representation). So the concept itself becomes a form of personification, in whose very character is implicit the dramatic interplay of lack and of a supreme orgasmic moment. The language of psychoanalysis will be used to fill out this personification, to create an area of psychodynamics which is relational and explanatory.

While there are extensions and variants which enrich and elaborate, the simplest underlying structure is three-way: the movement from features of language that can be semiotically described, to features of the psyche expressed in psychoanalytic language, to public dimensions which have their economic and social determinants. And these relations are reversible, can be read in both directions, or indeed in several. The 'textual logic' is reflexive.

So the formula of Lévi-Strauss 'Who says man says language, and who says language says society' can be reversed. Perhaps such an understanding is banal enough, but one possible aspect of such a reversal seems to surface in practice, in an awareness that 'man' in the abstract is too thin a form of representation, and therefore there must be persons invented to explain the features of language itself. In Kristeva the movement towards formal analysis in which the characteristics of language can be given in terms of the internal workings of a system is cut by the necessity of balancing descriptions in which analogous relations appear in human terms. This is partly done through the psychoanalytic language itself, partly through a form of fictionalising which works out the relations of the shadowy feminine figures of Mallarmé (Hérodiade etc.), to the use of explanatory schemes that expand upon them. Yet Kristeva's persons cling to that abstraction 'man', or especially 'woman', while Empson's, if equally hypothetical, are the imagining of what might have all of the solidity, if further ambiguity, of a Shakespeare, or Southampton, or simply someone we have had the bad luck to know.

One can see a similar extension of Kristeva's method in the handling of the diagrammatic analysis of 'Un coup de dés': the sequence 'A Throw of the Dice' is already putting into consecutive words a passive trans-formation. The constituent phrase is 'X throws the dice' (*RLP*, pp. 276–91). The 'X' is of course invented, perhaps on the reasonable ground that dice do not throw themselves. Yet the invention of 'X' suggests both the necessity of a human sequence involving causality and of an implied syntax within the poem's ostensive evasion of it. Although we are far from the Empsonian *dramatis personae*, the effectively real fiction required for 'A Throw of the Dice' is an implied subject for the sequence of connections the poem has been at pains to suppress. The elaboration of the ship-wreck and other fragments of suppressed narrative remain, like the throw, indeterminate steps in a mental process, finding a shape in the sides of the die itself ' ... which makes possible a constellation, a trans-linguistic device turning the semiotic into the symbolic, the game into the argument, chance into unity .... In sum, the text breaks the lines of the normative phrase and substitutes for it a syntactic polymorphism' (*RLP*, pp. 287–288).

The commentary on such a poem necessarily lives out its own paradoxical task. Insofar as the poem is to be made intelligible, 'explained' however brilliantly or badly, the very things that the poem avoids or suppresses are necessarily reinvented and articulated. However closely or loosely it may correspond to the 'text' it enters into a more conventional set of syntactic relations. If Mallarmé's obliquity is expressed in difficulty, a refusal of readability, avoidance, discontinuity, absence, emptiness, these find form in the fragments of consciousness designed to incarnate them: Hérodiade and her nurse, a satyr, Igitur, etc. And these in turn require further construction, a figuration which brings us closer to the common stock-in-trade of languages with more fixed relations and referents.

Certainly the poem itself poses a difference which pushes a limit of critical explanation. The disposition of particular words creates a radical ambiguity through the uncertainty of relevant modification. 'By the arrangement of the page, which makes the syntactic function of particular items ambiguous, Mallarmé indicates that the position of the elements determines their semantic and syntactic values beyond their presumed category' (*RLP*, p. 282). This, of course, is quite different from Empsonian ambiguity where the difficulty is derived from the claims of multiple contexts – as we have seen, at least up to 4096 possible movements of thought are determined by contextual decisions. Here the positioning, the blanks and spacing deliberately build another order of uncertainty where contextual determination is deliberately suppressed. Rather than 4096 possibilities it is more like zero to infinite. But the effect is that, in 'A Throw of the Dice', a radical uncertainty of meaning has become part of the meaning in a sense that sets out to defeat any decision about the possibility of honestly deciding what is important.

What I have described as a three-way set of correspondences by which language, psyche and society are seen in terms of each other, poses in Kristeva's handling of them a series of potential shifts in the level at which explanation occurs, and the interest in this often develops in terms of the intrinsic interest of the explanatory schemes themselves. Consider the shift with respect to 'mystery' in its linking of a subjective and social function. We have been drawn from the 'mystery of Mallarmé' in terms of a problem of poetic language where the underlying music shreds the syntactic guarantee of meaning, to mysteries which are 'signifying practices of antiquity'. What is the force of 'bring together' in this passage? Are we to deal with a double text, one of Mallarmé and one of some structural characteristics of particular mysteries? The ground of the correspondence is never quite clear, for the remarks on initiation rites which follow seem pursued largely for their own sake, and the notion of 'mystery' is handled at such a global level of generality that the possibility of direct relevance seems lost in its very scope. 'Within the mystery, woman represents that heterogeneity susceptible of violating the social code...' In pure anthropological terms this cannot be the case in other than restricted and highly qualified senses. In any large analogy with the role of the language of poetry in subverting social codes this seems to hang on the vaguest of resemblances. The method of super-imposing schema on schema means their exploration for their own sake, and the text of Mallarmé becomes the still point of a turning mass drawn from half a dozen systems of knowledge.

This reflects the structure of a project where the meeting point of multiple frames of reference is the essential constituent of the architectural whole. To a certain extent what is complex in matter and dense in argument contains distinct threads that are simple and clear. But the surface complexity stands out. *The Revolution in Poetic Language* is constructed rather like the Beaubourg, with all of its functional features, its framework, struts, conduits, heating pipes, ventilators on the exterior, so all of its working aspects are continuously present. What looks like a digression or centrifugal move is merely a cross-reference to another aspect of an all-encompassing intellectual frame. We can complicate the series of correspondences already suggested: language, psyche and society also embrace history, anthropology, history of religions, economics, with somewhere an ultimate, if also often tangential, point of reference, acting both as a crux and a clue, in the literary text. But this crux, and clue, may be the central point of a *logic* which cannibalises and employs other logics, and this 'ultimate point of reference' is only such in being an occasion rather than a ground. The text is not the basis on which other things come to rest in a fixed point of ontological stability, but rather the point of departure, as well as variable centre, where in the theory at least of the *textual* the multiple eyebeams cross. All of the sources of this focal point themselves exist in language, in independent discourses as necessary and as contingent as poetry itself. If for the moment, often a moment that slips uneasily past in the course of 700 pages, the special features of poetic language catch the critical working of the circumscribing languages, it is with the effect of unfolding their own character as a fully articulated dimension of the cultural matrix.

If, indeed, in any sense, 'A book is a machine to think with ... ' Kristeva's shows well-articulated machinery with an integrated intention behind it. Richards apologises for the 'lengthy excursion into theory of value, or into general psychology', partly because of the unfamiliarity of the ground, partly because of the felt uncertainty of the connection. By contrast Kristeva's multiple frames seem to belong to the same general enterprise, substantially through the implied connections given by the focus of historical crisis.

From the point of view of understanding, the frames exist as concentric circles around the text, of variable distances to be sure, and with an interchangeability as to the most immediate proximity. And the centre of attention may well not be the still point of the text, but the relations among elements of the frame. The variables of positioning continually change the focus. For the centre shifts – the discourses play upon each other, and the form of 'intertextuality' they suggest is one that deflects outward as well. The evocation of interdependence mingles with the character they have in their own right. For they may operate as perspectives in the manner of Booth or Abrams. But their presence is more active and more substantive. The movement from historical to psychoanalytic to linguistic spreads out reflexively. Mallarmé is often only present by implication, and may move on/off stage as the shifts of the centre require, like a final cause whose universe spins outward according to many laws. So an attempt to use particular texts as the continuous critical point of reference would be to concentrate on textual interpretation in a narrow and alien way. Hence, to ask, for example, how crucial to the understanding of any particular text of Mallarmé is the acceptance of the role of symbolic castration in ego-formation, is somehow to put the matter wrongly – to adopt an alien language-game.

The historical context predominantly shapes the whole. What we are observing through poetic language is the break-up of a social code enshrined in a traditional rhetoric, and inherited conceptions of what constitutes sense in language and suitability of figurative decor. The revolutionary refusal of poetry to participate in a deadening and repressive bourgeois order is manifested in the dislocation of syntax, in negativity, in *rupture* (sharp breaks); and in the power of *jouissance* (climactic pleasure), which in its excess, ecstasy, etc. is not assimilable to the traditional code. Much of this draws on the commonplaces of the development of French poetry from the 1850s, from Nerval through Rimbaud and Mallarmé himself. Yet the connections formed in the break-up of any such 'code' rest upon extension, and speculative extrapolation from linguistic features to implications at a high level of generality. No doubt, to ask too closely about the role of '*jouissance*' in Mallarmé's texts themselves, for all of the richness of ambiguity in the complex symbolic action, would be somewhat crass. It would be to single out an aspect of the figure in the carpet that is really only visible in terms of other aspects, and defined by other figures. '*Rupture*' is treated more as a pervasive feature of a semiotic field than as something locatable in a particular text which can help focus our understanding of that text.

The texts in question therefore do not present themselves as part of any final truth but as markers and indicators, as transformational 'practices'. We do not so much read Mallarmé through the multiple surrounding frames, as use him to embody and define the significant changes in those aspects of the world that the frames themselves describe. So one must remember, if it sometimes seems that Kristeva's text itself is swamped by the proliferating Freudian jargon, and lost to view beneath the subsequent speculation, that the Freudian language is less an end than an occasion. The text itself has become the interpretative device; the light flows from it on the composite world of which it is a symptom and for which it is a clue. We have in a sense invented dimensions of persons, if in abstract and highly generalised terms, to fill out our understanding of the poem in order that the poem may feed the system through which persons are examined and explained. So, when one says 'One would be able to read each text of Mallarmé as a dramatic representation of the feminism enigma ... ' the act of 'reading as' establishes a reciprocity in which one moves outwards from the text to the general enigma, yet back to the point of reference which the text provides – with the 'scene' itself constructed of those frames through which the understanding of the text is conceptualised.

Similarly the Mallarméan concept of the literary work itself is alien to the world of normal powers and institutions, which precisely makes it a danger to those powers. Any analysis of its intrinsic nature would have to embrace this mixture of apartness and subversive action. Mallarmé's very conception requires dual, or multiple, languages that move between intentionally reclusive features of the text and the dimensions of the world in which it participates in spite of itself. To what extent should we call these quite separate and different operations 'critical' languages? Perhaps in this context we are indifferent to the sort or degree of stretch the pressures on such a concept would require. Some formulations might account for the indeterminate character. Consider Paul de Man's assertion that 'the notion of crisis and that of criticism are very closely linked, so much so that one could state that all true criticism occurs in the mode of crisis'.[4] 'Mode' is a flexible word, and one will consider 'crisis' in another context. But here it links its Mallarméan ancestry in 'The Crisis of Poetry' with the global structure of Kristeva's project: crisis in language, crisis in psychic structures, crisis of political and economic forces, all embodied in the poetic texts of the moment when 'the act of writing is scrutinised right to its origins'.

Can we adapt such a consideration to *Some Versions of Pastoral* as well? We have looked at it on the level of detail which its method requires. And the general design takes us to a genre which mixes formal aspects with historically derived conventions, a mixture which Empson sees clearly as inherently unstable and continuously readapted. The few, usually rather off-hand, general remarks about the genre formulate this in different terms. In the context of *The Beggar's Opera*: 'It is this clash and identification of the refined, the universal, and the low that is the whole point of pastoral'

(*VP*, p. 50). 'Clash' and 'identification' summarise that meeting of opposites that, from Guarini on, have made the genre a disputed ground. It is the implicit challenge to orders of appropriateness, where the necessary resolution is both an instance of order but runs contrary to established order that makes it a natural vehicle of conflict. Norris is right to see this in widely social terms, although those terms are not as easily focused conceptually as those of Kristeva's revolution. This is partly by way of Empson's reticence with respect to general formulae, partly through the unsystematic darting about through unrelated historical contexts, and partly through the way in which pastoral appears indirectly in those cases that give it a cumulative if uncertain shape. But the use of pastoral certainly suggests a system of relations for the inner and outer dimensions of what we could reasonably enough call crisis.

In 'They that have power' this is explored through the extension of the possibilities of irony to the point that the pastoral necessity of resolution and of limit is almost an arbitrary imposition in the name of sanity. The vertigo of irony must be contained. 'Man is so placed that the sort of thing you do is in degree all that anyone can do; success does not come from mere virtue, and without some external success a virtue is not real even to itself' (*VP*, p. 114) Infinite possibility ends up in a 'queer sort of realism'. One must accept the establishment of one's social being, as a critic must honestly decide what is important. And if pastoral is a matter of putting the complex into the simple (*VP*, p. 23) this realism of appraisal does not abolish the ironies but subsumes them in a recognition of 'some limited life'. A sense of limit forced on the critic himself by the necessity of creating a reasonable description corresponds to the working through of possibilities that versions of pastoral may give form.

If the sense of pastoral is not developed through further explanations of an abstract kind, it nevertheless shows the operation of a controlling concept evolving out of the most apparently diverse of cases, with a quite disarming lack of interest in making grandiose claims, or arriving at far-reaching conclusions. There is a circling about and working through of the unresolved element in the case with only the most diffident indication that there is a general subject to be addressed with a systematic explanation. Yet in another way this is deceptive: the conception is there and poses the three-way relation of a genre with the cultural conventions that accompany it, a vision of the inner life that such a genre is best tuned to reveal, and a sense of the form of a world where social demands require a subtle series of adjustments. But the triple forms have no schematic existence in their own right beyond the cases from which they have been derived. To seek out their form is to examine and re-examine the cases themselves. If we were to invent for Empson his 'textual logic' it would rest not on the presumed interlocks of three different types of schematism, but on the descriptive language which evokes the implicit connections on the concrete ground of the case in question, or on the force of the analogies that arise out of them. And our judgement of them would depend both upon the felt presence of the text and the value of where these analogies lead us.

This is of course not to point towards a literalist use of descriptive language, or some tidy correspondence theory of the relation between descriptions and the texts they are meant to describe. It is simply that the comparisons, the analogies, the extrapolations, the fictions are visible in terms of those texts, rather than having an alternative life in another intellectual framework from which they might be derived. Thus we judge of the interest of the 'little plotter' in terms of Shakespeare's sonnet and the way in which it extends the contours of what we see as Empson's project, but not in terms of whether or not it makes plausible use of psychoanalytic theory, or of possible biographical or historical conjecture. And we may find him illuminating, preposterous though he may also be: illuminating in that suggestive filling out of the possibilities of the poem, whether or not carrying any very powerful conviction. One can see bits that are clearly wrong, and equally are valuable.

If, again, one reflects on the 'crossroads', it enacts as a figure one of Empson's strongest claims about the working of metaphor: 'this process of interaction between metaphors which acts like a generalization ... ' (*VP*, p. 102) implies that extended understanding which generalization is meant to claim. But it does so in resisting the movement down one of the possible roads to find 'one plain meaning'. Is it this very resistance that makes metaphorical interaction a working substitute for conceptual general-isation, but a substitute that avoids the very explanatory ease which would arise from the single road taken? If so, it would be by refusing to release us into that conceptual field, but would return us to that nexus which the text has created. The operative effect of these intersection points is to insist that the many directions are only of interest to us in terms of each other.

I have argued that Kristeva follows many roads by way of conceptual languages which simultaneously delineate the multiple aspects of the revolution. Further, the use of these languages has a synoptic force, implying that the combination of these approaches, all of which are seen to complement each other, would give a comprehensive account of the matter. Looking at the possibilities of irony in Empson is a process of separating out, of making distinctions – if also using that fusion of opposites that such concrete hypotheses as the invention of persons may allow. Kristeva's vision is of a totality, and two questions arise as to its viability. The first is whether or not the analysis of such a thematic element as the feminine in Mallarmé loses its critical dimension in the very movement through those psychoanalytic, sociological and other languages that develop it. The second, perhaps consequent on the other, is whether or not the totalisation is possible, whether or not the multiple languages in question add up to a 'logic' in any intelligible way. And would such a 'logic' be merely the sum of its parts, something merely additive, or become a single system through its textual ground, something which is suggested but not entirely explained?

The answer to the first depends on whether or not the opening up of the feminine enigma really works by way of Mallarmé, or rather embodies a theoretical construction on psychoanalytic grounds for which the various texts simply provide convenient illustration. There is a tension in this which Kristeva has perhaps not fully accepted, in the degree to which the spelling out of the psychodynamics involved in, say, Hérodiade is awkwardly literal-minded, and alien to that precise Mallarméan concern with the elusive and evanescent in the moment of poetic realisation – above all perhaps with the feminine. The translation into a structuralist and post-Freudian jargon, with a heavy Marxist overlay, falsifies what it intends to unfold and transmit. But then, she might reply that this indeed is criticism: the full rational explanation, as in that of psychoanalysis, and necessary to whatever rational procedure is applied to the elusive and difficult text. The enigma can no longer remain quite simply that. And how is it analysed and explained in all its psychic and cultural complexity and yet retained? It is possible that Kristeva's treatment poses the question more forcefully because the polystructural explanatory systems become so deeply self-involving, and surround the text with such extended elaboration that the opacity of the text itself shines more vividly. The essential act is always to step back and consider the outer circle of theoretical displacements, which in turn give us further maps of the course taken by the revolution, but in doing so turn away from the intractability of the 'mystery'.

In the end the text becomes a forum or meeting place rather than a unifying ground – a space (*chora* perhaps), certainly, but one where it itself is absent. In all of this the 'textual logic' does not arise out of the internal workings of a text of Mallarmé, but through the correspondence of languages drawn from our own historical moment. We may find aspects of Mallarmé through such a moment, but hardly in it. Text has become absent and logic a figure.

Pastoral perhaps has its own quite different form of obliquity. It becomes a controlling presence by fleeing its own central ground, and by travelling precariously around the margins of its limits.

# V    From 'wit' to 'astonishment'

An important passage in Eliot's essay on Marvell proceeds through the contrast of 'wit' and 'magniloquence' with a subsequent sketch of some possibilities of wit which help to delineate the nature of Marvell's own affinities. And it is part of a larger 'placing', as Leavis would say, in which a characteristic employment of wit finds its role in turn in the larger literary tradition. It also is presented with a certain grandeur of elaboration, a growing awareness of scale, a richness of reference, a fullness of one's sense of the possibilities of the uses of wit, to give the impression of wit as viewed through the manner of magniloquence itself. The aim is to elicit contrastively versions of the blend of these opposing qualities in the late seventeenth century, but the sheer force of comparison develops its own *élan*, and one plunges forward in time and beyond the limits of the original distinction:

The wit of the Caroline poets is not the wit of Shakespeare, and it is not the wit of Dryden, the great master of contempt, or of Pope, the great master of hatred, or of Swift, the great master of disgust. What is meant is some quality which is common to the songs in *Comus* and Cowley's Anacreontics and Marvell's Horatian Ode. It is more than a technical accomplishment, or the vocabulary and syntax of an epoch; it is, what we have designated tentatively as wit, a tough reasonableness beneath the slight lyric grace. You cannot find it in Shelley or Keats or Wordsworth; you cannot find more than an echo of it in Landor; still less in Tennyson or Browning; and among contemporaries Mr. Yeats is an Irishman and Mr. Hardy is a modern Englishman – that is to say, Mr. Hardy is without it and Mr. Yeats is outside of the tradition altogether. On the other hand, as it certainly exists in Lafontaine, there is a large part of it in Gautier. And of the magniloquence, the deliberate exploitation of the possibilities of magnificence in language which Milton used and abused, there is also use and even abuse in the poetry of Baudelaire.[1]

There is no suggestion of a typology of wit, but a series of touchstones that unfold alternative aspects (perhaps nothing would have led us to disgust if there had been no Swift?), with a use of negative examples which nevertheless have an additive effect. It is the ingenious use of negation that enables Eliot to establish while appearing to deny. For the denial suggests an oblique form of participation: no, of course it is not as in Pope or Swift, no, not entirely. Affinity and difference are subtly combined. And the lateral effects of the choice of examples suggests a range of marginal intentions which one merely brushes past. The appearance of Mr Hardy as the model of the modern Englishman proposes an irony not wholly under control. But the build up through a series of instances implying further mixtures of same and different, of affinities and distancings, is a miniature portrait of the cultural continuity in which wit finds its moment, and then seems to lose it – through Romanticism and its aftermath. It is selective: no Byron. And it is elusive: for a transient moment the Caroline poets seem to hold the centre with 'a tough reasonableness beneath the slight lyric grace'. Which perhaps excludes the outrageous: no Rochester. And is some strange centrifugality at work by which magniloquence is almost lost, only to be recovered in an unheralded meeting of Milton and Baudelaire? Yet the power and vitality of the notion of wit itself derive from a rhetoric which fuses limit with extravagance.

It is prolonged by a rhetoric of a different kind. The definition of wit interlocks more disturbingly with 'Puritan' than it does with magniloquence, if partly to account for a thread in Marvell's life which attaches him to important aspects of his age. But the negative characterisation turns into a rich and inverted Arnoldian pastiche, in which Zeal-of-the-land Busy and the United Grand Junction Ebenezer Temperance Association evoke a ludicrous puritanism which is carefully distanced from Marvell but whose sobering element also in some way qualifies wit. The comedy is oddly and effectively used to include and exclude at the same time, presenting Marvell as a man of his century, inconceivable without puritanism, rather than a puritan. The most abbreviated steps move from puritanism to another voice in its instance of the 'Coy Mistress'. By way of Shakespeare, Herrick and Waller another set of affinities is established to that deep tradition of *carpe diem* stretching back to the ancient world, where the transitory and contingent nature of love contrasts with 'Deserts of vast eternity' ... a tradition in which a 'whole civilisation resides' (*SP*, p. 163). The movement is from the possibilities of wit to a cultural whole, in which those possibilities have carefully if eccentrically nuanced places. It is the richness and cultural complexity, the interplay of language and politics, that situate the particular poetic powers of Marvell, that give some claim for his special character in a feeling of its fullness and its depth. Yet so traditional an effect is represented in terms that surprise.

The total effect, for all of the twists and turns, qualifications, ironical asides, its shifts from tentative definition to historical context, is cumulative, the effect of an extended rhetorical structure of seventeenth-century prose. Yet paradoxically, beyond the complex evocation to which the notion of wit has led us, the further effect is to return from multiplicity to simplicity in a gradual bearing down on the single great thing in which wit participates and towards which it points. An overwhelming concentration is effected which could not be represented in a more abstract language.

Of course, concentration may artificially exaggerate the effect. The aim of showing something as part of many things, as taking identity from a totality, combines as its focal point that richness and impetus in an historical sense that is wholly committed to its value. Compare an antithetical method working an analogous ground in a commentary of Poulet on a passage from Marivaux:

A philosophy of history which rigorously ends in the destruction of all history, since one always sets out again into the new. Neither Nature, therefore, nor humanity, nor the individual being ever grows old

I am seventy-four years old, as I write this, I have lived a long time: a long time indeed, alas! I am wrong: properly speaking *I live only in this instant that passes*; there was another which already is no longer, in which I have lived, it is true; but in which I no longer exist; and it is as if I had not been; thus *could I not say that my life does not last: that it is always beginning*? thus, young and old, we would all be of the same age. A child is born as I write, and, as I see it, aged as I am, he is already as old as I. That is how it seems to me; and on this basis what is life? a perpetual dream, except for *the instant one possesses*, and which *in its turn becomes dream*.

In all the literature of the eighteenth century it would be difficult to find a page in which the consciousness of the ephemeral is more clearly expressed. Perhaps La Fontaine and Keats, in other centuries, have been the only ones along with Marivaux who have had at one and the same time enough courage and suppleness to seize the slightest furtive instant of their existence and place in it all their faith, all their desire, all their spiritual exigencies. On the other hand, it would be a grave mistake to confuse the thought of Marivaux with the banal *Carpe diem* of the imitators of Chaulieu and Horace. It is not a question here of profiting from the moment because the moment is the place of our pleasures. It is a question of recognizing in the instant which lives and dies, which surges out of nothingness and which ends in dream, an intensity and a depth of significance which ordinarily one attaches only to the whole of existence. For Marivaux, as for Aristippus, Pater, and Gide, the instant is all, for it is only within itself, and not in time, that something happens and ceases to be, which is all our destiny. Our being is a rapid sketch, an immediate gesture, a cry of astonishment that mounts to our lips.[2]

It is not so much that we are sketched an alternative tradition in the realisation of the temporal moment, that time has a different presence and different echos, or even that we have a somewhat more casual view of tradition – the presence of Aristippus, Pater and Gide is rather a throwaway, while the line of Horatian descent is hardly a role of honour. Nor is the experience in question something which reduces the moment to a form of simplicity: 'A thousand shapes are glimpsed in the shadows of the mind. A thousand thoughts at once cross the troubled waters of our soul.' But it is not the varied and conflict-ridden contents of our moments of consciousness that engage Poulet, but the intensity of that moment of consciousness itself, in what amounts to purity and isolation. A descriptive language is developed that works by stripping down, by cutting everything away to reveal the impact of that moment of awareness and its far-reaching consciousness. This is partly to say that there is another kind of dramatic intention:

– I don't know what is happening to me.
– What does it mean ... Who can protect oneself from such a happening?
– Is what is happening to me conceivable? What an adventure! O Heavens! What an adventure! Must my reason perish in it?

Here we see the Marivaudian being rising up out of non-existence in undescribable astonishment. He *is* this astonishment. Without the slightest moment of gradation, in a lightning flash, he has passed from his negative state of habitual stupor, which is the state of sloth, to an entirely different sort of stupor, an essentially active stupor which is the stupor of being. What has happened to me? I have come to be. But I still know nothing about the event which has happened except that it has happened, that I cannot distinguish it from myself, and that it now forms a part of my very existence. More than that, when confronted with this event, I forget everything except this event and myself, and that this event is myself. I am that which is happening, although I am also the one to whom it is happening. I feel and apprehend myself in this instant in which unquestionably I unite my consciousness of being to this event's being. Yet all this only increases my astonishment, for I know that if what is happening to me is I, myself, on the other hand I know less than ever what is happening. My consciousness of being is at one and the same time a knowledge and an ignorance. What I know is that I am. What I do not know is what I am. (*ID*, pp. 6–7)

The steps here are not associative but logical. The movement, like that of Eliot, drives us forward, not through what we attach in passing, but through the continuous narrowing and tightening of focus. Everything turns back to the insistence on intensity: 'Habitual stupor ... an essentially active stupor ... the stupor of being'. Here there is no external reference, no touching upon cultural affinities. No one is present but Marivaux. The development is internal, and the language of Marivaux is mirrored in the language of the commentary. 'What is happening to me? I happen to be.' It is as if some honing and paring had reached the point of a Marivaudian essence, isolated, precise, concentrated in a moment of 'astonishment', in the sudden blinding moment of awareness reached through uncertainty and doubt. What remains is to draw the consequences of this awareness in terms of an elegant inversion of the Cartesian *Cogito*, the use of the most fundamental Marivaudian awareness as the basis of a negative self-knowledge, of a strange awakening to a form of being of which one can say nothing, a moment of illumination which is a moment of absence:

One no longer knows where one is, one is lost, one no longer comprehends, one is at his wit's end, one knows not what to decide and feels as if he were struck stupid. This is an astonishment which allows us no margin for reflection. In contrast to the Cartesian *Cogito*, the Marivaudian *Cogito* is purely negative. I do not know what I think, nor even if I think. And if I spontaneously recognize that something is happening to me, that is very simply because it is happening to me. I cannot get out of this. It is given to me to be the one to whom something happens. It is given to me to be, that is all. (*ID*, p. 6)

There is a startling sense of finality in 'that is all'. The possibility of thought through negation, of the sense of self in the absence of self, and in a revelation in which passive receptivity is caught in the momentary awareness is largely 'the flash of negative knowledge' from which other and further steps seem impossibly remote. We have captured the truth about a form and appearance of the self through that astonishment which is itself consumed in a pure sense of being produced by the moment of dislocation, and which flourishes in the pure paradox that one's knowledge is ignorance and one's ignorance knowledge. Awareness is pure, but it is purity without content; awareness and the void are one.

This is a descriptive *tour de force* in the effort to capture the meeting point of illumination and darkness, and create from it the point of departure to render the characteristic, underlying features of an oeuvre. But there is a self-cancelling quality in the language, fully acknowledged, and carried to what extremes it can reach: 'That is all'. The movement of language mirrors the problem it reveals, questioning the ground on which it might set up its own 'work of the mind'. Of course 'astonishment' and 'stupor' are psychological states which are describable enough. But certain externalised and extensively referential descriptions would be inappropriate to sharpening and intensification. Nothing must deflect, muddle or complicate.

A similar purity would seem to be the aim of Poulet's model of critical reading, in which a hypothetical *tabula rasa* is prepared for the impact of reading and describes a paradigm of critical awareness, again as in the case of Marivaux revealing a heightened awareness, an amazement in the presence of the 'other' – that alien consciousness that invades you in the form of a literary text, that somehow places another within one's self:

Also, I often have in my reading the impression of being simply witness to an action which nevertheless involves me and none of whose details escapes me. Whence, a certain astonishment on my part. I am a consciousness astonished by an existence which is not mine, yet which I experience as if it were mine.

This astonished consciousness is the critical consciousness: the consciousness of a reader, consciousness of a being to whom it has been given to grasp as one's own something which takes place in the consciousness of another being.[3]

Critical awareness of course grows and complicates in the multiple relationships of self and other, in the multiple forms of consciousness linking the critic to the text, which Poulet traces in *La Conscience Critique* from Rivière to his own contemporaries, Richard and Starobinsky.

Is this notion of the purity of consciousness more than a working hypothesis, and in the end a tactical device? It is not, of course, an innocent assertion of the mind's freedom from its multiple contents, or of the unintentionality of consciousness. All awareness is awareness of something. Even if that something is a gap or void in the flow of impressions to which we are accustomed. And in Marivaux those moments of dislocation in which the habitual patterns of consciousness are destroyed and realigned are those openings by which the contradictions at the heart of the period reveal themselves. There is movement, uncertainty, sexual and social surprise, disturbance and confusion lodged in the erotic gamesmanship of the *ancien régime*. Poulet's method is designed to reach through these moments of dislocation to those of pure consciousness and pure contingency in which the work of Marivaux reveals itself most profoundly.

The problem can be generalised in a number of ways. Wittgenstein remarks on the astonishment that anything exists.[4] And he connects this astonishment with the experience of the limits of language. We will see this problem of limits in several contexts, both in phenomenological criticism and in Derrida. And in this particular case it might look as if Poulet is pushing an extreme form of awareness which shocks the more deeply for being situated in a work to which it might on the surface seem alien. For one must remember the social comedy out of which this encounter with nothingness has been extracted. All of the quoted fragments of Marivaux have of course their context, which may involve pathos or despair, but also a richly figured social surface, and a pervasive sense of the relation between contingency and comic effect – and further, beyond the pathos, despair and comedy of manners exist in some dizzying but delightful equilibrium.

Certainly the metaphysical anguish and *bouleversement* goes beyond any obvious scheme of things which the comic sense of the oeuvre would suggest, even to the violating of tone, the feel of Marivaudian surface. But of course this is intentional. The starkness of contrast between that surface and the yawning 'inner distance' within the text which lie beneath the social working of manners and feelings is the point of this narrowing and concentrating. The world of human vanities and illusions, of idleness and folly may surround the 'indescribable astonishment' and it itself is describable enough: a formal configuration, a plot, a tale. To arrive at the depths of the passive awareness of the '*Cogito Marivaudien*', caught in the whirl of contingency which produces the 'stupor of being', one looks to the intensities of mental states revealed by the accidental flicker of dislocation shifting in the intangible and unpredictable movement of chance itself. The limits of language pressed are both those of Marivaux and Poulet, and the challenge of 'indescribable' is met through negation; from what the text cannot describe the critic can distil those fragmentary indications of evanescent and dissolving states of mind.

When one looks back to Eliot the richness of descriptive means is thrown into relief. So also the extraordinary indirection in the ways by which details are accumulated, the variety of pointers to multiple cultural contexts, nuanced combinations of similarity and difference. This can stand as a case of what Clifford Geertz has called (following Ryle) 'thick description', in which the simple and perhaps ludicrous case of the wink is turned from the mere contraction of the eyelid into a 'piled-up structure of inference and implication'. 'Thin description' is an account of the twitch. 'Thick description' is the full sense of what is implied: 'a strati-fied hierarchy of meaningful structures in terms of which twitches, winks, fake-winks, parodies, rehearsals of parodies are produced, perceived and interpreted ... ' For Geertz it becomes a model of the ethno-grapher's problem for the relation between observation and interpretation, in which 'winks upon winks' stand for the structures of signification that analysis must sort: 'What the ethnographer is in fact faced with ... is a multiplicity of complex conceptual structures, many of them super-imposed upon or knotted into one another, which are at once strange, irregular, and inexplicit, and which he must contrive somehow first to grasp and then to render ... Doing ethnography is like trying to read (in the sense of 'construct a reading of') a manuscript – foreign, faded, full of elipses, incoherencies, suspicious emendations, and tendentious commentaries ... '[5]

We do not need ethnology to complicate the critical task, but the relationship between literary and other cultural forms of 'reading' produce some useful connections. Here, in the case of Eliot, the simplest component of his argument, the most rudimentary sample of wit in whatever context, is already fraught with thickness. A cultural density is evoked in a pattern of implied descriptions, where the form 'wit of' trails its flow of allusion. And behind each of these lies a complex amalgam of forms of wit, the language that embodies it, and the cultural expectations that give it that localised force out of which Eliot's grander design emerges. In a sense Eliot has produced a chain of implied descriptions, in which the features which lie in the background need not be produced. The allusions create clues enough, and we need not unpack them as we go. The multi-layered thicknesses produce their own further effect.

If we were to try to dismantle one of the components of this layering, the process would lead us beyond implied literary history into those elements of which any complex culture is composed. Their multiple connections form part of that totality that Eliot conveys – albeit with enormous selectivity of that high European and Latin culture which provides the depth and eloquence of Marvell's wit. And even the unpacking of one of the components would perhaps be insufferably tedious. It would certainly involve the description of language, of persons, cultural situations, and of relations of many kinds. In many stages of the evolution of a literary tradition, linguistic conventions and cultural variables, popular verbal expectations would only be the beginning point. The most detailed accounting of the 'seventeenth-century background' or the historical evolution of the Horatian tradition, or the psychological foundations of the possibility of wit, would barely touch the surface of any such dismantling, for the simplest elements of such components are already so immersed in relations that the notion of a simple thread that could be straightforwardly described might seem to be mythical, to exist only as a hypothesis that some pattern of explanation was thought to require.

We expect as much, of course, as Eliot does. But it is the obvious thing from which other things follow. I shall mention four threads without seeing them through exhaustively (or even substantially) on this particular piece of ground. 'Thick description' suggests the piling up and concentration of critical language which increases almost exponentially the number of relations, both within what Ryle called 'established codes', between such codes, and in respect to new codes or even areas where codification might not be clearly and easily established. The case of 'wit' might suggest all of these possibilities as there are both uses where the context seems reasonably determinate and the place in a 'code' might be relatively uncontroversial, yet others which might be more difficult to place. So when one thinks back to Wittgenstein's remark about reasons in aesthetics taking the form of further descriptions, one must take care that the 'further' is not restricted to descriptions of the same kind. Nor does 'further' necessarily imply a linear sequence of a logical kind (although of course it might), but many possible forms of 'further'. We have already seen in the case of Empson's irony the deployment of that notion along several axes, including those of gradation and depth.

Others of our terms also convey in other ways a similar deepening: in thickness itself, or layering, or the imagery of surfaces and depths that I have just used of Eliot. One can pose the problem of such a construction in terms of what lies necessarily behind or beneath, to be uncovered by the

appropriate analytic moves, whatever they may be. There is a sense of
'further' that would get to the bottom of the sources of wit, either in the
prehistory of speech, the structure of the mind (as perhaps, rather
fancifully, in Lévi-Strauss), the panoply of cultural conventions which by
their very pile-up can be played against each other, giving the shifts of
awareness that wit requires – constructed in Eliot's case out of multiple
denials. And it is out of his knowledge of how expectations are formed to
be qualified or denied that one draws on a ready-made world of established
cultural arrangements, to .be flattered, exploited or shocked – as in the
sprightly packaging of Milton and Baudelaire.

But the notion of a beginning point, an isolating of the fundamental
strands, the nucleus about which the thickening accretes, may be illusory
but usefully so. The 'bottom' itself may indicate the necessity of
postulating the end one will never reach. Geertz gives a version of his own
explanatory process reaching for but disclaiming its fundamental terms in
a little tale:

There is an Indian story – at least I heard it as an Indian story -about an
Englishman who, having been told that the world rested on a platform which rested
on the back of an elephant which rested in turn on the back of a turtle, asked
(perhaps he was an ethnographer; it is the way they behave), what did the turtle rest
on? Another turtle. And that turtle? 'Ah, Sahib, after that it is turtles all the way
down'.

Such, indeed, is the condition of things. I do not know how long it would be
profitable to meditate on the encounter of Cohen, the sheikh, and 'Dumari' (the
period has perhaps already been exceeded); but I do know that however long I did
so I would not get anywhere near to the bottom of it. Nor have I ever gotten
anywhere near to the bottom of anything I have ever written about, either in the
essays below or elsewhere. Cultural analysis is intrinsically incomplete. And, worse
than that, the more deeply it goes the less complete it is. It is a strange science whose
most telling assertions are its most tremulously based, in which to get somewhere
with the matter at hand is to intensify the suspicion, both your own and that of
others, that you are not quite getting it right.[6]

Eliot provides a locus for the representation of depth in its intrinsic
incompleteness. But it is not a tremulous hand that ties the knot on our
bizarre package of magniloquence, but a master of multiple games whose
magician's hat produces not a white rabbit but a brown owl. We will
therefore think of hate quite differently and revise our views of...
magniloquence, Baudelaire, cultural continuity, Europe, the ways in which
aspects of language can be used or abused, the relation of 'deliberate
exploitation' to 'tough reasonableness', hatred, disgust, and many other
things that begin in wit which itself begins nowhere in particular.

Perhaps there are ways in which the example is extreme, and the
conjunctions so deliberately exploit those mixtures of similarity and

difference as to be a touch mannered in self-conscious virtuosity. And insofar as Eliot is 'placing' something, with every allusion the plot thickens. The comparisons open a sequence of doors leading in many directions rather than one. If the cumulative effect is to bring us closer to Marvell, it is by way of such paths that lead through Marvell as the nexus which in turn contains many others: of those literary works, persons, linguistic features that radiate outwards. The intrinsic incompleteness of the analysis however does not qualify its force. What we want from the overall force of the cumulative effect is not a single and incontrovertible conviction about one aspect of one particular thing, but the related explorations of many things which revise our understanding in a larger sense. 'Placing' is not the precise affixing of Marvell through tough reasonableness and lyric grace to the vocabulary and syntax of an epoch (or vice versa), but something more diffuse in which poet, poetry, poetic tradition are far-reachingly reseen. We do not move one feature with respect to the legends and contours of our map, but traverse a movement in which all features are rearranged, and none of them permanently. Incompleteness is both quantitative and temporal.

A further implication of such a necessary seeing of everything in terms of everything else is that there is no uninterpreted feature of any component of this scene. There is nothing described in a way that does not imply such relations with other elements that the understanding of it is not conditioned or 'placed'. This need not of course be in an abstract conceptual structure. But there is no description without interpretation. This need not mean that the projects of those like Susan Sontag who wish to abandon the wilder shores of interpretation for a more modestly conceived and more narrowly descriptive critical language have no point at all. Theirs may be reasonable reactions to various institutionalised extravagances of interpretation. But it is difficult to see how any remark in an essay like Eliot's could become so stripped of significant context as to become a kind of simple and matter-of-fact description. Or if we wish to call a certain range of critical remarks 'simple descriptions' it would still require writing a large sense of context into such simplicity. It is hard to find winks in critical discourse that would qualify for a rigorous form of 'thin' description. This may well reflect a difference between critical language and that of social analysis. Or perhaps a difference between Geertz and such social theorists as Runciman who believes that criteria can be given for distinguishing between reportage, explanation, description and valuation in a stratified, schematic way. And Geertz is somewhat ambiguous as to whether or not there is any serious use of 'thin' description in the social sciences. He does not seem to want to treat such simple elements as useful. A twitch understood as such involves interpretation, decisions made, a substantial reading of contexts. But is it something on which 'thickness' builds, or simply a theoretical construct which throws it into relief?

Certainly 'thick description' takes on a substantial measure of interpretation, and the thicker the description the more the interpretation may satisfy varied criteria of adequacy. This means in turn that it involves a high level of resistance to generality. By this I do not mean that general concepts do not play an important part in many aspects of a richly descriptive piece of critical language. Indeed, as I showed in Chapter I it is impossible to exclude them. Eliot makes no very direct use of general concepts in this instance, but of course they are implied in many ways. The most basic terms 'technical', 'syntax', even 'lyric' draw upon general schemes of things. General implications may stretch from them, and the notions of historical and formal relations are not theory-free. But while Eliot may employ such dimensions indirectly there is no overall scheme at a high level of generality to which this kind of discourse assimilates. And its very thickness and answerability to such varied criteria makes difficulty for generality in whatever further description we might give.

Finally, such a language does not respect the differences in talking of texts as linguistic structures, poems as works of persons and even of persons themselves as they reshape in language their relation to images, moral reflection, even 'the English mind'. The apostle of 'impersonality' situates himself in the dilemmas of persons, especially as poets labour to find what part of their tradition they can assimilate and put to their own use. My point is not to revive any focus on pervasive intentionalism – Cioffi has shown how widely and subversively such pervasiveness works – but merely to observe that these contexts all imply each other and no sense of their possible separation crosses the horizon. States of mind are present, if we lack Poulet's immediacy of concentration on them. On the other hand, the apparent concentration of Poulet on revealed innerness implies a density of its own. The very stripping down process invokes the elements which surround the moment of awareness and carries the concentric circles of the psyche's inner world with it, in the long run no less 'thick' than Eliot's cultural accumulation.

And there are deceptions. The series of negatives assists the assimilation of wit to the grand and terrible and reveals it as a pathway to the most profound and universal of themes, where that theme is renewed through 'the variety and order of the image', and where it forms the 'crescendo and diminuendo of a scale of great imaginative power'. And by a subtle alteration of direction the historical sequence is used to demolish, almost in passing, the distinction between imagination and fancy. Yet in doing so covertly Eliot uses it to give some measure of where Marvell's imagery may go wrong, where some images may slip over the edge through the very excess in precision or figuration into the unintentional error of taste. Wit itself remains to be identified with the conjoining of opposites in Coleridge's account of imagination, and is manoeuvred by way of negatives again (not erudition, not cynicism) towards a general formula: 'It involves, probably, a recognition, implicit in the expression of every experience, of other kinds of experience which are possible ... ' (*SP*, p. 170).

After the force of the examples this seems deliberately flat, as if embarrassed by generality and inclined to allow such formulation to fade out in a shrug of diffidence. It is so loosely framed as to suggest that such a translation into the nomenclature of our own time is a very approximate business, and that rendering the many concrete occasions in such an open way is fundamentally distasteful. But there is a further necessity in the recognition that there is a thread, a common element to the versions of wit – if not a sufficient condition for a definition, a suggestive focal point. One dimension of the problem is analogous to the problem of the general meaning of 'pastoral', where one is balancing the similarities and differences within a specifically literary tradition. But the notion of pastoral has little meaning outside of literature (its use in the visual arts is clearly dependent on the literary tradition). To think of it having a substantial reference to pastoral societies and forms of life would be to confuse it with a distant source, while wit in poetry is part of wit in general. Eliot's diffidence, like Empson's, may spring from a reluctance to engage with general definitions, but their procedures are different. Getting the complex into the simple relates the character of poetic language to a conventional form of literary structuring. Although much of interest happens on the way, even where the thread may seem to be lost, the concept of pastoral itself comes to life when its limits are pushed. The common usage is tested by the extreme case. The danger here is the temptation of the bizarre. Eliot, however uneasily, is moving towards a centre, indicating an essential core. The further danger is that stated on such a level it may seem empty. Yet even if an essence cannot be conceptually isolated, there is assurance in the sense that it is, roughly speaking, there.

However, both share the double movement of fleeing generality and invoking it, refusing an involvement in abstract reasoning, yet finding its use. Compared with such tortuous evasiveness there is something almost shocking about Poulet's directness. Perhaps the phenomenological point of departure so concentrates on the immediacy of consciousness that the very moment of critical notation is an enactment of one's theoretical commitment. The critic can touch that flash of awareness in which being or becoming are revealed as a shared and recurring form of the *cogito* as in the Gidian instant in which one's being appears through the fluttering succession of moments of consciousness: 'Framed between sudden appearance and vanishing, appearing only in order to disappear, the Gidian world exists only in the very fluttering of its reiterated being'.[7] Perhaps Marivaux provides an especially vivid series of such moments of 'fluttering', where every step in the sequence of instance is a further moment of discovery, of total alteration of consciousness, in which awareness is found, cancelled, recovered or reconstructed out of loss. 'My thought is reduced to astonishment. Astonishment at being what happens to me.' Each moment is one of uncovering a new psychic state. And critical awareness corresponds to this artistic concentration of our psychic life in its moments of change, in the realisation that something is different from what it was before, the critical consciousness reliving each moment of transformation.

The assumption of this translatability from mind to paper to the critical recovery seems perhaps too easily made. But I think it must be taken as the essential given in Poulet's work. The isolation of the moment of consciousness, the awareness of it, the response to it in another moment of consciousness, is fundamental to Poulet's project. As is the idea of the succession of moments, the subsumption of them into the flow of time. '"I do not depict being", says Montaigne, "I depict passage."'.[8] And the work of Proust begins 'with a moment *empty of all content*. It completes itself in a series of other moments of impressions truly *full*, those which are outside of Time.'[9] From the first discrete moments of isolated awareness, through their temporal flow into the final transmutation that lifts them out of time, 'the Mallarméan poem is thus composed of a spray of small ephemeral durations which engender a continuous duration, through which there appears and in which there is finally made incarnate a nontemporal reality, Fiction' (*ID*, p. 276). Somewhere among 'ephemeral durations' the moments of Marivaux are witness to the hazards and uncertainties of a contingent world. Yet contingency also enters into history, and the multiple relations of being and style have their historical coordinates. 'Perfect marriage of being and word, flung into the same adventure! But is not that also what the Mallarméan poem will seek to realize? But the one and the other by the sole virtue of language seek to mime all the variations of being. The play of time and of chance becomes a marvellous "play of words".' (*ID*, p. 28). And this play of words enters into the thickening of historical sequence as in the forms of 'wit'. And the capturing of those moments in a sequence suggests a critical transcendence of the fragments of human time in its own form of consciousness.

# VI 'Fool' and '*pharmakon*'

'Ambiguity' like 'irony' has so long been a common instrument of modern criticism that its use may well have sunk into the totally routinised. Yet its capacity to find new forms of defamiliarisation, to resurface through other conceptual languages such as the 'polysemy' of Barthes or Derrida, may show the ease with which certain underlying preoccupations about language may be naturalised in conceptual schemes of different sorts, with their wider implications of quite different kinds. It is the echo of this naturalisation, and what it tells us about the theoretical structure that uses it, that may help measure the force of such theories themselves, show something of their degree of reach, and their illumination of the richness and congestion of meaning to which they address themselves. For the exploration of the possibilities and limits of the multiple senses of 'complex words' has seemed part of our understanding of language in general, but most especially of the language of literature where that complexity seems a constitutive principle. And in an adjacent form of discourse Derrida sees something equally constitutive in the ambiguity that arises through translation and marks what he calls 'the very passage into philosophy'.

What happens when one tries to measure the passage by way of translation, with all of the multiple senses such passage may contain – including the translation by which we express our understanding of a literary work – or the analogous path by which the exploration of the richness of language may be found in the cultural depth of a key word? If I am concerned here with two kinds of investigation, the analogy may have some use in giving intelligible dimensions to an enduring problem in critical thought. And a point of departure can be found in the difference between Empson's treatment of ambiguity in *Seven Types* and the effort to ransack fully the cultural matrix of more open contexts that characterises *Complex Words*. For Empson's treatment of the Shakespearean 'fool' goes beyond what a typological analysis can do and talk of types of equations vanishes in practice. That might give sense to the working of 'a type' with the somewhat reductive effect that its characteristic feature is distinctive boundaries. To set up a model of the relations between types would in turn imply a falsifying map that the open-ended procedures of the later book had to redraw, in following through to the end the fullness that a key word or concept in what its multiple contexts can reveal, and doing so with respect to a great work where the resonance can be most grandly and consequentially felt.

Certainly one feature of this change in his own method is registered in the distinction between those meanings which are 'imposed by the immediate context' – difficult as the criteria for establishing this may be – from 'the compacted doctrine', where the word itself 'seems to put the doctrine into our minds'. It is the difference between the variables that context may determine, and the further variables that lie like 'traces' one might say, of its many commitments within the word itself. These words seem to carry what Empson calls 'equations' as an internal relation. These equations are certainly formulated in terms of another typology, but rather than the typology being the framework through which the possibilities of complex words are studied, it is as he says something devised after the case studies, so he is 'more sure of the general literary account than I am of the classifying fitted onto it'.[1] The investigation preceded the rationalisation and ordering of its components. One effect of this *post facto* approach to the more general levels of argument is to suggest an almost arbitrary imposition of pattern. It suggests that the classification is given more as a helpful ground plan than as an operative principle. And certainly the relations between the types play no active part in the ways in which the equations themselves evolve, but are mentioned as reference points, rather in passing. One will invoke references as an aspect of the way in which they might illuminate context, rather than as interrelated features of a system. This seems partly an awkwardness which follows from an attempted resemblance to the model of *Seven Types*, when in fact the similarity is superficial.

An awkwardness also attaches to the notion of equations themselves. Here a mathematical, and sometimes overbearingly mechanistic, way of explaining the relation of a referent to its complex properties becomes – somewhat as with Bloom's ratios – an artifice most honoured in the omission. The two elements taken together seem like an experiment in scientific description which is evoked but seldom applied. And the same may apply to the nagging presence of Richards's distinction between cognitive and emotive language which looms so large in the more theoretical chapters. These somewhat misleading pieces of theoretical apparatus make it look as if the interest in the work is back to front, while the most important aspects of theory arise from the case studies where the implications of the particular can unfold. I do not suggest that this is akin to de Man's notion about critical blindness to one's presuppositions, but simply the mistaken impression given by attempting to formalise one's procedure in a counter-productive way.

The discussion of 'fool' is set naturally in historical context, and in the paradoxes that arise directly from it:

'This fellow's wise enough to play the fool, and to do that well requires a kind of wit' (*Twelfth Night* 111.1.67). The conception had to be built up gradually, both in his own mind and for his audience, before he got to the terrific uses of it in *Lear*. On the other hand the clown who bases his effects on 'you are a fool too' was certainly not a romantic invention of Shakespeare's ... To make the characters theorise about the clown was to insist that he was part of the play. This may also explain why Shakespeare tends increasingly to say fool rather than clown; the stage comedian was called a clown but the court clown was called a fool, and Shakespeare wanted to insist that he was representing a court fool not letting loose a clown on his stage. According to the N. E. D., something important had happened to the word just before the Elizabethans took it over; the earliest affectionate use for a dependent is dated 1530 and the earliest use for a mere imbecile is 1540. How the introduction of these two further meanings into the word was necessary to complete it as an instrument ... (*CW*, pp. 114–15)

It becomes an instrument in its subtle power to join opposites, to catch both the fusion and the distinction in the versions of wisdom and folly. The power implicit in its fully conscious use was created both from the ambiguity that Erasmus had already explored, and the steadily complicating uses that the N. E. D. records, in which the colloquial, courtly, legalistic and theatrical streams of use combine unevenly, and where the predominant sense shifts in the historical perspective. The effect of mapping this sequence of accumulating uses on to a non-English tradition, is to develop a permutation system in which different uses combine, but selectively, and the reservoir of possible meanings is sufficiently present to enable us to ask what of a large number of possible meanings is predominant in any one case. Does 'fool' mean idiot, or clown, or object of endearment? Is it used derisively or affectionately? The narrowly exclusive sense would hardly ring true to most of the Shakespearean instances, and the context can throw multiple aspects of the primary, secondary and 'trace' elements of the meaning into a variety of reliefs. The 'adventurous stage' of trying 'to codify the process of combination' (*CW*, p. 39) which relates the supposed 'head sense' to the 'immediate context' (*CW*, p. 46) gives rise to the puzzles of which Empson is so immediately aware: both 'head sense' and force of context are impossible to state with any certainty in a clearly codifiable form for any occasion of a complex use.

The equation system in *Complex Words* goes further than the open world of possibility in the analysis of 'They that have power' towards establishing a relational pattern among the possible meanings, which can establish a degree of primary force in context which subsumes those pressures generated by the possibility of alternative or even quite opposed senses. There may in this be a superficial resemblance to the structuralist *combinatoire*, in which an analytic model is created for the relational functions within narrative or linguistic structures. However, the structuralist aim is at a higher level of generality, and the Empsonian equations do little more than condense a description into notational form. Rather than an analytic instrument they are a form of shorthand which aims at clarity through tightening the terms of the description by the very effect of numbering types. If one asks whether a certain use really fits under type II or type III one may be largely engaged in an effort to pin down the variables of context sufficiently contrastively to define other variables so that they can be seen in terms of each other. The uses of 'fool' fit all types of equation by turn, and to some extent the confusion created by somewhat arbitrary classifications is acknowledged (*CW*, p. 117). But the seductions of this urge to system do little more than embroider some peripheral nuisance. The genius of Empson lies at least partly in his capacity to move from one context to another with the awareness of how they reflect and qualify each other. The combinations are not so much codified as lovingly and ruthlessly explored, with an eye to what takes flight and eludes as well as to the bed rock. And perhaps the very notion of open-ended permutation gives to any thought of system that very feeling of the mind in movement, travelling the circuits of possibility.

I have two criticisms of the equation system itself. One is that the determinants of the particular uses are so elusive that 'head' and subordinate senses cannot be tidily fixed upon to provide a relational system that is both convincing and stable. The drawing in of another comparison or the seeing of another aspect of context would shift the combination like a kaleidoscope. And Empson's sensitivity to this comes out pervasively in the qualified language through which the system is operated: 'it seems to me', 'I suppose', 'we may suppose', 'I suppose it would be fussy to', 'not always in quite the same way'. This tentativeness is attractive insofar as it represents an exploratory 'trying out' habit of mind which is then partially cancelled by the necessity of fitting itself to some type derived from the notational system. And this reflects the second criticism: once the pattern of accumulated meaning is translated into the notational system that system does not communicate anything of interest additional to the input. So the comment 'Such a twist of thought seems a fair case for the question mark sign: $3c + ?\ 2 = 1a$-. $1\pounds1$.' leaves the question mark buried in a formula that is only useful as part of a further explanation which must be made in another way. Empson's notational codes have something of a Rube Goldberg quality, although they are perhaps not much more preposterous than Lévi-Strauss's efforts in the same line: they are merely abbreviations that are useless until decoded and even then add nothing to the argument.

Perhaps the difficulty comes out more clearly in the essay on 'wit'. With 'fool' the system is not worked very hard, and the schematic layout of the possible available meanings for the Shakespearean repertoire of uses (*CW*, pp. 111–12) may at least have the value of a kind of display in which the elements to be combined can be spread out and seen in a sequence. This represents a development which is a series of qualifications of one sense by another. And the altering or piling up of combinations with the qualifications implied gives the ground of the possible movements of mind. It is from the Erasmian tradition of praising folly that arises the paradox on which variations can be played. Upon this base the simple senses inherited from the older tradition may push against the paradox and insinuate the substitutions which multiply the variants. And part of the process of multiplication is created through the drama itself, in the growing audience awareness, where for example 'a new head sense could be established temporarily as part of the "style" of the play'. If common or legal usage is the source of a meaning, it is dramatic context that enables not only the deliberate transmutation of one sense of 'fool' into another, but places the fool upon the stage to comment. Action's fool is reflection's man of wisdom. And mixed folly and wisdom from the same source complicates the awareness of possible senses.

In normal practice Empson's method tries to determine which of the meanings from the original permutation repertoire is primary (sometimes this is the 'head sense' but not necessarily), spelling out the multiple accretions to it, while at the same time selecting those critical differentiae and perhaps even marginal aspects of the usage that give it its peculiar distinction and flavour. 'Clown' is on the path that leads from affectionate dependence and imbecility to 'fool', part of the development which leads towards the completed instrument. Yet judgement is all, and Empson's procedure moves from describing the accretion of complex meanings to selecting out the prominent and those whose interest reaches further. There is a double movement of mind – in this case Empson's own – between the growth of possibility of meaning through complexity, and the selective cutting across or breaking down of that complex amalgam of meaning. Both historically and procedurally it is as if synthesis preceded analysis. For analysis to take effect the variables must be assembled; this resembles a linguistic natural history which records and classifies the elements of a complex whole. Then one can begin to pull apart in various ways, discriminate according to a variety of interests and principles or senses of relevance. The movement is from a general picture – itself carefully constructed – to aspect seeing with a more localised focus, which catches the figural force of important intersection points within the repertoire.

The problem of this figural force comes through the recognition that any one use can become a metaphor for any other, so that the simple substitutions of 'fool' and 'clown' create in the first instance the figurative expansion, for if you reflect about a foolish man that he is like a clown 'the effect is then that you call him a clown metaphorically'. The move from particular to general can be doubled as in what he calls 'Mutual Metaphor' and the process of figuration seems to have no limit. But the choice between meanings that this opens us to must be determined by another principle, even if an unstable one. Even the movement in a single direction seems to push the meaning open in ways that must be otherwise shaped and contained. Consider the way in which one metaphoric movement presses against the Erasmian doctrine:

If then a Shakespearean use of fool is not a metaphor from the clown, I class it as a rather generalised memory of the Erasmus doctrine; but if it is, as most of them are, I maintain that it brings in the darker and more tragic picture that he got from his madmen. The two structures need not conflict, though they seem normally to be independent; and I think that *The Merchant of Venice*, which has a good deal of medieval feeling in its central allegory, gives a rather special case of a combination of the two. The negro prince represents pagan splendour and the lust of the eye; he chooses the gold casket, and finds only death in it, but nobody calls him a fool. The admittedly undeserving suitor who gives and hazards all he has (and all his friend has too) is apparently to stand for the triumph of the humble Christian. Only the conventional man between them, who chooses reasonable silver and is too much of a gentleman to ask for more than he deserves, is met by a picture of an idiot and a schedule calling him a Fool. Erasmus would no doubt have liked the thing as a whole, but I doubt whether he would have rubbed the idiot in so firmly. And what the allegory meant to Shakespeare was probably something rather different from the Christian interpretation; I think it was that you ought to accept the realities of life courageously even if rather unscrupulously, and not try to gloss over its contradictions and the depths that lie under your feet. I do not know how to symbolise a direct fusion of the two structures. (*CW*, p. 124)

I suppose the failure to symbolise represents a limitation of the equation system. But it also seems to indicate some larger conceptual difficulty. The relating of a 'darker and more tragic picture' to allegory opposed the disorderly open-endedness of metaphor to the 'generalised memory' which contains both traditional narrative forms and ordering conventions. So, what 'the allegory meant to Shakespeare' may be distanced from a Christian interpretation, yet there is something disturbing and unresolved about placing the Fool at the heart of the reasonable life. It is as if the allegory proposed a series of relations, an order of values. Yet that order contains an element that runs amok, that refuses to keep its place, and in the end is not assimilable into the allegory. And this parallels the problem of the two structures.

If Empson fails to find a way of representing this disturbing or subversive force in a rather schematic and self-contained allegorical scene, the problem is more complex in *Lear*. For if here 'Fool' suggests the uncontrolled element in an ordered scheme, in *Lear* he presses against the very uncertainty of order. Of course the source of disorder is palpably there: 'it is the Fool who causes the beginning of the storm against Lear' (*CW*, p. 129). The offence against Goneril is against that newly established and conventional order whose evil we will soon know. But he is the catalyst to a chain of disturbing consequences: Fool offends; gentleman chides; Lear strikes; Goneril responds in the name of her own established rule and interest. Of course the measure of 'fool' in the uncertain order of *Lear* is developed by way of Empson's rejection, often implicit to the point of being taken for granted, of any overall allegorising or Christianising view of the play. This puts a number of possible determinates quite aside, and key terms lack that solidity and certainty of placing themselves that an allegorical scheme might have given. They are less precisely outlined in the abandonment of any conceptual order which might lend itself to allegory. This relative indeterminacy may also partly account for a more open explanatory structure in the essay, largely abandoning the equation and permutation systems to engage with the colouration of that 'darker and more tragic picture' which derives from certain dimensions of 'fool'. The description of that colouration takes two general forms. One is an index of the degree to which the relation of oneself to one's world has gone awry: 'the natural fool of fortune' or in playing 'fool to sorrow'. This is something of a rag-bag of uses for which Empson attempts no typology or precise genealogy. The family resemblance draws on the way in which a moment can reveal a gap or discrepancy; or ironic perception of the action leads to the substitution of 'fool' for whatever the normal identity of a character might have been. The variety of effect is startling but somehow does not push the limits of resemblance: Edgar in disguise, Cordelia hanged, Kent in the stocks, and of course Lear himself both identified by the Fool as 'fool', and in the end truly one – 'he is genuinely a Fool now and has a right to the title' (*CW*, p. 145). In what is called a 'universal accusation of folly' to become a fool is to deny or lose oneself, or step into something alien, an abyss. But there is also a normative element in it, a black alternative condition which draws on disparate meanings that join worthlessness to madness. Beyond this there may be worse as the Fool implies to Lear: 'I would rather be anything than a fool, and yet I would not be thee'.

But this is the Fool's voice, and it is the principal vehicle for the other aspect of Empson's description. An intensified awareness coming through that mixture of diversion, hard truth and subversive implication in the Fool's commentary, requires continuous revision of one's understanding. One sees not only 'this great stage of fools' but the dislocation of it from the Fool's own vision. Taken together the two forms of description provide inner and outer forms of irony, a double vision of folly set in the dramatic irony of discrepancy and the discrepant appreciation of it.

Much of the argument moves between alternative explanations of how the intricate reflexivity affects both particular uses and the 'head sense'. But the applications within a play are of course on the part of characters in it. In this perhaps the Fool may have a privileged role in his incarnation of the multiple displacements that calling others 'fool' implies. But the sense of any such use depends upon the understanding of its source, and with the characters in a play the construction of some form of hypothetical psychology, some general understanding of what their words and actions mean at any one point in the action. But there is also some fuller sense of what they would be like, if one could really have a comprehensive view, even if we see it only in fragments through the dramatic action. The implied whole is a construct, even more than the particular dramatic moment. And this differs for serious readers, for the obvious mixture of personal and historical reasons. To see Lear much as Bradley, or much as Orwell (or Wilson Knight, or Jan Kott, etc.), the 'much as' indicates that sharing is qualified, if always imaginable. That a bent of mind, or feel for one's own contemporaneity, both shapes imagining but can be modified and manipulated goes without saying. As does the possibility of self-deception and the counter-productive: 'The determination of Bradley to bring out the best in the good characters sometimes makes his judgements rather brutal, oddly enough ... ' (*CW*, p. 131). This is also an example of trying to overdetermine and limit the possibilities, with an indication of its attendant cost.

So one dimension of the understanding of 'fool' works through the understanding of persons, but in a way which draws on dramatic circumstance, which makes the use more complex than the analogous case of 'They that have power'. For the use is qualified by the presumed understanding by the speaker of his object, a secondary and wider understanding of both speaker and reference, as well as the change of meaning as the action unfolds. That is, it might not only mean something quite different at the end of the play from the beginning, but have gone through intervening transformations. But the single case can pose different kinds of variables. When Lear says of Cordelia, 'And my poor fool is hanged' the reading depends not only on the historical resources on which Shakespeare might have drawn, but presumptions about Lear's state of mind and present understanding, the alteration of Cordelia's fortunes, the relations of innocence, folly, madness and endearment, to pick only the main lines of possible meanings. The most primitive grasp is a meta-fiction built on a fiction of Lear, trying to overcome its intrinsic opacity. And this construction no doubt requires the corresponding invention of an audience which will be a sounding-board for the diversity of this process. Here 'fool' becomes the focal point where understanding and confusion meet – relation and disorder.

While others are of great interest, there are two aspects of Empson's method that have consequences that I wish to isolate. One is that procedure through the invention of persons and their invention of each other that I have tried so briefly to describe – something which resembles the procedure used with 'They that have power'. The other lies in seeing the metaphor from the 'fool' stretched to the further reaches of its implications:

The foolish Lear can compare the storm and the heavens to himself, and the stock metaphor from the clown and the lunatic can be extended to include the cosmos. Such is the impression from a literal reading, I think, and critics have either evaded it or hailed it as being anti-Christian. But, if you take it as simply a result of working out the key metaphor as far as it would go, you need not expect it to have a clear-cut theological conclusion; the problem for the dramatist was rather to keep such a thing at bay. The effect of the false renunciation is that Lear has made a fool of himself on the most cosmic and appalling scale possible... (*CW*, p. 155)

Here the use of dramatic form works in another way, to qualify and ironise metaphysical commitment. How specific this is to Shakespeare is unclear, and certainly the balance of effect in other dramatists is not entirely the same. There is a formal theological conclusion to Faustus yet it is rich in ambiguity and a strange openness strains against the allegorical, while the splendid carnival of punishments at the end of Volpone leaves no doubt about the rigour of moral conviction. Perhaps this is one reason why, for all his brilliance, there is a residue of ugliness in Jonson which appears precisely in this literal-mindedness. Even at Shakespeare's crankiest (Empson is quite straightforward on the streak of sexual revulsion) a world is created which is not quite reducible to a hard-nosed opinion. This raises the question of whether or not the Empsonian pursuit of metaphor would work as well in a world of more fixed and tidy views. (In *Complex Words* Pope is the case where the brilliant deployment of uses is not played out in a metaphorically extended way.)

In 'working out the key metaphor as far as it would go' Empson at least partly indicates that Shakespeare has used it at fullest possible stretch, that Lear has appeared as somehow the ultimate fool, which combines the notion of the most extreme case with the confluence point of the richest sources of meaning. Somehow they do not cancel each other out, although accretion may change its aspect as emphasis, selection and modification work within it. In this case 'as far as it would go' also suggests completeness, that all the possible resources have been ransacked, and that they are somehow all present in the supreme 'fool'. Yet this suggests an essentialism that is wholly avoided. Various criteria for the determination of 'as far as' are hinted or implied: extreme extension, saturation, completeness, etc., but no essential yardstick. Much of the implication is of the inexhaustibility of metaphor. And there is no fixed measure.

The inexhaustible possibilities of 'as far as' of course would not imply that some meanings are not suspect and that their marginality cannot be made clear. Empson rather shies away from the notion of the Holy Fool with its transcendental trappings, as he does from anything which might give the play too well defined a metaphysical force. The various *obiter dicta* with which the essay ends have a methodological diffidence which would seem to put such a force rather outside the reach of his own way of seeing, even if something is there that must be acknowledged: 'by being such a complete fool Lear may become in some mystical way superlatively wise and holy. It seems hard to deny that this idea is knocking about yet I think it belongs to the play rather than the character' (*CW*, p. 157). It is a view which pushes away from doctrine and belief and towards experience and desire. 'And the scapegoat who has collected all of this wisdom for us is viewed at the end with a sort of hushed envy, not I think because he has become wise but because the general human desire for experience has been so glutted in him. He has been through everything' (*CW*, p. 159).

So the final terms are naturalistic and psychological rather than transcendent or metaphysical – glut more than understanding. These are given features of the human condition: hardly describable, much less encompassable, ready to resurface in unexpected ways with another surge of feeling or flicker of appetite. Yet wisdom and holiness are 'knocking around' in aspects of 'fool' that do not adhere to Lear, perhaps partly because if there were an aura of holy folly it could not be possessed by him alone. One may vaguely think that the play generates certain moral or religious atmospheres with which it then does nothing decisive. These things are felt and present, but hardly located with respect to any distinctive pattern of belief. And to go further by way of Empson would be pure speculation.

A more characteristic indication of how the method works is given through the selectivity of senses: 'What the key-word or "pattern" approach brings you to, I submit, is a fundamental horror, an idea that the gods are such silly and malicious jokers that they will destroy the world' (*CW*, p. 156). This is not quite akin to saying that the real force of the play comes through its subliminal message, but that the cumulative effect of the language transcends particular occasions. Yet this too must be treated with reservation. He is sceptical of Caroline Spurgeon's more classificatory and additive approach, for the frequency of a figure may not be the indication of its importance. 'Gold' as an implied metaphor in Timon may outweigh the rarity of its direct use. On the other hand, he has not made an attempt to measure the cumulative effect of the forty-seven manifestations of 'fool' or to decide which act metaphorically and which do not, although he may assume that the substitutions implied are so pervasive that all of the manifestations are metaphoric to some degree while the literal references to 'gold' in Timon are simply that.

The thought of accounting for implied metaphor takes us further still from clear contours to a method. The difficulty in extracting a programme from this comes out partly in the imprecise relations between 'key terms', 'master symbol', 'double symbol' etc. ('dog' is a double but not a master, while 'fool' is a master). Sometimes the force of these distinctions is clearly visible and sometimes not. 'Metaphor' is often used loosely for almost any sort of figure, although very good reasons could be given for this. He treats Richards's quite open definition as unduly restrictive (*CW*, p. 332). So 'working out the key metaphor as far as it would go' – which seems almost as programmatic as Empson gets, bar the equational system – has both an openness as to what constitutes the right sort of key, and as to how one determines how far one should go, as well as the liberality conveyed by the highly indeterminate 'working out'. All of these depend ultimately on the depiction of such aspects of context that 'what is important' is clearly seen. And in the depiction of these multiple contexts and the power of transformation which they operate Empson's descriptive invention continually rediscovers the possibility of meaning.

In this the two great Empsonian themes of ambiguity and irony make their return to the foreground. Both derive their effect from an openness of possibility that goes beyond the particular case, yet which has not found a description at a more general level. Complex words are open to continuous mutation – the historical record is evidence enough – and employ a combinational freedom that contexts draw from them. It was through this that the creation of 'fool' as instrument became possible. What Empson's example shows is the degree to which the interest is rechargeable with that shift of context, with the discovery of the new dimension in an example, a way in which the background of the complex word opens to another shaft of light or turn of screw. In the most direct possible way the ironies of 'fool' arise from such complication, where the most concrete version (clown) and the most grandiose implication (cosmic) serve as ironic comments on each other. The effect is to give further and further dimensions – like new vistas appearing on the stage and scenery changes – to the enormous complexity arising out of particular circumstance, so as to provide another ironic contrast with the downbeat simplicity of the conceptual machinery and its absence of general claims.

To relate this effect to Derridean irony is to evoke a different mode of the relational. If one looks to the 'complex word' *pharmakon*, the terms in which its transformations are seen have more precise lines of directional control, as if every element were part of a more structured design, even if to call that structure in question. For the design relates movement, change, uncertainty within a world of carefully controlled connection.

Hence, for example, the word *pharmakon*. In this way we hope to display in the most striking manner the regular, ordered polysemy that has, through skewing, indetermination, or overdetermination, but without mistranslation, permitted the rendering of the same word by 'remedy', 'recipe', 'poison', 'drug', 'philter', etc. It will also be seen to what extent the malleable unity of this concept, or rather its rules and the strange logic that links it with its signifier, has been dispersed, masked, obliterated, and rendered almost unreadable not only by the imprudence or empiricism of the translators, but first and foremost by the redoubtable, irreducible difficulty of translation. It is a difficulty inherent in its very principle, situated less in the passage from one language to another, from one philosophical language to another, than already, as we shall see, in the tradition between Greek and Greek; a violent difficulty in the transference of a nonphilosopheme into a philosopheme. With this problem of translation we will thus be dealing with nothing less than the problem of the very passage into philosophy.[2]

This sense of 'passage' derives partly from the transformational power in the ambiguous substance which denies its substantiality in a self-contradictory nature. The account is rich in indications of transition, of multiple forms of movement from one state to another: passages through languages and cultures; through magic, alchemy, medicine into what may be health or death; from non-philosophical concepts into philosophy, from myth into truth. All of these transitions are representations of movement: 'from ... into', 'from ... to', so repeated that the movement itself seems to predominate over any final term or destination. And indeed 'The pharmakon is the movement, the locus, and the play: (the production of) difference. It is the *différance* of difference. It holds in reserve, in its undecided shadow and vigil, the opposites and differends that the process of discrimination will come to carve out' (*D*, p. 127)

As in the created ambiguity of 'différance' where the insertion of a temporal and logical gap into the distinction from which meaning is derived is conveyed by neologism, the cross-currents of *pharmakon* come from a calculated over-determination that does not arise from the *Phaedrus* in the way that the ambiguities of 'fool' arose from *King Lear* where the natural nexus of combinations created the complex instrument. There is a nexus, but its most important features are arranged through coordinates brought to bear. I do not mean that Derrida could have got his argument under way without natural ambiguity. And the ambiguity is rich enough without his reinvention of it. But of course it looks more tangential in the *Phaedrus* where it seems so often an indeterminate metaphor of trans-formation, and where its richness in context is but a distant point of allusion. That richness is reinscribed so that the multiple natural meanings – 'remedy', 'recipe', 'poison', 'cure', 'drug', 'philter', or even 'charm' or 'spell' – all are through the fact of translation the representations of the mysterious signifier in what can become alternative areas of understanding, or structured lines of thought.

So the 'malleable unity' in question 'or rather the strange logic that links it with the signifier' is already shaped by the kind of self-consciousness that works through meta-languages. (Here I take the signifier to be the word itself, and the 'malleable unity' the collective possibilities of the multiple signifieds.) Are these ways in which this 'strange logic' is analogous to the process by which 'fool' has gathered its depth of meaning? If the latter has been followed through the wild course of natural process, subject to hazard and uncertainty, revealing glimpses of the unexpected through the unpredictable course a word has taken, the masked and obliterated unity will still be the subject of something regular and ordered. Any such analogy will compare the description of a jungle whose rare fauna may be caught in flight with a more conceptually controlled environment, a philosopher's Garden of Adonis perhaps whose arranged magic is valid for a season – ultimately to be jettisoned like last year's ladders – and where the seeds and specimens have known identities and predictable promise, a controlled and ordered polysemy.

There seem to be two senses in which the understanding of such a polysemy is opened up. One lies in the sequence of more or less approximate translations that the various contexts may draw upon thus evoking different decisions in the translation, sometimes as radical as the choice between the 'poison' and the 'cure'. In this sense the 'passage into philosophy' is similar to the breaking down of some mythic nucleus which can be dismantled into analysed components, involving us in discrimin-ations, choices, critical procedures – deciding what something means. The other lies in those senses that involve a form of symbolic displacement, as in the identification of the *pharmakon* with writing. Of course the latter may work by way of the former, as is straightforwardly the case in the treatment of *Phaedrus* 274e where ambiguity so appears 'without hidden mediation, without secret argumentation'. But this process has begun with a reference to the written oration hidden beneath Phaedrus's cloak, where the hidden argumentation exists in Derrida's assertion, a step necessarily suggested through reading backwards: the riches of argument were already there.

This is only to suggest two rough tracks on which the polysemy might be deployed. Derrida's argument moves on quite other and more various paths. But the notion of translation poses questions that are not wholly resolved or, at least not in the instance of use, revealed. I mean that the *pharmakon* which lies behind its translated versions derives from them a mythical unity; it seems to stand behind all of its incarnations like an 'ur' concept, the guarantor of the unity. There is an assumption of something constant behind the translated terms that we have found in our own natural and conceptual language so that however variable the possibilities of reading there is a point to which they return. Does this very presence of the underlying *pharmakon* imply at least a semblance of essentialism, even of that aspect of Platonism which does not wholly disappear with 'malleable'?

I should like to follow in a selective way some aspects of the various paths. But consider first certain of the conditions that govern them like 'indetermination' and 'overdetermination', which themselves seem to imply the possibility of essential meaning which is either diffused in the indeterminate or over-narrowly specified in the overdeterminate. Over-determination might have its ordered regularities if one saw it as the attempt to contain the possibilities of meaning, to give it the tidiness and distinctness of limitation. That any particular translation of *pharmakon* would require the terms of a determining context to give shape to the necessary 'head sense' would be understood. In the passage mentioned, 274e, Theuth clearly means that writing is a cure for the memory, yet Thamus's reply, which does not mention the word, argues that it is not. Is a deep indetermination introduced by this further consideration, which shows without saying so the danger hidden in the therapy, the poison in the cure?

Yet indetermination would seem to have no characteristic use of its own, but be simply the loss of determinate meaning in any one context; it introduces the shadow world of the many uses that we have for the occasion rejected, and whose existence as trace elements may appear to haunt us as the slightest perspective changes. But is the indeterminate only intelligible in terms of the failure of determination, and is there any way in which a regular and ordered account of it could be given? It is hard to see something that goes beyond simple structuralist oppositions: order and disorder, regularity and chaos, which coexist as *definienda* of each other. After all, as Wisdom says 'What is oneness without otherness?'. But it is otherness that poses the difficulty in having only a negative identity.

It is not part of Derrida's aim to remove such difficulties, or to unpack

in a satisfactory way the contradictions in relating order to the indeterminate, which is merely inherent in the 'irreducible difficulty of
translation'. There is no way in which 'irreducible difficulty' can be
resolved in smooth rearrangement. His method is to follow the stages and
problematics of the irresolvable as Plato's text provides the ground of
devious paths. 'Operating through seduction, the *pharmakon* makes one
stray...' (*D*, p. 70); and again 'the leading astray' (*D*, p. 71). This
'ordered' straying is in some senses Derrida's own literary form, and the
relations between ordering and straying, between sequential and oblique
movements, constitutes at least the external form of a game in which the
nature of one's own discourse is continually, if not exactly systematically
or seriously, put in question. The shifting of types of discourse within the
essay enables a number of kinds of language game to coexist, and to extend
the treatment of *pharmakon*: analysis, description, side comment, narrative, parody, a mock fictionalising, all play part in the larger sense of
language appropriate to its divine inventor. For 'His propriety or property
is impropriety or inappropriateness, the floating indetermination that
allows for substitution and play. *Play*, of which he is also the inventor...
' (*D*, p. 93). The effect of this is drawn out more fully in a passage that
examines the non-substantial character of the *pharmakon*, which 'cannot
be handled with complete security, neither in its being, for it has none, nor
in its effects, the sense of which is always capable of changing' (*D*, p. 126).

The pattern of movement is from the 'floating indetermination' to the
transformational possibilities of play to the systematic analysis of
ambivalence. But this ambivalence is at least partly unlike the ambivalence
of 'fool', in that it is not substantive. 'If the *pharmakon* is "ambivalent",
it is because it constitutes the medium in which opposites are opposed, the
movement and the play that links them among themselves, reverses them
or makes one side cross over into the other (soul/body, good/evil,
inside/outside, memory/forgetfulness, speech/writing, etc.)' (*D*, p. 127).
There seem to be two levels that are not indicated separately. One is of
primary ambiguity where two or more meanings may coexist in indeterminate mix. The other is a somewhat stricter notion of ambivalence as
the conjoining of opposites, although the pairings mentioned include
opposites of quite different sorts and hardly form an intelligible class.
Certainly the primary ambiguities are subject to the further variables of
being read according to context, where the predominance of one meaning
may efface others, in varying degree; or as in the case of 'fool' carry their
doubleness (or multiplicity) with them.

If one proceeded through an inventory of the relatively natural
meanings, it would be moderately restricted in its possibilities, although
contextual instances would, as with 'fool', qualify each other. To the

process of symbolic identification there seems no limiting principle. However it is the non-substantive nature of the *pharmakon* that enriches the possibility of complication. 'Without being anything in itself', it is the 'medium in which opposites are opposed', as well as being the inexhaustible reserve 'diacritical, different, deferring', from which 'contradictions and pairs of opposites are lifted'. Part of the problem of this arises in the passage of the *pharmakon* from what is essentially a substantive characterisation – poison, cure, drug, spell, etc. – through a symbolic substitution – writing, forgetfulness, etc. -to the non-substantive matrix from which discrimination, dialectic and contradiction derive. And one will have to ask in the end whether or not in the course of this passage logical problems arise which are damaging to the enterprise.

This is clearly a highly figurative portrait of this matrix, of this beginning point which can hardly be described in itself, but must be located, researched, dramatised through what spills out of it. Only the consequences have the suitable degree of definition, are separable as identifiable pieces of language and argument – at least insofar as we take the notion of insubstantiality substantially to heart. The cultural, mythic, literary and philosophical components that have spilled out from the 'medium' unfold through their appropriate differentiation and are culturally specific according to their own modes. We can say all sorts of things about them. But theoretically, we can only reach the *pharmakon* through the products of this possibility. The 'medium', matrix, *chora*, etc. becomes a hypothesis only reached by way of what follows from it. Yet for Derrida it is incarnated in a word, '*pharmakon*' whose multiple uses and meanings, which echo through the Platonic dialogues in rich and varied ways, provide a medium of another kind, a ground of figurative transformations.

This means two kinds of development are directly possible. One is through the numerous Platonic instances of a word whose multiple meanings lead directly to the figuration that composes a substantial part of Derrida's own 'argument' about the nature of writing. Whether or not this development supports his general argument, or could do so, does not concern me. (I happen to think that it does not, and could not. But here it is not a relevant problem.) What does concern me is the intrinsic interest in the process of unfolding, in the complex and devious ways through which an 'instrument' is created. And the process may tell us enough about the nature of that instrument that we might have some sense of its further use. If it is the beginning point of a sequence of 'movements of mind' we might reach some understanding of the drift and consequences of such movement.

The other kind of development is the dark mirror of the first. It simply consists in a number of things that Plato did not say. They may come to us by way of Plato in that they are represented as arising in the interstices of what he did say. Or they may circulate more freely as implicit in the kinds of concepts in play: *pharmakos* does not exist in Plato's text, indeed is 'strikingly absent'. The 'forces of association' may powerfully suggest the importance of terms not actually present but communicated through the lexical system (cf. *D*, pp. 129–30). And the 'pharmacy' of Derrida's title seems largely a construction of his own, an extension of the notion of *pharmakon*, something evoked by it to give a sense of the depth of reserve. 'It is also this store of deep background that we are calling the *pharmacy*.' This concept is interesting partly because the depth of background will bring the essay close at many points to the historical and etymological dimensions of Empson's complexity. So it is out of the extension of concepts, the elaboration of cognates, the construction of further members of the verbal chain, that the dimensions of meaning and possibilities of argument will move.

The justification of the evocation of *pharmakos* clearly gives some difficulty. More than one would expect, as one hardly took the essay to be a strict reading of Plato in the first place. The important move seems to be from the sense of the density of the textual setting to the metaphoric freedom that the construction gives, a freedom based on Derrida's awareness of the far-reaching use of Socrates as scapegoat. It is characteristic, of course, that this is a metaphoric step, another figurative aspect of the instrument.

Indeed, the whole method by which the unfolding of *pharmakon* proceeds is a process of figuration, which may or may not parallel a conceptual argument for which it provides the articulation, or which, if seen the opposite way, is followed by certain conceptual implications. Even if what Derrida is doing is a form of philosophy, he seems to begin 'within the limits of this tissue: between the metaphor of the *histos* and the question of the *histos* of metaphor'. That web may be the product of centuries to be undone, yet it is undone through the construction of a pattern of figures, a web in a sense of his own, and one in which a series of figures are described by others. A sequence of figural substitutions is inaugurated, in the first instance by reference to the role of example, which will be seen in terms of further example. And so it will proceed through stories, myths, rituals, customs, visual examples from painting, family relationships, politics, gardening, and others, including the possible multiplication and subdivision of such categories.

Have the many stories become figures which may represent each other in such a way that the figuration of figuration dissolves all meaning in metaphor? We shall look at this possibility in the end. But certainly the openness of play as opposed to the closed-circuit of the game is posed for Derrida both in terms of the Platonic appropriation of play, and its own openness as figure. The reduction to game means a subordination to rules, so that one can say 'it is part of the rules of this game that the game *should seem to stop*' (*D*, p. 128) The force of 'seem' in this may blur the edge of a necessary decision. And indeed, is 'this game' *his* game? For the sense that the *pharmakon* is 'caught' by philosophy suggests that his own play has been tied to a game which by its built-in rules should have to stop. But is it illusory? Is Derrida caught in a game posing exit lines that he knows are arranged, 'overdetermined'? It might be a consolation compared with the indetermination of play. Does one sense that of the multiplication of metaphors there is no end and much figuration is a weariness of the mind's eye? Or is it the vertigo of freedom in the face of implicit overdetermination?

It is tempting to see in this an analogy to the Empsonian problem of where to put the common-sense limits on the open-endedness of permutation. But Empson's 'system' is conceived in what can be expressed as quantifiable terms, and its limits are those that a natural historian might find in counting specimens or deciding how many more examples were necessary to establish a general rule. Mutations may continue but they are not infinite in number at any one point, nor precisely and finitely containable. Derrida suggests rather a closed system in which new meanings are generated through contrast and opposition, something which may reflect fairly directly his Hegelian and structuralist inheritance.

The empirical habit of mind, of seeing things as much as possible for what they are and not what they are not, finding one's way among the individual cases with a close eye to their circumstantial character and carefully discerned uniqueness, contrasts sharply with seeing things defined by opposition and by positioning within a relational system. This suggests that there is, to put it paradoxically, a systematic indetermination built into the empirical approach. A new example might turn up, a new circumstance alter the perspective on what had seemed like more limited uses. And the 'post-structuralist' character which seems rather literally identifiable in this aspect of the treatment of *pharmakon* conveys some distinctive determination through this very fact, which inserts some element of game in whatever movement towards play.

Yet, if in Empson there is no stopping point other than the exhaustion of interest, in seeing that the permutations run into the sand as there is less and less critical light to be found in looking to further cases, the difficulty with the proliferation of figure lies less in its diminishing returns than in the centrifugal force of the further dimensions its re-creation involves. The movement into a predominantly figural expository mode makes narrative, myth, metaphor shift so radically that one game seems to have become another. We cannot decide whether or not the same rules would apply, or where in the series of substitutions we come to feel that the connections have become lost, and irrelevance or inanity yawn before us. So the other face of 'overdetermination' is metaphor roaring out of control, and the 'ordered' yet indeterminate polysemy has produced a consciously self-mocking but intellectually fatalistic conjunction of randomness and design.

Rather than following a metaphor as far as it will go, the multiplying of metaphors in a sequence of substitutions outflank each game as the shape of the game begins to seem determined. Is the creation of the semblance of a stopping place in effect to describe the metamorphosis of the game, and hence the reality of the stopping place? Or is there no final outflanking movement by which the others are contained? For if the very nature of the game lies in a limitless reinvention of itself it rules out the possibility that the game stops. The seeming stopping point will simply be the lightly touched pencil marking which indicates what we hope is an intelligible segment, a point at which *we* at any rate have to stop, and where the flow of games is punctuated by some appropriate sign, like the curious little fiction with which Derrida's essay ends. There is no end and there can only seem to be one.

Arguments which work in such a fashion bring us to two of the principal difficulties that are frequently pointed out in what has come to be called 'deconstruction'. One is that the indeterminate possibility of substitution leads to an infinite regress in which nothing is ever finally explained, nor can ever be. One moves from the semblance of an argument through a story, a myth, metaphor or related figure and back without a sense of where the satisfactory level of explanation may be found. Even if one restricted oneself to steps which were of roughly the same form there would still be no way of saying this is the point at which we now have an understanding. This is clearly intended, but can it be coherently stated and held?

The second difficulty lies in the implicit reflexivity. For Derrida's own text must itself enter into the game – or even play – and its own authority cannot be other than assimilated to the same standing as the text on which it comments. There is no way in which the comment can stand outside the process it describes and claim any form of privilege with respect to it. These considerations lead far beyond the present case to what has been thought the implicit nihilism in these games containing games, founded on nothing but each other and caught up in a contingency of language which is recognised in a 'playing on the play within language'. The consequence is best described by one whose idiom is close to that game, J. Hillis Miller:

'Deconstruction' is neither nihilism nor metaphysics but simply interpretation as such, the untangling of the inherence of metaphysics in nihilism and of nihilism in metaphysics by way of the close reading of texts. This procedure, however, can in no way escape, in its own discourse, from the language of the passages it cites. This language is the expression of the inherence of nihilism in metaphysics and of metaphysics in nihilism. We have no other language. The language of criticism is subject to exactly the same limitations and blind alleys as the language of the works it reads. The most heroic effort to escape from the prisonhouse of language only builds the walls higher.[3]

The verbal gyrations which follow and try to indicate the way in which deconstruction may yet point to a region beyond metaphysics need not concern us. It is the question of interpretation which does.

We have been looking at a reading of certain aspects of the *Phaedrus*, or at least at the exploration of certain issues by way of that dialogue. Beyond a series of tentative seeming manoeuvres which combine diffidence with assertion, the text is gradually reached through, among other things, a recognition of the impossibility of its being directly perceived. The 'rules of the game' are hidden. And the text itself lost to the present except for the regenerating power of reading, that tissue of decisions which undoes the web of centuries. We must enter into a necessary game which we can never master, 'by the logic of play'. We take and follow a thread – continuing the figure – creating a web, a supplement if one likes, playing a game without known rules. Is our reading, like Derrida's, like any, creating through decisions, discriminations even, which sketch that fragmentary understanding called interpretation, which must in the end be identified with the text in question, in effect the only text we have? Perhaps in Derrida's case the philosopher and critic have become one in the making of the web, in this meta-commentary become speculation which remains text. If so, what has happened to the passage into philosophy? For the philosophy we have reached through being caught in discrimination, dialectic, etc. seems no different from interpretation. This in turn ends in the ironic tale in which the echo chamber disarticulates speech into the illusion of a dialogue 'Full of meaning. A whole story. An entire history. All of philosophy' (*D*, p. 170).

Such reinvention is less a violation or rearrangement of the text than a signal that the original ground is incomplete. The normal procedure through much of the essay is to take the philological, historical and anthropological evidence quite seriously in a perfectly conventional way, while shifting the angle from which the text is seen so that the necessity of interpretation forces a more and more radical figurative characterisation. After all, the philosopher moves through multiple games and interpretations, from the simple breaking apart at the beginnings of dialectic to the indistinguishable blur of buzzing voices which surround the last incarnation of the *pharmakon*: the doubleness of an attack of demonic possession and the cure against such attack. The philosopher's recognition of his contradictory self is a form of madness, yet which bears within itself its cure: one keeps writing.

The ambiguities that surround acts of philosophical utterance, the passage into philosophy by the simultaneous assumption and demolition of the myth of itself, do not make it easy to decide how such a commentary – interpretation as Hillis Miller says – fits any version of critical understanding that is consonant with itself. Insofar as it was perfectly clear that Empson was involved in a critical reading, one must acknowledge the degree to which such a reading accepts the authority of an historical conception of meaning. But contingently so, not in the sense of claiming some special epistemological character for history. And the lowest level of implied metaphysics would be hard to identify beyond an Enlightenment rationalism that is attached to process and not to substance, or an experimental outlook that is relatively humble in the face of its given. Derridean interpretation in a sense has no given. What one interprets becomes something else in the moment of mentioning it.

His works are neither philosophical nor literary. His strategy refuses to be governed by concepts of ends ('a teleo-eschatological horizon'); rather than ordered relations of means and ends his strategy refers to the play of the stratagem itself. Rather than names having a precise conceptual meaning they represent a 'system of predicates', a conceptual organisation centred on a predicate, with the use of a name (indeed old words, old names) being 'a kind of *lever of intervention*' through which such organisations are grasped and transformed.

Hence the extended use of *pharmakon* as both conceptual centre and lever of intervention. It is an old word of course, and one which attaches by *écriture* to others, one which has been carefully surrounded by the radiating circles of multiple meanings, by its mysterious past, cultural exoticism, its innate capacity to be used against itself, to the old word banalised by familiarity, eroded by use, yet requiring its own rediscovery as the guaranty of philosophy's only possible 'ultimate' term of reference and point of departure.

I am quite aware that I have avoided in substance any consideration of the ostensible theme of Derrida's argument concerning the relation of *logos* to *écriture*, or any consideration of his elaborate dismantling of the Platonic assumptions: words name things, which are so namable because they in turn represent essences which in turn have their metaphysical foundations. From this a long tradition of metaphysical realism with respect to universals follows. There are two reasons for this omission. For one I am convinced that there are other ways of disposing of this metaphysical baggage without going by way of this contrast of *logos* and writing. Secondly, I am not convinced that the reasoning about supplements etc. succeeds in its own terms. But for my purposes it is not necessary to argue this case. It enters only indirectly through the characterisation of *pharmakon* as the antidote to that metaphysical primacy. For it is the figural centre of a descriptive system, an account of the non-essential nature of naming, of the non-substantive picture of language, and my concern is not with whether or not such an account establishes what it set out to do (in fact I think it does not) but with the nature of this figural instrument.

But if of the making of figures there is no end, the vehicle for such figures is writing, and there is no point at which the comment on a text naturally exhausts itself, or reaches a point where the account, or our understanding, if you will, is complete. Rorty remarks: 'For Derrida writing always leads to more writing, and more, and still more – just as history does not lead to Absolute Knowledge or the Final Struggle, but to more history, and more and still more. The *Phenomenology's* vision of truth as what you get by reinterpreting all the previous reinterpretations of reinterpretations still embodies the Platonic ideal of the Last Reinterpreter, the *right* interpretation at last. Derrida wants to keep the horizontal character of Hegel's notion of philosophy without its teleology, its sense of direction, its seriousness.'[4]

As with figures, so with interpretations. There is no way in which the lever of intervention can make a move that is more decisive than other moves. Interpretations are not justified, but simply are. They may serve our understanding if we accept their relational and transitory nature. But then, if no criteria for justification can be given, no criteria for failure are present either. For indeed, if all teleological considerations are abandoned there is no end by which comparisons might be made. The way in which a figure may illuminate another may be seen, but hardly explained. That there should be any difference between 'the right interpretation at last' and relative rightness in limited contexts for which at least partial criteria would be statable could not provide Derrida with the fixed necessary fulcrum – that would be too dimly quotidian, too deeply dispiriting altogether. And the moment of settling on it would be fatal to it.

However, even if 'relative rightness' is not the matter of the project we may accept it as its aftermath. Like Malraux's '*monnaie de l'absolu*' there is the tissue of the possible in the proliferation of 'small change'. For the relative rightness that comes through makes up the working hypothesis to serve a further understanding, in a continuous process. Perhaps there is some degree of rapport with the natural history of 'fool' in which the accumulation of senses never quite comes to rest, the perspective is altered with every occasion of its use, and the totality will always reveal its provisional nature. Relative rightness will serve, if no stated version of it will ever be acceptable. For even if we give up in our pursuit of 'fool', accede to that moment of awareness that the music will have to stop, we never lose our conviction that perhaps another interesting move may be made. And for this possibility the word 'relative' simply stands as a marker.

If *pharmakon* is a lever in a flux where no leverage is possible, 'fool' is a key where in the end there is no lock. In Empson there is no riddle, and in his own way, no end. The pursuit of 'fool' leads to something quite different from the buzzing in Plato's head, but as deeply palpable in the experience of pain. Or perhaps it is an end of a most unanalysable Anglo-Saxon kind to find the terminus of an analytic process in experience itself. So our two cases may point in quite different ways, with the instruments of ambiguity and polysemy shaped by quite different procedures, yet in the comparison have analogies of value. Empson has moved through the pathless wilds of a natural language where the uncertainties of connection, qualification or predominance of an aspect leave judgement or decision on a 'darkling plain' where the glut of experience has no precise measure. Derrida works through the artifices of hypothesising and then eroding controlling structures.

Both have moved through radical uncertainty of meaning with wholly different concerns in the management of its consequences. One takes the recognition of the randomness of things as a fortuitous and natural fatality which is the underlying condition of life. The other forces randomness upon us through dismantling the false structures and makings of sense which our fictionalising mentalities have shored against our ruin. For Empson the dramatic irony of *Lear* is a mirror to men's hearts where the truth of folly is a concentrated and terrible moment on which the mind may come to rest. For Derrida the mirrors reflect each other in an endless exchange where nothing comes to rest and the eye must simply follow to the vanishing point.

# VII 'The monstrous clarity'

Mallarmé's shadow of the soul's journey begins before a text. The path through the darkness of the self points for Igitur to an indeterminate end, where the *clarté chimérique* – the monstrous clarity – of the flickering candle's extinction falls upon a closed page.[1] Indeed, the closing of the book in *Igitur* follows rather abruptly upon its disclosure, open in its 'pallor' upon the table. Perhaps we should expect no more from a work which has been pared to its symbolic overtones, where Midnight is the moment of 'clarity', and the light falls on the page in the darkness of pure dream. No doubt to such purity of paradox we must bring, as Mallarmé suggests, a few of our own 'stage trappings'. Certainly Poulet has found in the opening of the 'dramatic' fragment a heightened paradigm of the consciousness of the reader: 'In an empty room on a table, a book awaits its reader. It seems to me that this is the initial condition of every literary work.' Before consciousness approaches it is an object. What is on Mallarmé's page? Does it connect in some way with 'an ancient idea'? Or is the page blank? We shall not know which *tabula* is *rasa* and how consciousness will transform this encounter. For Poulet the image suggests a *locus classicus* of the text's otherness, of the entry into one's awareness of a consciousness which is not one's own, and whose alien presence startles through its very existence. Our awareness may bring the book to life, but the awareness through it of another being is a primary moment of astonishment which becomes the ground of criticism. As we have seen: 'This astonished consciousness is the critical consciousness.'[2]

Hence one's account becomes the filling of an empty room, the 'chambre vide' of Igitur, the 'page at Midnight' (*M*, p. 435). Poulet's description becomes an extended metaphor, in which the evolution of consciousness becomes the filling of a space by the mind's moment of shock, discovery, identification, loss and recovery of self, in registering the presence of another, an *other* defined and opened through the pages on the table. Is the critical enterprise the appropriate filling out of the dramatic possibilities for a reader's intelligence, a response to the invitation on the title page? As

one might expect Mallarmé' himself closes off the moment of confrontation. We are not told what happens before the closing of the book,
nor given a sight of the pale pages. Do they suggest the long obsession with
whiteness, the contrast with pervasive dark, transformed into the *grimoire*,
the book of riddles and sacred knowledge, of indecipherable ancestral
traces, where the *alter ego* finds the model of all critical beginnings and
interpretative tangles? It is such a confrontation that Rorty draws from
Nabokov's phrase in *Pale Fire*: 'Man's life as a commentary to an abstruse
unfinished poem'.

Abstruse, unfinished, with the added uncertainty provided by the way in
which notes and alternative versions qualify each other, the invitation to
the intelligence of the reader invokes something which is almost the
reversal of Poulet's primary astonishment at the other, for the 'other' is as
close as possible to absent. The text may open itself, and ask us in as an
integral part of a necessary life, as if some such complement were essential
to its being. It is not only the elusiveness of a literal sense that requires what
Mallarmé calls 'a noble complementary operation', but something which
introduces, however deeply immersed in ironies or indirections, the need
for an external world to give life. *Igitur* is implied theatre with all that may
require in adding 'stage trappings', strangely matched in Mallarmé's
concern with another theatrical art where implication dispenses with
language altogether. 'Ballet gives little away: it is the imaginative genre.'
Choosing to balance the 'point philosophique' on the dancer's points is to
gesture towards the elusiveness of music or the transitory character of
movement which becomes 'as one wishes in art itself, in the theatre, fictive
or momentary' (*M*, pp. 295–6).

If the noble complement exists, and is not to be dissolved in irony or
brutalised by external claims upon it, the conception may be expressed
more as indirect indication and casual practice than as programme. What
follows in *Crayonné au Théâtre* (*Noted at the Theatre*) is of course not
criticism in the academic sense of the word, nor is it theory – although it is
expressed at a high level of generality – nor is it occasional appreciation.
There is rather a meditation which draws on everything from the sense of
one's personal circumstances – indeed the setting, the chat, the desultory
observation are part of an atmosphere which helps compose the grand
metaphor of theatre itself – to 'the idea', 'the passion of Man', 'the
Mystery', which lie over the horizon of the moment but are part of the
essential terms of critical play. 'Crayonné' of course – pencilled in –
somewhat casually, perhaps on the back of a programme. And the
'complement' moves through circumstance, figures that represent the
engagement of one's own mind, in a meditation that strays and turns back
on itself, in a form no doubt of its own 'divine malaise':

Taken as an enterprise, criticism does not, cannot have a value, nor can it approach the level of Poetry or bring to it a noble complementarity other than by holding in focus, directly and proudly, both the observed world and the universe. But in spite of this, perhaps because of its quality of a primordial instinct buried in the secrecy of our dissimulations (a divine malaise), it yields to the attractions of the theatre – which to those who don't need to see things as they really are offers no more than a representation! – of the play written on the folio of heaven and acted out with the gesture of his passions by Man (*M*, p. 294).

This grandiose throwaway catches both a duality and a necessary deformation in the critical project. The complement derives its value from what is a simultaneous involvement with the world and its substance and the infinitely seductive power of the representation. Such a doubleness may at least partially help account for an obliquity which is itself a creation, a capturing of the intellectual movement, or movement of feeling, in an interplay in which the fundamentals of reception theory are subsumed, and in which its ponderous mechanisms are largely erased. The relationship between language and silence, the powerful evocation of what lies beyond speech, finds its medium in the arts of mime or ballet, where the problem of the literal sense of the action is avoided by the primacy of a logic of suggestion, perhaps in its indefinable way as rigorous or ineluctable as the tracing of consequences in the *code civile* but as inaccessible as the 'primordial instinct buried in the secrecy of our dissimulations'.

It is this movement of mind that one might reasonably wish to account for, in a sequence which is submitted to time, to the succession of moments which is also the essential condition of music, which becomes for Mallarmé the model of an art which may escape language yet still pose its 'point philosophique'. The reality of such an art resists the vulgarisation of any reduction to the coded and formalised languages of interpretation which are the normal fate of the performing arts. The established vocabulary, the professional bow-wow, the expected categories and clues, appropriate references or evaluative comparisons are either rejected or ignored. Everything derives from a reciprocity which lies beyond the conventional work of explanation, and suggests that the 'complementary operation' however indicated by a gesture towards a corresponding mental process is never one of spelling-out, or of reducing to an identifiable public code.

Perhaps the implied participation in what may exist 'thanks to our lucidity' has a seductive power, which may have tempted Poulet, among others, to see the 'complementary operations' as an allegorical analogue, writing what is the necessary version of a page that has not fully declared itself. In a sense the page of the text is never fully written and always calls for another. The commentary becomes the complement which by aiming 'directly and proudly' at things themselves and the world itself, becomes in turn the text, one's own, alas necessary, comment on that art and that life which form in the end an indivisible continuum.

Certainly such a doubleness is conveyed, however diffidently, in Mallarmé's critical language, where behind the literary dimensions of a 'Crisis in Poetry' lie problems of the relation of language to the world, where a crisis in literature is an indicator of a cultural process, of the transformation of one's world. Obviously, one writes now in another historical situation where criticism has become an immensely elaborated amalgam of interlinked disciplines, which respond to those circumstances with an intensified self-awareness developed in them. If I have talked, in what has become something of a cliché, of a crisis in criticism, and referred to de Man's sense of criticism as intrinsically linked to the notion of crisis, I now wish to explore the notion in three ways. First through a problem in the interpretation of Mallarmé himself, in Derrida's sceptical account of Richard's study *L'univers imaginaire de Mallarmé*, which raises fundamental questions about the possibility of criticism. Secondly, through Paul de Man's use of the notion of allegory as the 'impossibility of reading' as a model of reading in his work on Rousseau. And finally, I wish to look at the ironic effect of Derrida's form of reasoning in the construction – *faute de mieux* perhaps – of a critical *esprit de finesse*. These are, as an ensemble, three aspects of our inheritance from Mallarmé, and three ways of looking at the crisis of critical language.

## 1  The double complement

One thing that Derrida has realised quite fully, perhaps without exactly saying so in this kind of context, is that the very existence of the commentary poses not the notion of definitive understanding, but is testimony to the indeterminate multitude of other understandings. 'It's like this, isn't it' means that the alternative is already on stage (and much of the rhetoric of Leavis is devoted to the control of those other possibilities that the invitation invokes). Indeed, what can a complement be but another voice, and then another? There is no way in which the notion of complement could ever be definitive, always suggesting that something extra, that addition, a filling out which is never completed. And for Derrida's 'The Double Session' another complement is already in place. Or more than one if one thinks first of the style of Mallarmé's own figurative commentary: the 'fictive or momentary' displayed through the shifting light on the facets of a crystal chandelier (as in impressionist painting, a radical breaking apart and refocusing of mimeticism) in which a 'dramatic work shows the succession of external features of action, without a single moment preserving the reality, and in which, in the end nothing happens' (*M*, p. 296). Such asides, suggesting art is both presence and nothingness, pose the evanescence of the performing arts as model of the transitory nature of the artist's gesture, and to Derrida a further model of the critical subject.

The second refracting complement is in the work of Jean-Pierre Richard which poses a substantive construction of meaning, and which will become one of the models of the possibility of a critical language, and which will be systematically considered as the case of the 'most rigorous need for the "critical" operation'.[3] The work of Richard is one of interlinked systems, of relational moves which work through the implicit areas of coherence (*D*, p. 248), through the resolving of the tensions within the text into a satisfactory 'equilibrium' (*D*, pp. 247–8), a world of pressures and balances expressed in a language in which a vocabulary analogous to that of the Anglo-Saxon new criticism is discernible. It gives an accounting of the relation of disparate elements to intelligible wholes, of diverse and suggestive images entering into formal and coherent relationships, in *thematic* analysis. In one example of it that Derrida quotes 'it is actually the multiplicity of lateral relations that creates the *essence* of meaning here. A theme is nothing other than the sum, or rather the putting in perspective, of its diverse modulations' (*D*, p. 250). For Richard this allows for the hope, the 'dream', of reaching a sum and of determining a perspective, even if the modulations are infinite. Such a sum or perspective would enable us to define, contain and classify the different occurrences of a theme. In effect, a systematic form of critical understanding could so be based.

Derrida argues against this possibility, partly on the ground that the aim is for a totalised and comprehensive reading that the text will always exceed. And Richard poses at least one kind of test case of the possibility of criticism. This issue is unfolded in the Mallarméan context on at least three levels: in terms of the kind of crisis of literature that Mallarmé's own text reveals; more particularly that movement through the Mallarméan text of the uncertainty of the ground of critical remarks; more narrowly still in examining whether or not the thematic criticism of Richard establishes a viable critical understanding, what Richard calls – though Derrida has given it a rather specialised context – the possibility of 'a sure revelation of meaning'.

I shall not try to give a comprehensive account of this negative demonstration, but follow up three aspects of Derrida's attack that have far-reaching consequences for the 'crisis' in criticism and for the possibility of constructing a rational critical language – above all in the sceptical treatment of critical description.

A number of Richard's critical terms, largely those linking the structural aspects of poetry with psychological states – a list is given on page 248 including those remarks about equilibrium which I have already quoted – are said to commit one to a kind of psychologism which implies the reification of mental states. This issue is not argued but simply asserted. And one complication in it is that the notion of the 'real' existence of mental states is consonant with a variety of possible metaphysical commitments. One thinks of I. A. Richards's use of poetry as something to assist in the ordering of mental states, which is applied in the context of a materialist and mechanistic psychology. And a special difficulty in the case of Mallarmé is the strong evidence that, whatever he thought the metaphysical implications to be, there is a pervasive evocation of such states in his talk about poetry. One would have to distinguish here between the use of phenomenological language on Richard's part, and those aspects of Mallarmé's thought where the reality of the mental states seems implied. Consideration of the latter is inseparable from the oeuvre. One could argue that Richard's use of them in critical explanation is no doubt simply a hypothesis, a means of talking 'as if' something were the case for the sake of the description, to appear a critical operation without metaphysical commitment. This question seems open.

Two features attributed to Richard's method, dialecticity and total-isation, are rejected in analogous ways. Dialectical structure is held incapable of accounting for the concrete elements which it comprehends, and the totalising effect is exactly that which creates the semblance of the theme by merely seeming to imply it. For Derrida totalisation also contradicts Richard's own commitment to the 'differential or diacritical' concept of language by which the making of a marking, or critical distinction, implies the totality within which differentiation is made. This is of course to say that the metaphysical implications of Richard's version of phenomenology are present in every case of its application. It is difficult to tell about this, but the assertion seems to go beyond what is required in understanding Richard's method itself. One could argue that certain aspects of phenomenological criticism are not wholly dissimilar from their more empirical equivalents, and one can conceive of the total thematic sequence as being open-ended. There could always have been further instances and the theme could always be identified indirectly through language in which it was not expected. Totalisation would not make a limit, but simply represent our sense of the thing seen as a whole, a perspective.

There is also the question of how precisely the marking of a theme lends itself to a discrete identity. Derrida's underlying argument is that a 'theme' is ultimately an unintelligible concept. But this seems not to mean that thematic elements are not diacritically identifiable. Only that the consequence of diacriticity 'prevents a theme from being a theme, that is a nuclear unit of meaning'. This implies that the possibility of diacritical discrimination will continually break down the linguistic units of which themes are composed, so that their instances may come apart. This is the other side of the argument about totalisation. One argues both that themes are unintelligible because their instances come apart and can have no primal integrity, and that they do not add up to the whole picture of what they intend to describe.

Derrida attacks both through his example of the fan, the Mallarméan *éventail* which appears so frequently in his work and which we might loosely think of as supplying a 'theme'. He is largely concerned with the succession of 'blanks' and 'folds' as the fan is opened and shut, and the complex pattern of associations that are intertwined with the fan. First the direct figures of wings, pages, veils, folds, etc.; then the more complex figurative dimensions these take on through the 'tropic twist' of analogy, metaphor, etc. These 'semic units' in their complex movement would not only tell against the nuclear unity of the theme, but to conceive of the totality of their relationships requires something further: a 'surplus mark', 'margin of meaning' or 'supplementary valence' (*D*, pp. 251–2). It 'marks the structurally necessary position of a supplementary inscription which could always be added to or subtracted from the series'. So (I shall try for the most part to phrase these arguments without employing all of the terms of the jargon) the totality of a thematic description can never be given, for the very conceiving of it is to imply an added element, the series plus one. Hence the impossibility of a complete and determinate series.

It will be important to look more closely at the 'blanks' both in Mallarmé and in a series. If the sequential character of the series is indeterminate, the internal thematic valency is more radically so. Hence one could not mark a series containing them in a way which could be intelligibly totalised. These blanks are of special importance to Mallarmé, as the spacing on the page in certain poems is an essential part of the poem. The question arises as to the blanks: are they identifiable signifiers? And if so is a larger blank somehow a different one? And what is the relation to the meaning? Derrida argues that 'This non-sense or non-theme of the space that relates the different meanings to each other (the meaning of 'blank' or 'white' among others) and in the process prevents them from meeting up with each other cannot be accounted for by any *description*' (*D*, pp. 252–3).

This places a heavy weight on 'accounted for'. Clearly certain literal accountings were exactly what Mallarmé's language set out to avoid. That there should be spaces between words, as between the stars as Valéry observed, or spaces within consciousness for that matter, and that the variables of these spaces should alter the fundamental relationships between the elements in question seems intelligible enough. That some description is possible is clear from Derrida's own account which touches on the dislocating effect of the blanks, their associative filiations, their necessarily indeterminate effects. If not exactly 'accounted for' they can be described, although certain features of that description may not have any very clear exactitude, and the description would be far from exhaustive. Yet an unease persists that the terms in which such describing may be done are fundamentally unsatisfactory. And there is no good reason to believe that we would be able to give any precise criteria for what would be a satisfactory description, or that it would be especially desirable to do so.

What Derrida draws from this is a consequential pair of false inferences. This is perhaps the point at which the screw tightens on the relation between a crisis in literature and a crisis in criticism. For if there is effectively nothing that can be accounted for by a critical description, does this imply that what one cannot describe itself describes nothing? So when he urges that it follows that there 'is no such thing as description, particularly in Mallarmé's work', he moves from a position with respect to critical language to an assertion about literary language and especially that of Mallarmé. Certainly this rests on a very narrow concept of description which confuses it with literalism. For one can easily accept that 'description' of scrollwork motifs in decoration is a complex metaphor. But this does not imply that it has nothing to do with scrollwork tracing at Versailles. If it is, on Derrida's reading about something else, this does not require that it does not also 'describe' and there is no doubt that Mallarmé employs a descriptive means.

The second inference while equally shaky is germane because through it he comes closer to articulating the difficulty of such poetry. If the 'blanks' indicate reading something to which no signified corresponds, we would be approaching and trying to describe, by way of themes etc., something which we cannot touch by these means. Something will escape from a descriptive system such as thematics. This seems almost certainly true as an indication of the limits which any descriptive system may encounter, and equally untrue in suggesting that description is neither possible nor useful – that is, takes us nowhere that we might wish to go, even if there are places it cannot take us. Is 'articulating the difficulty' itself a form of description?

This relation of the limited world of giving accounts to what lies beyond its reach, of the critical enterprise to the unbounded possibilities of the text, is taken beyond the context provided by Richard towards two general laws. One follows from the notion that 'If polysemy is infinite, if it cannot be mastered as such' (D, p. 258). This is not because a finite reading fails to exhaust 'a superabundance of meaning'. Rather it is because the 'law and structure of the text' is reconstituted as a displacement of finitude. In this the blanks are central in a way similar to what has just been described. They destroy the possibility of constituting or closing a finite series. The second is what he calls 'the general law of textual supplementarity through which all meanings are dislocated'. This latter is present, but is not clearly placed. This may be because the action of supplementarity is too loose a concept to state effectively. It is pervasive, perhaps for Derrida seen everywhere, but cannot be intelligibly stated.

However, let me approach such aspects of generality or what would constitute general laws by way of what concerns the possibility of critical reading. There seem to be only two points of substance and they are relatively simple: one is that if the gaps in any series are counted as part of the series, and these gaps are indeterminate in size and distribution, then the series, semantic in this case, must remain incomplete. This connects with the further argument (related I presume to supplementarity) by which any such series may have either another unit at its end, or another blank whether considered as unit or otherwise, to which another may be added, and so *ad infinitum*. Its critical force is that no account is ever complete, or text exhaustible. Yet as a reason for this the arguments seem weakened by adhering to an adaptation of a mathematical problem about the nature of infinite series, and thus setting up a false criterion for what a critical account might require, or for what might be to Richard a 'sure revelation of meaning'.

One must look at one or two features of the way in which this version of the bed of Procrustes is designed. Perhaps there is a simplified model of a basic sequence of Derridean moves that goes something like this:

(1) In order to say anything about anything you must see an utterance as 'marking' what is asserted and hence related to it. So
(2) the seeing of this relationship becomes assimilated to, or the condition of, the original assertion.
(3) Therefore a double movement takes place by which the various 'markings' become part of the discourse they purport to limit, while further markings are necessary to define a previous meaning, and so understanding vanishes, inevitably receding in an infinite regress.
(4) Hence one effect is a 'general law of textual supplementarity through which all proper meanings are dislocated'.

Such dislocation would incidentally apply to the language in which it is established, as well as those which it marked in its own fashion, and the very activity of establishing it would be entrapped in its own procedure, denying its validity in claiming it. This is of course a commonplace objection to 'deconstruction' which is more general than the question of the revelation of critical meaning. But if such reflexivity is seen as the destruction of the notion of establishing anything, it has the effect of becoming an example of what it claims, and the argument must be accordingly qualified.

A further question however arises as to whether any such general laws would derive from more ordinary uses of language, or whether their proper locus is in the special kind of difficulty posed in Mallarmé's own poetic language, with its elaborately multivalent meanings and conveniently indeterminate gaps. Does his own special method create the invitation to the sort of theory which, if generalised, would have to show its relevance to less difficult poetic methods? Yet of course, his is the paradigm case of the crisis of literature, the register of its moment of break with naive mimeticism and common sense, of its full challenge to the possibility of rationalisation and understanding. To deny that the elaborate thematics of Richard can account for such a literature seems to deny that any account can be substantially complete or even approach a sure revelation of meaning. It is also to assert that one is locked into a double supplementarity by which the text is always both less and more than the comment on it, and the comment is conversely both less and more than the text. Hence four axes of misfit are available to, and probably present in, any one moment of application. But who would have thought otherwise? The critical enterprise has never assumed that degree of reductivism by which the language of commentary produced such precision of match. Its very explanatory value lies in difference, the difference implied in one's very move into such an alternative language with its own constitutive features. As in Derrida's own. In this case the failure of 'translation' is its telling point. And what looks like a destruction of the critical process is in effect itself a description, the very necessary, if in turn incomplete, 'opération complémentaire'.

When such a poetry as Mallarmé's is revealed in all its difficulty and confronted with a description of certain features of the thematic method one can then point to areas of resistance: of particular features of that poetic language to the construction of the theme; of any totality to being comprehended through such a method – it always stretches beyond; of such systematic descriptions operating in a world in which descriptions do not operate at all; etc. But of course this refusal of description must operate through descriptions of one's own, both implied and direct. For in characterising why they do not work the reasons must refer to the special nature of the poetic object to which they cannot apply. So, 'in marking itself out, it [the blank] makes us take agglomerates for substances. If thematicism cannot account for this, it is because it overestimates the word while restricting the lateral'. Now Richard has, as we have seen, certainly been concerned with the possibilities of lateral connection; what such a comment in effect produces is an opening to an alternative version, a revision of Richard's argument which works on the same level, even while denying it.

Several things are run together which can be separated out when so needed. One line of argument runs counter to the possibility of critical descriptions; a second is directed at thematicism itself; another seems intended to counter particular aspects of the way in which the thematic analysis is done. The attack on overestimating the word touches this particular level (although Derrida has already quoted Richard on the possibility of breaking words down, as Mallarmé's trait of concealing some words within others would suggest, into 'a phonetic phenomenology' of key words) (*D*, p. 255). But at each of these levels there is a degree to which he adopts the form of discourse whose possibility he would deny, and affirms by implication the possibility of the project he has put in question.

If they were successful the arguments of Derrida would have established the impossibility of criticism in three senses: the innate incoherence of such central critical terms as theme; the impossibility of fitting such a thematic language to the cryptic heart of Mallarmé's text; finally, the necessary radical incompleteness, or otiose excess, in 'accounting for'.

I have so far been concerned with difficulties which arise in the course of these arguments, but I should like to look further at problems in the very coherence of their own formulation. For the attack on the logical character of 'theme' is to place a false requirement on the concepts used in critical language. The notion of the theme as 'a nuclear unit of meaning' like a Democritean atom could be replaced by one of strands, nuances tied by family resemblance into intelligible bundles, overlapping and complementing, almost like the fabric of the nervous system. Perhaps Richard has to some extent encouraged an excessive belief in the explanatory power of the themes. But one can still distinguish between establishing the logical boundaries of the concept in some pure nuclear form and working out its critical function. The use of 'theme' will have a different ground from that of establishing its logical identity. In practice 'theme' is only an indicator of the particular theme, whose internal principle of resemblance is not one which imposes a hermetic isolation. Rather it has shifting borders and is a class with relational contents. Derrida sees and notes this, and uses it against the intelligibility of the notion. And indeed accepting the nature of these variables (as perhaps in the case of Empson's 'fool') may lead us into a world as uncertain and relational as Derrida's own, but hardly on the same kind of pseudo-logical grounds.

The problem of completeness seems artificial in another way, in its dependence on the manipulation of the concepts of infinity and of series.

The notion of the infinity of polysemy seems itself rather loosely handled, as the temptation to speak of infinitude (rather inexactly) derives not from the multiplication of further meanings in serial order, but from the subtle adjustment of meanings in changing contexts which, like 'fool', make many alterations within an accepted range of possible meanings. Such a number of changes is probably not infinite in the mathematical sense, but simply incalculable, and the degree to which such variables 'cannot be mastered as such' is subject to no mathematical or logical principle. Partly because mastery is in use.

Consider the analogy of the game of chess. If the total number of possible moves is greater by some substantial power than the total number of particles in the universe, there may be a semblance of infinitude – can one not always make another move? – but even if the number is finite, it is unknown, and probably unknowable. The analogy to a Richardian thematics would be the invention of a descriptive system of aspects of the game that had been explored, a system which could both indicate something of its limits and of the lines of extension which it had not followed. But if the 'infinitude' is hardly touched does this mean that we cannot understand or master the game? Certainly the descriptions move from the simple mastery of the mechanics and rules of play, through enormously complicated case law, to the highly speculative. Understanding means something different at every stage, if not discretely so. In a sense the game is mastered – easily, and by any of us – and not mastered – ever, by anyone. And we would find it difficult to give hierarchical logical stages for a path to understanding or a clear picture of what understanding would be. There are many paths and none in particular. The infinity of possible moves spirals off entropically while the mastery of the game lies in the moves that are consequential – as Empson was 'honestly' concerned with what 'seems important'. But the last thing we would begin to seek is a totalisation, a sense that all of the possibilities could be so contained, that such would be the measure of 'mastery' which would not be achieved without it.

One further implied aspect of such a picture of the impossibility of criticism is an obvious and far-reaching sense that the 'crisis' of literature bears most deeply upon the impossibility of constructing, however intelligible the concepts employed may be in themselves, a recognisable reading of what dissolves before these concepts, in the literary 'object' (cf. D, pp. 244–5). Our misgivings about the literalism of both description and explanation are mixed unevenly with the naturalness with which we turn to it. 'One does not explain Mallarmé, one feels and loves him' (M, p. 431), writes Dr Bonniot in the course of some notes that contain among other things some reasonable explanations. The most demanding poetry calls for a response in language that is not its own, which by comparison is alien and banal. And those who will attempt to create their own 'theatrical setting' can hardly be expected to do so in the poem's idiom. When one understands that the very nature of the poet's work enacts the resistance to the spelling out of any 'meaning', will all literal-minded languages of explanation evoke a suitable mixture of laughter and disgust? If one presumes that a critical language makes clear, makes intelligible what was inaccessible, difficult and obscure, one accepts the necessary and impossible simultaneously.

But what is literal? Derrida's description of 'the constellation of "blanks"' where 'the semic content' remains practically empty, demonstrates an effect of what we have seen as a law of supplementarity:

If polysemy is infinite, if it cannot be mastered as such, this is thus not because a finite reading or a finite writing remains incapable of exhausting a superabundance of meaning. Not, that is, unless one displaces the philosophical concept of finitude and reconstitutes it according to the law and structure of the text: according as the blank, like the hymen, re-marks itself forever as disappearance, erasure, non-sense. Finitude then becomes infinitude, according to a non-Hegelian identity: through an interruption that suspends the equation between the mark and the meaning, the 'blank' marks everything white (this above all): virginity, frigidity, snow, sails, swans' wings, foam, paper, etc., *plus* the blankness that allows for the mark in the first place, guaranteeing its space of reception and production. This 'last' blank (one could equally well say this 'first' blank) comes neither before nor after the series. (*D*, p. 253)

This takes us back to the point where the making of metaphor had to stop – or rather did not. Here the effect of supplementarity is an unfolding of figuration which of course destroys it. Would not this in turn destroy the difference between the most extravagant poetics and the most banal explanatory language in a kind of terrifying linguistic entropy? If rhetorics have no margins they have no limiting and distinguishing features. If Derrida's rhetoric in the end both destroys and describes, the ambiguous nature of the critical complement is established in the very fact that the 'rigorous need for the "critical" operation' can therefore never be marked.

## 2    Allegory and the rhetorics of crisis

Multiple versions of the 'crisis in criticism' abound, and there is one in de Man's work which shows this problem at least partially naturalised in another scholarly and critical tradition. The movement towards a more and more adequate rhetorical description finds a necessary and consequential incompleteness in that description, just as the careful adjustments to a conceptual design may lead to the understanding that no such conceptual structure can ever be adequately stated. One development of this difficulty comes through the transformation of the notion of allegory from the indication of a fixed relation between a form of narrative and the conceptual order it is intended to represent. A traditional allegorical narrative might stand for political, ethical or theological concepts in such a way that the correspondence between those concepts and their narrative representation may be directly understood. That it might require interpretation, that images might be dark, and repel the casual or ignorant reader, that the narrative might be governed by a code which is only partially revealed, or where the compounding of the reader's errors are part of its strategy ... all of these move slowly towards an institution of hermeneutic contradiction, where the correspondence is not with a discoverable conceptual order, but with the very failure of order and understanding which is the modern condition. Such steps may take us at least part of the way on the path which leads to de Man's conception of allegory as the 'impossibility of reading':

The paradigm for all texts consists of a figure (or a system of figures) and its deconstruction. But since this model cannot be closed off by a final reading, it engenders, in its turn, a supplementary figural superposition which narrates the unreadability of the prior narration. As distinguished from primary deconstructive narratives centred on figures and ultimately always on metaphor, we can call such narratives to the second (or the third) degree *allegories*. Allegorical narratives tell the story of the failure to read whereas tropological narratives, such as the *Second Discourse*, tell the story of the failure to denominate. The difference is only a difference of degree and the allegory does not erase the figure. Allegories are always allegories of metaphor and, as such, they are always allegories of the impossibility of reading – a sentence in which the genitive 'of' is itself to be 'read' as a metaphor.[4]

How much of a more traditional sense lies beneath the surface of this? We can hardly, however sceptical, accuse de Man of a perverse misuse which transfers an arbitrarily invented meaning to a word by which we have always meant something else. How does he employ (consciously exploit?) the strangeness in the use of a term which has given a form to one of the 'sense-making' functions of literature in turning it to a stark denial of the possibilities of sense? Old affinity and connection is clearly evoked in a radically altered fashion:

But in the allegory of unreadability, the imperatives of truth and falsehood oppose the narrative syntax and manifest themselves at its expense. The concatenation of the categories of truth and falsehood with the values of right and wrong is disrupted, affecting the economy of the narration in decisive ways. We can call this shift in economy *ethical*, since it indeed involves a displacement from *pathos* to *ethos*. Allegories are always ethical, the term ethical designating the structural interference of two distinct value systems. In this sense, ethics has nothing to do with the will (thwarted or free) of a subject, nor *a fortiori*, with a relationship between subjects. The ethical category is imperative (i.e., a category rather than a value) to the extent that it is linguistic and not subjective. Morality is a version of the same language aporia that gave rise to such concepts as 'man' or 'love' or 'self', and not the cause or the consequence of such concepts. (*AR*, p. 206)

If morality and allegory are language aporias, they embody not under-standing but the failure of it, the incarnation of conflict, where two incompatible systems embody their point of difference. A narrative representation might have a corresponding resistance to the surface coherence which would offer itself up to reading. And secondary narratives may no doubt point at the discontinuities, interstices, the 'blanks' if one will, which indicate the failures of connection both in the primary narrative itself and in relation to it, effecting the defeat of the enterprise of intelligibility. This secondary status suggests characteristics of criticism, of a language which is always above or between, 'floating', always too much or falling short, too aware of the metaphorical structure on which its secondary self is based to undertake the simplicity of a reading.

But let us consider the point of entry into allegory. In looking at the second preface to *Julie* 'the point at which the allegorical mode asserts itself is precisely when R. admits the impossibility of reading his own text and thus relinquishes his power over it'. In the main text of *Julie* 'the value system and the narrative promote each other's elaboration'. But with the discovery of unreadability there is a reversal, and the value system and narrative syntax enter into conflict. Rather than saying all too directly and copiously what it seemed to say, we find in the narrative an uneasy relation between a practical message and an intellectual reserve. The 'stock characters in a sentimental tragedy' working through expected polarities their conventional demands on the reader's responses are resituated through Julie's recapitulative letter. Yet what is the effect of the recognition that the discarding of certain expectations and understanding means that 'the entire narrative has to be reconstructed along different lines'? The newly discovered world of 'holes', 'traps', 'errors' is itself a 'new network of narrative articulations' or 'a narrative chain'. And the image of the chain goes on to a 'chain of substitutions' and 'chain of transformations'. But has not this chain been followed and the network of articulations been read?

One can see the critical value of what has been read, discovered and described. It rescues Rousseau's text from the sentimental and didactic *longueurs* which have afflicted other readers, to indicate a more interesting world of conflict, contradiction, tangled identities and uncertainties. But what does this reveal about the method, and our beginning point in allegory?

For one thing it is the vehicle of reversal, and hence of the dramatic revision of understanding. How this defines the character of allegory as a mode is unclear, but the movement from the highly readable to the unreadable is somehow shaped through it. The narrative commentary on itself shifts the false sensibility. 'The readability of the first part is obscured by a more radical indeterminacy that projects its shadow backwards and forwards over the entire text. Deconstruction of figural texts engenders lucid narratives which produce, in their turn and as it were in their own texture, a darkness more redoubtable than the error they dispel' (*AR*, p. 217). But if the end of allegory is critical darkness? One can see the form of a movement from an understanding to its falsification to the awareness that understanding is impossible. In *Julie* it might be said to parallel the failure of awareness in constructing Julie's new world through the very figuration it would reject. We can envisage concentric circles of darkness: the character's, the author's, the critic's, each representing the illusion that one could somehow surmount the original condition of one's saying to an intelligibility that lay beyond it. One way of constructing the sense of allegory is to see it as a model of these successive failures, if it were not that its discovery creates the very contradiction that puts these procedures in doubt. Unreadability has become a form of reading through recognition and identification.

The problem of interpreting unreadability is given a somewhat simplified form in the consideration of the *Profession of Faith*, which begins with a direct enquiry as to whether or not it is a theistic text, and decides that it both is and is not. 'A text such as the *Profession de foi* can literally be called "unreadable" in that it leads to a set of assertions that radically exclude each other.' This is derived of course from a reading, subtle and largely persuasive, that is clearly not designed to 'deconstruct' or invalidate itself. But the notion of 'readability' implied has both a specialised and a generalised sense. Specialised in that it does not include a surface or casual understanding which even the educated reader might have, but an understanding that is more complete and exhaustive, which has a depth and textual grasp – a sense that the depths are there to be plumbed, and the reading undertakes that. And generalised in that 'readability' refers to a capacity which is expressed as a logical possibility, as if it were an abstract quality that a text either had or did not. But is the conflict of theistic or non-theistic readings in this case one which challenges the possibilities of reading in this total way?

The fact that we can give two constructions might simply imply that the text was irreducible to either of two intellectual stances that might be thought to be derivable from it. And is this irreducibility equivalent to unreadability, or is it simply an awkward feature which must be taken as read, even if it violates our expectation that the matter should in the fullest sense be resolvable? Has de Man in effect given criteria for 'readability' which correspond to a particular and rigid notion of what it would be to have really read it? Is the acceptance of something indeterminate which might be expressed as ambiguity, or a profound incoherence which might destroy the effect of the work as 'exhortative' performance nevertheless something which has shown the 'impossibility' of reading? The assertions that lead us in opposite ways both 'compel us to choose while destroying the possibility of any choice'. Yet has not this agonic stress-point itself been read?

If we cannot hold either of the possible consequences which the text might imply, either conversion to theism or its rational rejection without contradiction, de Man is ambiguous about where the difficulty lies. Is it an incoherence in Rousseau? A form of bad faith in the posing of metaphysical alternatives in a way in which they are self-cancelling? The former would be a reasonable psychological hypothesis, the latter a hypothesis about the text's flight from a metaphysical concern which is nevertheless its pervasive obsession. But such a problem is not rare or strange. One may immerse oneself in questions that are never resolved, and the holding of such conflicts in the mind's eye does not so much indicate the impossibility of apprehension as the irreducibility of that apprehension to a decisive version of one of the implied arguments or determinate aspects that might be derived from the text. The impossibility of reading may in a sense indicate the rejection of all possible versions or accounts, points at which the mind can come to that partial resting place: 'It's like this isn't it ... ?' In that case the constitutive nature of the text cannot be vested in a systematic ambiguity which can be 'read' as such. The impossibility would then be placed somewhere beyond the notion of the ambiguity itself, in the unacceptability of that as a form of 'reading'.

Here as in Derrida there seems a demand for a definitive and complete notion of reading that sets the targets at a step beyond the means, wherever the means may take one. Does this imply that the notion of unreadability is based upon an absolute concept of reading, a totalised finality which by necessity is never achieved? Nothing could then ever be read. Or are we concerned with the more modest criterion which selects out certain of those problematic texts which test our powers of reading and find them wanting? It is unclear what de Man intends. It is unlikely to be the former, but this is the kind of criterion which seems to be used when working out the implications of the latter. And remember that 'impossibility' does not admit of degree.

Consider a text that does not on the surface of it seem to lead us into the tangles that end in the impossibility of reading, say, *Tom Jones*. In the rather relaxed empiricism of its outlook the world is as it is and is not as it is not. There is natural goodness in young men of lively parts, but there is also natural nastiness and viciousness about, and indeed a vulnerability to deception in the presumably wise. Men of choleric disposition lose their temper and behave irrationally for no other reason than the nature of that disposition. In this loose baggy monster (no looser of course than *Julie*) the disparate elements rattle about together without posing such contradictory paths as to suggest serious difficulty, and indeed the ironical tone of Fielding's commentary so mediates for the reading process as to indicate a natural perspective. The kind of contradiction that appears in *Pamela* between an absolute deontological commitment to sexual virtue, and its ruthless utilitarian exploitation as an instrument of social ambition, which marks the problematic, is absent, as is any suggestion, as in Sterne, that the accompanying reflection doubles back upon and subverts the narrative. It rather leads by way of commentary to a sense of wholeness in diversity as the onward movement of the text involves the reader in a sequence of pleasures and responses which propose not division but a reasonable if untidy unity.

Unless, and yet ... We can find contradictions if we only look, difficulties that pose irresolvable problems, perhaps in the very relation of the naturalness of the world to the complex artifice of coincidence through which the highly polished mechanism of the plot works to its all too fully predictable romance conclusion. No doubt from this, and perhaps other interstices of narrative and commentary, an 'unreadable' *Tom Jones* could be constructed. But in doing so would the transparency, and perhaps for some perversity, of its construction – as opposed, here let us follow de Man, to the ineluctable cross-purpose proposed in Rousseau – seem all too deflatingly obvious?

'Impossibility', 'unreadability', Barthes's 'illisibilité', all convey the quality of intention by which critical language declares its involvement in difficulty. It is after all where the intellectual interest of literature lies, or at least has done from the new criticism onwards. But our problem here is partly in asking whether or not this difficulty, translated into impossibility, is the necessary condition of critical reading, or simply the extreme to which critical reading under the greatest pressure from the most recognisably demanding texts responds. In one view all literary phenomena, from the blank spaces in Mallarmé to the hoppings of Christopher Robin (as a small masterpiece has already indicated) are the problematic stuff of critical enquiry. In the other there is a canon, indistinctly defined perhaps, of works which pose their unreadable status as part of their identity. This may be the effect of intention as with some modernist texts, or simply the expression of some deep and unresolved cross-purpose as in Rousseau.

One can imagine two different kinds of rhetoric of crisis proceeding from these alternative views. One would see the pervasive fact of unreadability as the natural and unavoidable condition of the modern reader. No text is unproblematic; no straight reading is possible. The most simple and transparent work forces its obscurity upon us; the process of reading is the confrontation of the tangle which separates us from the other, and commentary is the record of struggle. According to the second the magnetism of the difficult stands out against the ground of more accessible and less interesting works. Defined by features that reflect one or another of the great 'paradigm shifts' of history, or by extreme versions of the constitutive ambiguity of literary language, they elicit from the commentator a doubling of awareness as to where his uncertainty lies between historicised self and an indeterminate other. In practice such rhetorics may seem indistinguishable. And de Man gives no clear indication of the reach of uncertainty. One can only suggest that the first view would destroy the meaning of 'impossibility' by its indiscriminate use. Of the second there are many versions. But by admitting of degrees of difficulty it implicitly qualifies the meaning of 'impossible' or 'unreadable' and turns their absolute use into a figure. They are the subject of their own allegory, the distant, marvellous, magical representation which stands for everything and explains nothing, perfect in their ultimate irreducibility.

This opacity in his own 'allegorical' dimension recalls a definition of Benjamin's which is quoted in *Blindness and Insight* as a void 'that signifies precisely the non-being of what it represents'.[5] For the notion that allegory represents the unreadability of a text comes to stand for the deepest aspect of literary language in the opacity of the figurative. The basis of such allegory is the ultimate uninterpretability of metaphor, hence of the irreducibility of the figurative, through however many layers of metaphorical substitution. The representations of representations, however ingenious the means, have no end – as we have seen in the case of Derrida. And there is no solution to the problem of figurative language, either at the level of particular reading or at that of the possibility of an overall frame for such localised understandings – the antithesis of which is expressed in the term once applied to such general interpretative frames, in allegory.

Hence rather than supporting an understanding that is relational or systematic the study of figure undermines and destroys it. Its consummation in allegory is untranslatable and intransitive – if literature works through figure and figure is not assimilable to any general scheme of explanation or understanding. Allegory is a space that can be indicated, but never filled. Those untranslatable figures spell the impossibility of a continuous critical discourse when the individual critical movements of mind end in 'failure', 'impossibility' and acceptance of the unreadable.

Yet the commentary on Rousseau is astute and profound. The reflexivity by which the problems of the text have played back upon the language of commentary mirror the Mallarméan crisis of literature in a crisis of understanding in which the language of criticism has its substantial commitment in the marking of its own inadequacy.

The triple crisis, of culture, of literature, of criticism is therefore an interlocked series of denials:

For the statement about language, that sign and meaning can never coincide, is what is precisely taken for granted in the kind of language we call literary. Literature, unlike everyday language, begins on the far side of this knowledge; it is the only form of language free from the fallacy of unmediated expression. All of us know this, although we know it in the misleading way of a wishful assertion of the opposite. (*BI*, p. 17)

In the opening pages of *Blindness and Insight* de Man sketches the problem which is fundamental to his own discourse. 'The rhetoric of crisis states its own truth in the mode of error. It is itself radically blind to the light it emits' (*BI*, p. 16). This is stated as a general law, yet it is hard to see how its formulation links with the possibility of demonstration. And both this formula and others which amplify it seem to rest at the level of assertion. Consider: 'a constitutive discrepancy, in critical discourse between the blindness of the statement and the insight of the meaning'. And again, the interaction between such blindness and critical insight is shown by way of Derrida 'as a necessity dictated and controlled by the very nature of all critical language' (*BI*, p. 111).

But the scope of such claims is not matched by the argument that follows about the misreadings of Rousseau. For if Rousseau is 'systematically misread' would the notion of system require a level of internal development which proceeded from any effort to say anything about Rousseau – or one supposes any problematic text? In such a schema, to criticise would be to project system. But such a notion disappears into a catalogue of ways of going wrong, of 'the diversity of the tactics employed to make him say something different from what he said, and of the convergence of these misreadings towards a definite configuration of meanings' (*BI*, p. 112). It is uncertain whether this convergence is one or if the one stands for many. For it is clear from the wider context that there are many ways of misreading Rousseau. In fact one seems to oscillate between stronger and weaker claims. The strongest would imply that any criticism must by necessity misrepresent its object, indeed do so largely and fatally, while a weaker would require only that the distinctive ambivalence of Rousseau's texts is a trap for wrongfooting the unwary. Does the use of 'mis-understand' and 'misread' imply the possibility of their opposites, proper understanding and good reading? This too can be stated in a weakened form of at least more respectable understanding and more plausible reading. Certainly the standard form of the trap is discernible in the propensity to see and represent Rousseau in terms of one's own scheme of things and not of his – a trap with many forms and degrees of error. And degree is possible in the value of commentary: Starobinski is better than most and has cleared away mistaken *idées reçues*, and Derrida may sometimes be right: 'Derrida seems altogether justified in seeing Rousseau as ... ' (*AR*, p. 126).

I break off at this 'as' because of course I do not intend to represent the complex mixture of involvement and distancing with which de Man approaches Derrida's argument, but merely to indicate that justification may exist. And indeed de Man believes his own justification exists in correcting Derrida on Rousseau's handling of the relation of imitation and presence: 'Contrary to Derrida's assertion, Rousseau's theory of representation is not directed towards meaning as presence and plenitude but towards meaning as void'. We are on the path that leads to allegory, but we know our path. It will pass through a brilliant reflection on music and silence, and again through *Julie*: 'tel est le néant des choses humaines qu'hors l'Etre existant par lui-même, il n'y a rien de beau que ce qui n'est pas' (*BI*, p. 131).[6]

But if critics can be both mistaken and otherwise what do we make of the conclusion that the reading of Rousseau by way of Derrida 'shows blindness to be the necessary correlative of the rhetorical structure of literary language'? One has somehow entered into a necessary aspect of one's work which relies on the force of a figure which is far-reaching, both in its attachment to multiple dimensions of the subject and in the reflexivity with which it decentres its own presentation. This mirrors the curious circularity in seeing the crisis of criticism as something intrinsic to criticism itself – thus blurring a current conflict within an institution and discipline with the essential character of the discipline itself.

'Blindness' as a description of the critical condition thus becomes another figure; powerful with visual connotation and redolent with the historical and mythical connotation of the seer it joins such figures as 'allegory' in proposing the ultimate impossibility of explanatory discourse. But insofar as it is the condition of a rhetoric of crisis it also marks the necessary failure of any such rhetoric to convey the truth of what that crisis portends. One asks uneasily whether the notion of 'crisis' represents the condition of an historical moment: our situation and our crisis. To a certain extent it is described in terms of the transformation which contemporary criticism underwent as the influx of new concepts and disciplines put in question the traditions of historical scholarship or the new critical practice of formal analysis. Or does it represent a condition endemic to academic thought about literature? For if 'all true criticism occurs in the mode of crisis' (*BI*, p. 8) perhaps one can also see the sense of the term with respect to Dr Johnson's prefaces to Shakespeare, that tortured assimilation of a turbulent world to the requirements of a sense of order. But in effect it provides a criterion which distinguishes real criticism from literary chat. Does it therefore again risk the circularity which would deprive it of its own historical force and turn it into simply the marking of whatever critical discourse seems significant? Does it too become ultimately figurative in its use? There seems a repeated movement of mind by which explanatory terms move out of their context to enter into a special world of figure in which they indicate the limit of the possible ways in which language can make an intelligible world.

## 3    Geometry finessed

We have faced two versions of a paradox which implies that the arguments used in critical thought work through a language which is diametrically opposed to what those arguments require. The effect of the analyses we have seen, employing what de Man has called the 'power of inventive rigor', has in his own case been the attempt to transcend the necessity of misreading through an admission of the impossibility of reading, postulating, however uncertainly, some shadow of critical truth which lies beyond impossibility on the far side of our negative knowledge of what constitutes literature. And in that of Derrida there has been the demolition of the possibility of a substantive critical language of themes in a generalised form of argument that negates the possibility of marking the distinctive features and limits of the critical. One consequence might be that any possible criticism would have to escape or elude the world of argument. A corollary could be that Derrida has inadvertently marked the ground of critical *finesse* by the limits of *géometrie*.[7] For he has insisted on 'geometrical' rules of analysis that produce an implied description of what one cannot say. The denial of the possibility of systematic criticism has shown its effect against the concept of total explanation partly by the rigour with which it applies the concept of totality. The manoeuvre is here directed not merely against an explanatory system but against the possibility of such systems. And what might exist as criticism would have to exist in the interstices of our multiple geometries. The consequent irony is the creation out of such geometries of the necessity of *finesse*, the unpredicted complement.

I do not intend any element of a post-deconstructive imagining to mean that de Man or Derrida has set its terms, for I have given reasons to believe that such terms could only be self-cancelling. Yet if something has eluded the false models of understanding, as well as the deconstructors of those models, is there not a perspective from which it can be described? If one wishes to argue that the *finesse* of literature and of any sustainable talk about it is not to be contained in any geometry does this mean that it is totally inaccessible to the concepts through which any particular geometry may have been created? We can imagine certain of them – including that of 'theme' – used with reasonable obliquity as an imaginative correspondence rather than a totalising explanation. (One could indeed argue that this is what Richard has done.) Certainly it is characteristic of Mallarmé's own critical prose that the tentative and oblique movement of mind before thought, text or performance, proceeds without linear geometry or any systematic series of relations. It almost describes that movement of mind before the object as embodying an evasive and uncertain positioning before the intangibility of verse – or of dance – in a language especially marked by ellipsis, or by a pointer towards the possibility contained in an uncompleted thought. We could no doubt characterise this as a 'rhetoric', a rhetoric of verbal acts, manoeuvres, and distancings – a rhetoric of *finesse* if one likes, but one whose essential terms would not convey the structures and coherent relations of traditional rhetoric. The very impossibility of containing any systematic discourse within such terms does not undermine its descriptive power. And it has a vitality which is alien to more formal rhetoric. Take de Man's remark that 'the similarity between anacoluthon and parabasis stems from the fact that both figures interrupt the expectation of a given grammatical or rhetorical movement' (*AR*, p. 300n). This in a sense is true, but not in a critically significant way. It is the very nature of 'interruption' that cannot be given its systematic term, and indeed, like the blank spaces in 'A Throw of the Dice' cannot be substantively described or accounted for. Placed within criticism in this way there might be in that uneven movement between text, thought and further imagining, a rhetoric without margins. Or at least without the geometrised concept of margins we have seen in Derrida. But with focal points, where attention falls.

Such a movement of mind will certainly include the use of general concepts, but not entirely as those products of geometrising intend themselves. They give to aspects of the moment their semblance of shape. What may further be involved is their capacity to mark points of conjunction, however rapidly those may change their terms and reconstitute themselves. In some senses de Man's notion of 'crisis' is the precise indicator of such a conjunction, pointing to the instability in the quixotic task of establishing a mediating rhetoric of relations, with the determinate vocabulary such would involve – to face a richly indeterminate task with crassly determinate tools. In this of course I am imagining a rhetoric which goes beyond the description of particular linguistic phenomena and effects towards the interlinked vocabularies which would produce an impersonal substitute for synopsis.

Such a notion of relation has its sense in the desire to connect and interpret the flow of critical observation. Take Mallarmé's own movement from the things seen and drawn apart to the relation it has to another observed occasion, then to the hypothetical construct which evokes the 'idée'. What presents itself as a single form of discourse integrates at least three kinds of language game. And the levels of generality proceed from the most concrete to the most abstract as the games are successively superimposed. It is largely of that middle area of discourse in which the connections between observation and abstraction are so multifariously carried out that I wish to give a fuller portrait when looking at what I shall call, partly borrowing from Lyotard, 'critical paganism'.

The account that de Man gives of the entry of 'Gallic turbulence' into the native American critical moment represents an historical dimension of the 'crisis' which also introduces a process of accommodation. Hartman and others have noted, with suitable amusement, the theory-resistance of Anglo-Saxon criticism, without going on to a fuller account of its further transformation, conveying how the exogenous Gallic elements relate to any endogenous pressure or felt need. Of course there are significant endogenous sources for the growth of a theoretical dimension to criticism in the simple need for 'further descriptions', the explaining of oneself and justification of both particular readings and general procedures. The most passionate commitment to particularity may generate its crisis and its theory. But the 'endogenous' growth of theory out of the process of explaining oneself represents less of a charge of theoretical energy than those 'exogenous' implants. Certainly there is a glamour to novelty, and de Man himself seems dazzled by the flow within that vertiginous moment. What is difficult to assess is the extent to which one form of theory has simply supplanted another or whether it has been grafted on to or naturalised into another. In effect, do we develop different forms (even levels) of critical generality through the influx of incompatible epistemological and metaphysical commitments?

However, the notion of a convergence between two kinds of theory, one concerned with the elucidation and justification of a tradition of critical practice, the other formed in a general philosophical enquiry about the relation of language to the world, would be illusory. What has evolved is a community which is capable of reflecting on the conditionality of post-Heideggerian hermeneutics out of one side of its mouth and talking about poems and novels in a matter-of-fact, empirical way out of the other. Of course the most rigorous notion of practice can be devoured by the 'idea' as, say, Leavis's work is reduced to Leavisism. One sees very well how a resistance to generality arises from that sort of thing.

Yet it is the act of mediation, the middle discourse, whose conceptual character is most difficult to recover as it almost disappears into the interstices of the uses made of it. It functions like a momentary flicker to point the character of the immediate and passing. It is perhaps partly the effort to capture this movement of mind that gives de Man that mixture of loquacity and immobility before the opacity of figure. The flow of thought may allege 'impossibility' in the very passage about *Julie*, while in fact telling us a great deal about it. The problem of giving an account seems to depend on 'showing', on ostensibility, in a way that at least resembles the force of the Leavisite 'this'. Such in turn might suggest that critical *finesse* can only be identified ostensibly, and its operation seen as that immediate complex of relations is identified, but that further description is inevitably attached to a more theoretical language. In effect, theory is our only path to that middle ground on which the most immediate perceptions are shaped, related, arranged and displayed.

Hence it is through theoretical languages that such a discourse is interpreted, and only through the general concepts of those languages can it enter into any wider understanding. I mean this in two senses. One is the necessity of those languages to the formulation of any grasp upon the localised perspective – a basis of interpretation on which the most rigorous practitioner of the case-by-case method ineluctably falls back. The other is that it is through such languages that the place of case, text, literature itself is part of the larger culture. The model of 'paganism' that follows in a later chapter will sketch these relations. And as we have seen in certain case histories, such concepts are as unstable as the circumstantiality with which they may propose to deal. For one thing, if *finesse* always interrupts, always cuts across the interpretative scheme, always suggests an added dimension or aspect, the phenomenology of *finesse* cannot be fixed in the language of *finesse*. It does not lend itself to systematic construction.

This may suggest that a post-deconstructive imagining is an elusive movement of mind, complementary perhaps but incompletely so, for it is interpreted through a palimpsest of more general languages that make the 'noble complementary operations' take many and unpredictable steps. They will not fill out the blank page of *Igitur*, for the negativity of pure consciousness will no doubt disdain the vast proliferation of complements piled upon it and sourly underscore the law by which all such multiplicities inevitably exist in an ironic mode. Disdain also the mass of accommodations and domestications which Bersani quite rightly identifies as the aim of a traditional criticism. But beyond such domestications lie more radical constructs which are inevitably false, and beyond them the sense of absence. The complements vanish slowly on the wings of the night. For in the series of substitutions by which they succeed each other the critical consciousness accepts the full and grandiose irony of its own undoing. This would of course mean that all critical idioms (geometries) are equally valuable (or worthless) and the critic enters into a chosen form of discourse knowing it as auto-destructive as the next. De Man quotes Rousseau's *Julie* on the primary nature of imagination: 'In this world the country of chimeras is the only one worth living in'. But who is to choose among chimeras or find his way among fictional roads to the supposedly substantive but all too fragile fictions that lie beyond?

Mallarméan irony, at least in its critical form, uses its discontinuities as a defence against regress, in the very moment of representing it:

The occasion to say nothing doesn't come and I make no feeble excuses for the emptiness of this study or of all of them! A dead year: but the main problem lies in the primary defect of the spirit which a writer who has forgotten the incompatibility between him and his epoch brings to the undertaking of his work. 'Do you go to the theatre?' – 'No, almost never': to my question this reply by whomever, of whatever standing, that suffices, women or man of the world, to bring the furnishing of his dreams right up against life itself. 'Come to that, neither do I' I might respond, were it not that most of the time my disinterestedness here proclaimed itself in every line right up until the final void. (*M*, p. 297)

In the face of negative awareness voices are found – right up until the final void. Whatever inverted commas may fix the 'noble complement' there is also a necessity which transcends the placing of commas and the ironies they imply. I shall say more about how this necessity arises out of the nature of critical language itself.

What can be said about Mallarméan irony must again consist largely of negatives. But a remark of Bersani's invites extension: 'If his writing makes manifest the negativising moves of consciousness, it also makes negativity itself an object of irony'.[8] This is not a model of irony which, by the application of rules of 'inventive rigor', could find all discourse a failure including its own. The ironising process may, in some deconstructive uses, have seemed a game without significant issue. But here, the ironising of negativity has the suggestion of implying the possibility of further discourse – one marked by scepticism, by a second, and further, perspective on what one can identify as one's presuppositions. Each step is made in the awareness that it re-examines whatever steps have gone before, not to obliterate but to qualify. I have mentioned Bloom's citation of Schlegel's stricture on the wearying effect of irony, and his awareness of a vitiating negation in its use. But the Mallarméan example transcends any easy dialectic of the action of negation on negation. One has rather the sense that a subsequent movement of mind shifts a perspective and finds an illumination in comparison – a process that continually renews itself, but has in its continuous complication a conviction in its activity and movement. The uncertain and friable compound of the imagination's work calls for its own impingement on the blank space, and the creation of its own 'chimera'. But the outward movement entails a doubling back, and attainment of a 'monstrous clarity' takes language and its limits together, much like the ironic empiricism of Empson, as the unstable untrustworthy, all too alluring given.

# VIII   From 'ensemble' to 'exception'

## 1   The vanishing enigma

What one has seen in de Man has been transformed into a commonplace: we find in moments of contradiction the established and institutionalised features of our intellectual landscape – as 'irony' and 'ambiguity' were half a century ago – and which are now attaining their own form of domestication. What has been called 'absurdist criticism' has found its proper repertoire of moves, its canonical concepts, in 'indeterminacy', 'undecidability', 'impossibility', etc. A short précis by Leo Bersani can serve as a classic statement:

> Criticism, far from solving the enigmas of literature, has perhaps even put into question the very category of the enigma by dissolving it in a more radical view of literary language (a view to which narrative resolutions of enigmatic sense are irrelevant) as continuously performing the deferral, or the absence of its meanings. In a sense, the peculiar achievement of contemporary criticism has been to demonstrate the unreadability of the literary text.[1]

There is something strangely open and shut about this, as if the achievement were definitive and the force of demonstration conclusive. One thinks of the strength of 'achieved' in Bloom's 'achieved dearth of meaning', the hard-won product of the poet's art and negation in his utterance. One can see this point as one of no return, of the surrender of any possibility of reading to a meditation on the blank spaces that frame the intellectual space of the quixotic enterprise. Would the realisation of this point be the ultimate consummation of the de Manian sense of crisis, in the surpassing of incompatible modes of understanding to abandon it altogether?

Thus the idea of impossibility would become part of our understanding; all absences, blanks, contradictions become part of the solid matter of the critical tradition, and the impossibility of reading becomes another evolved aspect of 'thick description'. The moment of crisis, forever shifting in its cultural matrix, may represent the felt presence of a fissure, an effect of the 'minor earthquake', as Barthes says, in a given moment of time, or part of a perennial sense of the awareness of incompatibility.[2] For Hayden White the absurdist moment has always been implicit in our tradition: in the Platonic gap between the world of ideas and that of things, in the gap between the active and the contemplative life, in the philosophical gap between the phenomenal 'world and whatever reality might lie beyond it'.[3] And from our cases it has been clear that contradiction can be reached through different paths, that there are senses in which the failure of intelligibility in Leavis's resistance to general concepts is another form of the failure de Man reached and then asserted through a meta-critical course.

The movement from the enigma to the impossibility of its rational solution, to the difficulty of establishing a rational approach, turns the focus of thought back on the means. Of course Leavis could elude the reflection on means because of the felt assurance in the assumption of a direct and unmediated response in which the whole man could grasp the palpable presence of language in feeling which could, with suitable discipline, be conveyed. The dialogue with kindred spirits established the only 'means' of importance, and that consummation in feeling of the disciplined sensibility was far from the cold contemplation of one's speculative instruments. To have reflected upon them, or even to have realised their presence, would have meant turning away from the central thing of limitless value to follow a sequence of reasoning that would be inevitably abstract and find its appropriate dearth in the theoretical mode. Therefore one limit of discourse lies in ourselves, in the form of refusal which would isolate the critical subject and impose isolation from an examination of means, to insist upon using our language instrumentally without a reflection on the conditions which that might impose.

In the opposite direction lies the recognition reached through following the analysis of method itself, that the account one is able to give is fundamentally incomplete and that this incompleteness qualifies the validity of whatever form of critical project. But what is the force of any such qualification? If the thematic account that Richard gives of the blanks in Mallarmé's text is both incomplete and claims too much (we can follow Derrida so far) it might lead us to move too easily from recognising the force of the case as contingent fact to the claim that it is a constitutive feature of any thematic account. I have already noted this duality in Derrida. The notion that he is dismantling the strongest version of the thematic account seems an empirical claim about the text in question. The general inference with respect to the possibility of thematic reading would on the other hand indicate that there is a flaw built into the enterprise. I have given some reasons to doubt that this second and stronger argument is established. But even if it should be so what would remain would be a general but weak proposition to the effect that 'all criticism is approximate'. A fundamental gap would be built into the enterprise guaranteeing its failure, at least insofar as completeness is a criterion of success.

Does this touch at more than one point the criteria for a rational and acceptable account? If the analysis of the possibility of means, of the impasses of a method brought to the fullest account, shows this kind of flaw in its essential operations, to what extent does this so weaken any art of the approximate as to make those chimerical undertakings unacceptable by any rational standard? It is doubtful that Leavis in turning his back on philosophy would have denied the rationality of what he was doing, although he might not have conceived of rationality in abstract terms. If a model of practical reason is to emerge from the activity of criticism itself it will accept not merely a contingent but a constitutive incompleteness, a sense of its limitation as an art of the approximate. The *via negativa* pointed by Derrida describes essentially such a limit, but perhaps in so doing evokes a criterion that would be alien to such a model, and one must ask if built-in incompleteness and approximation can be part of a rational and acceptable account.

Consider a variant on Hume's distinction between rational and reasonable: we may not satisfy rational criteria in believing in the existence of the external world, but we behave reasonably in acting as if we do. The measure of a total readability is not the measure of a language of practice. The thematic account does not fill out the totality – it is a part of a thickening description. As such it is of course incomplete, for the description can always thicken, and the open-endedness of the process may invite that further move in which the 'blank', the 'enigma', will never be captured but will simply be seen that fragment more fully. In effect, the critical account does not admit of closure or of the definitive reading.

There the 'unreadable' text is a quite natural inheritance, in the understanding that we have not read through to the end, touched bottom so as never to have to touch it again. And we can accept the stronger version of Derrida's claim even if his own reasoning is essentially flawed; the crack in the fabric that is a constitutive feature of critical language may keep a certain vision of totality at bay, but hardly at a cost that the reasonable use of a language of practice would be unwilling to pay. In consequence it comes easily to rationalise the idea of unreadability in the language of practice where it is itself transformed into another aspect of description, another moment of thickening. As a logical marker 'unreadability' loses its interest even if established as an indicator of a theoretical limit. And indeed its use becomes largely figural, as both an aspect of critical instrumentality and of literature itself. 'Impossibility' becomes a form of possibility, a means of indicating not the end of a path but its nature, in a process by which, as Derrida would quite understand, the further move absorbs the marking of a process back into it. And this movement defines a body of practice, a point where the theoretical becomes the pragmatic.

## 2    From the awkwardness of theory to the banality of pragmatism

An uncanny confirmation of an assumption of de Man's seems to run through the cases we have examined. What theory in effect does is only obliquely related either to the intellectual sources of its legitimation or the precise bearing it is meant to have on the particularity of critical reading. I want here to look at the strength of theoretical claim, something which does not propose any typology but is simply a rough measure of force, of the strength of claim that impinges on generality, on the chain of implications that 'theory' might lead us to expect: either systematic poetics, conceptual aspects of the historical moment, or merely the roughly coherent grounds of critical working assumptions.

What is apparent from any survey of recent literary thought is the failure of 'theory' to construct what Culler once considered possible – 'a poetics which stands to literature as linguistics stands to language'.[4] Such an intention could be seen in those aspects of structuralism that lent themselves to systematising. This is a clear-cut case, even in the form of its presentation of theory as analogy, where one also is uncertain of the force the analogy was meant to have. The constitutive features of literary language – the freedom of substitution with respect to figure, the constituent ambiguity which Jakobson noted, the openness to invention of non-referential uses – do not lend themselves to the precise kind of differentiation by which the distinction between phonemes describes an absolute difference in meaning. For the latter, even if the combinations are effectively infinite, the elements that compose them are precisely describable, as are the principles of combination, so that an infinite number of possibilities may be conceived as a sequence of permutations within a closed system. There may be reasons for thinking that such conceptual tidiness is illusory. But the project is nevertheless statable in a reasonably systematic manner and the terms of such statement intelligibly defined. But if one turns from phonemes to metaphor the very components which enter into implied comparisons are more problematic to state. And to contrast metaphor with other forms of figure requires a quite different sort of discrimination, which is then problematic in a further sense.

Of course if the language of literature itself is constitutively ambiguous it does not follow that the language which describes and analyses it must be equally so. Indeed it would necessarily be of a different order. But the very difficulty of establishing the precise limits of the figural means that categories of explanation cannot be precisely defined. The tradition of establishing such categories through the formal rhetoric of figural types has always had its approximative uses. But we have seen in the case of Bloom's highly sophisticated version the problems which follow if such a 'poetics' is applied. Bloom has, with characteristic courage, picked one of the most difficult forms of case. But the difficulties were at least two-fold: for one thing the identification of the rhetorical feature within the poem was so very approximate as to cast doubt on its appropriateness. Secondly, such terms were sufficiently incomplete in themselves as to require both psychological and historical filling out to give the figure in question the distinctive character which implies an explanatory force. The full sense was a compound of elements of different kinds, with additional elements of diverse sources continually added to provide further understanding of the case, and added on what seems an eclectic basis. So the 'system' of rhetorical terms could never function self-containedly in its own right, but always reach out for explanatory features which extend beyond what one would normally understand as 'poetics'. Rather than analysing the constitutive features of literary language they would require the further entanglement with the human situation in more and more of its dimensions.

Whether this is done through a complication of rhetorical terminology or through the abandonment of a notion of a systematic poetics, the case points rather to a loose set of guidelines for overlapping descriptions. That these descriptions may be persuasive or otherwise would be indicated in two different respects at least, both for their localised context and the attraction of the general schema. The relation between the two might have its further specific appeal. And the appeal in a complicated instance might invoke more than one form of 'poetics'. This would in turn make the notion of a 'poetics' a component of further description, with certain features on which critical argument might draw, as it might on yet another version of 'poetics' which was in some way usefully complementary.

This problem has been seen clearly in a structuralist context by Todorov in his essay on James, where he recognises the effective incompatibility between criticism and structuralism in the conflict between the requirement of the particular case and the functioning of a general scientific law: 'criticism seeks to interpret a particular work, while structuralism, for its part, is a scientific method implying an interest in impersonal laws and forms, of which existing objects are only the realizations'.[5] He then justifies the use of theory not in terms of its critical value, but in terms of the value that application has for the refinement of theory itself. What then is the speculative instrument? In James's allegories of the artist where the 'real thing' is the representation and the model or source a secondary device, the 'primacy of the system over what it represents is a conclusion that poetics derives from the extension of the Saussurian model to the sphere of the grammar of literature; and now we find literature itself endorsing these conclusions'.[6] This is Ann Jefferson's formulation and she comments that this ascribes a special kind of content to literature which is form itself, and structuralist criticism is 'characterised primarily by this kind of reflexivity'.

If so, a law of diminishing returns sets in. For Todorov's astute reading of certain tales is not only a very partial representation of James – compare with the preface to *The Golden Bowl* – but is so specialised as to show the very opposite of what is intended. To attempt to universalise the theme of a narrowly selected group of tales tells powerfully against the possible generalisability of the method itself. And if the validity of the method depends on the possibility of universal use, Todorov's critical insight invalidates his theoretical purpose. What is shown instead is limitation, if not contradiction.

A larger use of theory lies in those general analyses that explore the conditionality through which literary language might exist, in which its historical transformation might occur, and which indicate that range of larger forces – psychological, economic and political – in which the determinates of that language may be seen. Strong versions of such conditionality may push towards the breakdown of the coherence of the concept of literature. In this respect consider the programme of Sollers for *Tel Quel* in 1967, which seeks to mark the implications of the 'practice of writing' as something which lies beyond the normative idea of literature. Of course taken literally this is a truism. Its use was to break into the institutional cocoon of traditional literary thought. Theoretical analysis must cut through the pseudo-continuities of this normative congeries to show the breaking points, expressed as 'rupture', as crisis (again) which is kin to social or economic crisis and affects the critic as a crisis of readability. We have seen other versions of such notions. But a true 'comprehensive theory' would indicate a nexus of crossing points within the historical field, putting in question the official continuities, seeing the literary text not as the familiar object of comfortable assimilation, but as a conjunction of activities of production whose plurality both enters into a 'monumental' as opposed to a cursive history yet simultaneously embodies a gesture of destruction: 'this destruction, this negation, are explained by theory which is therefore the language of this destruction of language ... '.[7]

I do not wish to overplay certain comedies of the sixties, nor to impose too crass an overview on this curious and chaotic document, so full of interest and confusion (and already marking the way which will lead from *ensemble* to *exception*) but to point to its unease in combining the notion of theory as a general form of explanation with the notion of theory as a destructive instrument – the means of both seeing a version of an intelligible whole and demolishing the inherited and false account of one's historical situation. This duality, and unease, seems the measure of the uses of theory that characterised the two subsequent decades, the awareness that in theory one has found the necessary cutting-edge of critical language, the means of reshaping its purposes both in terms of invention and of necessary polemic.

I have taken Kristeva's *The Revolution in Poetic Language* as representing this moment in terms of 'ensemble', that is in terms of the coalescence of a group of theoretical approaches around an historical crisis of poetic language named by Mallarmé himself, articulating that moment through four (at the least) theoretical perspectives: linguistic, psychoanalytic, historical and economic. One effect of this should be centrifugal. It should make the four theoretical axes responsible to the particular claims of their individual sources, to be justified in those primary and largely separate terms. Yet as interpretative axes they are seen in relation to a common purpose and are substantially transformed. They may seem to represent hypotheses about the intellectual circuits from which they derive, but the actual embodiment of them in their use, in what has become 'critical theory', has left their truth value with respect to their source irrelevant. So it does not matter that a certain model of linguistic science is highly contestable, that Marx's notions about the dialectical movement of history are largely fanciful, or that Freudian accounts of the structure of the psyche have no scientific standing whatsoever. As interpretative devices they are redirected in their instrumentality. Their use is all-important and their validity or lack of it wholly marginal.

In such circumstances theories of many kinds are used as aspects of understanding that exist in delicate and changing balance with others, exchanging and modifying relative prominence and degree of force. They may obscure one another, or be seemingly dropped to be recovered in another context. The 'ensemble' shifts its elements as aspects of a text surface to require further adaptation, deviance and revision of perspectives. Of course there are theoretical explanations of literature that do not enter into this instrumentality – one can conceive causal explanations that do not engage in a way we should want to call 'critical'. But the slightest attempt to illuminate the particular example may be fatally seductive and a pristine externality compromised. The committed Marxist or Freudian who is also a serious critic may, as we shall see further, oscillate between the rigour of his commitment and the qualification posed by the operational changes that are an intrinsic part of critical involvement. There are many versions of the conflict Todorov noted between the particular case and the general law.

Whether these multiple forms of general law could lend themselves to further totalisation seems put in question by the terms in which the little use one can see of ensemble operates. The shifting relations between the elements of the ensemble suggest the opposite, the continuous requirement for something complementary, as one theoretical consideration evokes another, and the possibilities of a unified field of theory slowly recede. What has become apparent is the destructive nature of critical engagement, its capacity to absorb and devour theory, and in doing so to demolish its essential structures for the sake of the fragment that will be turned to the use of the moment. To this end criticism admits both contingency and temporality. The fragmentation and sequentiality implicit in occasion are the solvents of conceptual structures. It is perhaps as parody of this all too friable field that Derrida marks out the conceptual limits of language games as the target of multiple paths of transgression.

Hence a paradoxical order arises in which those concepts designed to give intelligible unity, the level of generality and continuity that links the working of many instances, become ancillary to the particular resemblances and differences out of which a pattern of relationship can emerge. We may nevertheless argue as if the general concepts are the integument which connects the stream of particular observation, but insofar as this is so they do not enter into critical discourse but remain external to it. Their engagement in it produces the variable transformation that our cases have shown, in which the making of 'sense' lies in the moment of catalysis that a theoretical action may perform. Therefore critical discourse is essentially discontinuous. The relation between a theoretical concept as part of the overview and its instrumental use in critical discourse may represent this discontinuity even when it is masked by the assumption of homology.

If theory in critical use must be distinguished from its more general premises one consequence is that its value for criticism can only be described in terms of those operations. That is, one cannot reasonably think of the 'theoretical enterprise' as such. There are only particular theories and their uses. And it follows that there is no case against 'theory' as a whole, as there is no case for it. One could also perhaps put it that use 'pragmatises' theory by subordinating our understanding of it to an aspect of practice. In this I am thinking only of what one could call an operational pragmatism, not the epistemological neo-pragmatism which sees the grounds of understanding vanishing in an endless chain of interpretations of interpretations (turtle upon turtle all the way down). We are moving towards seeing the relevant fragments of that chain as a thickening description in which the predominant role of theory – or rather, of theories – is further dimension and cutting edge.

I shall also argue in a following section that the pragmatic characterising, this open-textured and operational version of pragmatism, is not incompatible with the normative undercurrent of a classicising tendency which, for all of its discontinuous character, is implicit in critical reasoning. For part of the thickening I have described lies in the fusion of theoretical implication with observed affinities, even if the sources of theoretical energy are quite diverse, and even if they contain what Sollers noted in the curious symbiosis of movement towards coherence of explanation and the creative necessity of disruption.

This does not mean contextual accommodation in the sense in which in the work of Murray Krieger 'contextualism' itself becomes a form of theory. Certainly the weaker senses of theory – which include something less than an abstract conceptual framework, such as simply an area of coherent presuppositions or even of public stances – lend themselves to a complex cohabitation. Eliot's mixture of social conservatism and traditionalist taste entered into the most radical aspects of modernism. And in Eliot's case there was no effort to reach the kind of conceptual sketch that would create a synthesis or totalisation in which these opposing aspects of his work would find their relational place substantially indicated. Did this mean the growing predominance of those traditionalist sentiments at the expense of creative energies? This question arises in the study and assessment of the *Four Quartets*. On the other hand, the refusal of any such theoretical synthesis is an implicit rejection of the idealist heritage of Royce and Bradley, a refusal to see one's work as a conceptual whole. Neither the tensions of a dialectic of opposites nor a weak form of contextualism where everything finds an appropriate place may have seemed a suitable resolution for the demands of coherence, which, whatever the concomitant difficulties, found a poetic form.

If one applies the test of coherence to the working of theory, notions of 'contextualism' would seem to be too weak to provide effective intelligibility, however pragmatically the internal relations of any imagined coherence may be conceived. It is in fact difficult to conceive of contextualism as a theory at all; the rich and substantial exploration of such a stance – in its belief in 'literary complexity' and 'distrust of universals', where human existence itself is 'enigmatic, beyond the reach of philosophic propositions, and needs an enigmatic literature to illustrate it' [8] – is a restatement of the tradition of Arnold, Eliot and even Leavis, in which the work of literature is complex and dense, somehow belonging to a different world of understanding and requiring different sorts of explanation from a highly generalised philosophical discourse. Contextualism also has a distant affinity with de Man's distrust of the smooth explanatory kinds of theorising. Both critics might be said to use theory pragmatically, but in quite different ways. Krieger's is an adaptation of the variety of explanatory modes to the contexts that use them most richly and effectively. De Man's is the use of theory to disrupt our flow of easy explanation which would too easily flatter our manners of making sense. But both respect the integrity and unassimilability of the enigmatic presence. A weak sense of theory which refuses the imposition of false coherence may also strongly suggest the amorphous boundaries of the subject, as the strong and disruptive use may cut through them at multiple angles. Both may put in question what their point of departure requires, the existence of the critical 'language game'.

Such a question is of course implied in Sollers' destructive action of theory, as it is in the relation between the conceptual dimensions of Kristeva's multiple framing of a crisis of poetic language. In the latter there can be no fundamental language game in progress to which the psycho-analytic or historical analyses make a contribution, nor is there a manifold in which the multiple frames are drawn together into a single area of understanding in which the 'ensemble' has taken on an identity of its own. It is more simply that the collaborative activity of several disciplines has a common point of application. That there should be a correspondence between their functions is not so much conceptualised in its own terms as simply assumed, not in the manner of a Baudelairian mystery but in the form of practice, a pragmatism which represents the point of convergence. But this need not be an artificial unity. If, as Barthes says, the text is plural, is not our understanding plural also? Such a plurality either devastates or banalises – we see the cracks in the possibility of an intelligible whole, the all too comforting 'readable', with appropriate terror. Yet the habituation of our sensibility to those 'minor earthquakes', the necessity of looking at the many dimensions of plurality, gradually evolves that tissue of complementarities by which the plural no longer shocks and the multiple movements of mind beckon towards each other as separate aspects, as complementarities. The 'earthquake' is the threshold of eclecticism. Plurality accommodates. The particular genius of de Man is to deny this accommodation in the elaboration of a practice that keeps the sense of crisis omnipresent, however tortuous the necessary means. But the usual form of accommodation is ultimately entropic, with the individual critical moves and their rationales separating themselves out, finding a diffuse plurality in which the scattered fragments beyond the 'earthquake' coexist in comfort.

Such an effect enervates and undermines pragmatism of whatever kind: Krieger's 'contextualism', what Christopher Butler calls 'contextual relativism ',[9] and common sense in most of its forms, at least insofar as they pretend to the status of a general position of any kind, or present themselves as *ensembles*. It may, for somewhat different reasons, erode the pluralism of Barthes. It is not an argument against them, but merely an indication that some forms of quite intelligible and defensible practice come apart at a level of generality that proposes an overall sense to the whole procedure. It is almost as if we can name an activity called 'criticism', identify its plurality of modes, the sources of its speculative instruments, extend our description of its practices, yet in attempting to grasp it as a significant whole, produce something useless and uninteresting.

Yet I have talked of critical discourse devouring and transforming theory as if there were such a primary medium of transformation. And also of the pragmatising effect of critical activity, in which a particular practice has an identifiable matrix. Can there be such a 'language game' that its plurality of elements suggests a collection of the most diverse rationales, yet has its distinctive features in the process of its operation? We have seen some of the difficulty in imposing a conceptual coherence which would shape that process through theory itself, as well as the way in which theories once applied begin to alter their own terms.

## 3      The illusory language game

One has the problem of representing a paradigm that embodies those very discontinuous features that I have indicated, which shows the effect of an activity through the very features that lie in the way of a univocal perception of a working whole. What kind of coherence does the working of the critical game require? Certainly the nature of such a game is not revealed in rules, nor in anything that can be described in terms of form. As a matrix where mediation becomes possible its somewhat negative shape lies in the working out of its application. I have noted as a lowest common denominator the group of moves which mark similarity and difference, which revolve about the old formula 'It's like this, isn't it'. But of course the 'this' may range from the most singular example to the largest general category. In Chapter I, I argued that the world of particular comparisons was incomplete to the point of being inoperable without the existence of general categories. Yet the recognition of observed similarity and difference between particulars may work by way of the implied general qualities – indeed the whole history of disputes about the nature of universals lurks in the normal use of the extended 'this'. And difference may be easier to state than similarity, because the role of the 'not quite' gives us the illusion of a particular distinction which eludes generality. The negative move seems purer, less cluttered with implication and unnecessary presence, yet is inconceivable without drawing the other in its train. Difference is always 'from' – whether from a ruthlessly ostensive 'this' or something which packs the total wardrobe of tradition. The game, however reduced, to whatever denominator, has a double movement. Yet such a simple paradigm draws upon all of the wide range of discriminations of everyday life – not simply between apples and pears, but between apples and other apples. Does the critical use have, so to speak, its own form of difference?

Certainly the area of its operation might define the possibility of imaginable effects, even if the moves are assimilable to a comparison like any other. The sense that the manoeuvre of a comparative kind is so casually reducible would give to any language game the character of a disappearing act, slipping off quietly into the most ordinary workings of ordinary language, and masking the radical force of the tyranny of particular occasions. Perhaps its strength is in a certain invisibility, as in John Bayley's use of 'division', the extreme example perhaps of Waissman's 'open texture' in its continuous repositioning in the face of varied objectives. 'Division' is, after all, 'division of'. Is there a far-reaching concept at work, a form of theory, however weak, and however diverse in its forms of application? We shall look at the possible commitments implicit in this. But certainly nothing theoretical is said. The notion of 'division' is neither defined nor described. Yet it begins in breathtaking generality, delivered in the most off-hand manner: 'Of course, the creative process always begins in division'.[10] Of course. But this 'begins' is a logical point of departure, not the threshold of a genetic account. Compare with what an Aristotle could do: 'Of course, the creative process begins in imitation'. This is the beginning of an explanation of a quite different kind. It is about beginnings: all men love to imitate, take pleasure in imitation, etc. This Aristotle would tell us how the whole thing came about, something which does not concern Bayley at all.

To begin in division is simply to posit the hypothetical past of a work from which its inner development proceeds. The work of art is the solution to a problem which could be of ever so many possible kinds. But it begins in the division – could one have said the 'difference'? – from which some kind of reshaping, ordering or arrangement is presumed to work towards unity, towards the healing of division, whether within men's souls, in the relations of persons, families, or bodies politic. Thus it assumes that we approach through representation the substance of literature, with a problem which generated the work, which poses itself rationally, and which indeed it would be wicked not to resolve. It is intentionalist in the pervasive way that does not worry about the precise intentions of authors, but merely assumes that they are there, engaged reasonably enough with the flow of difficulty and contradiction that arises from division in the human heart. Who could deny that literature is about persons and by persons, and works through describing what they say and do, and that without a sense of this it would not only be unintelligible but would simply not exist?

This direct contact with the substance of literature, with what it is 'about', does not prevent 'division' from being also a formal term, even if in the roughest sense of the relation of unity to chaos, or less radically, of what is shaped as opposed to what is less so. The assumption may be held without excessive precision about its terms that the very selectivity of literature is the first move of such a shaping process, and that such selection involves difference, instability, or some version of division. To be immersed in the happiness of happy families is not really a beginning.

So represented this seems comprehensive and banal, with all written matter present, and the very term the example of a critical vocabulary so casual and reticent as to be capable of shaping nothing of interest. Yet the whole awareness is put sharply in a modern idiom. We are not as far from de Manian crisis as might first appear. How alien this language would have seemed to any critic before Arnold. For Aristotle the achievement of unity lay in the ordering of action, not in the overcoming of conflict. And for Dr Johnson the chaotic world of Shakespeare, so pressing upon our natural craving for intelligibility and order, reflected the turbulence of genius uncorrected by close reflection on classical models, rather than some subversively generalisable notion like 'division' which cuts into the many versions of the coherence of our world, revealing that failure of fit within form, psyche and society like a small logical fissure, a miniscule 'earthquake'. And such division runs not merely through the works we contemplate but the act of contemplation; we cannot help entertaining a reflexive awareness of what the notion might imply, how the uses ricochet among the verbal structures we observe and make. For the recognition of division is the ground of interest, where the resolution of form is almost secondary.

Much of this further effect is indeed implied or indirect, because many of the 'uses of division' do not employ the word. It is said that Stanley Fish found seventeen meanings of 'division' in the book.[11] This not only seems a modest estimate, but one which raises the important question of how he counted. For many of the 'uses' are expressed in quite other words, or shown indirectly. Fish would have had to count 'not the meaning[s] but the use[s]' when they are not only not actually named, but can only be reached inferentially. The coherence of the multiple uses seems less underwritten by a universalisable essential meaning, but by certain common qualities of situations within which language works. When you look at this sort of case, and then this, etc. ... certain features appear, the common element more sustained by observed similarities of perhaps rather approximate kinds than by a quality of any sort that could lend itself to general definition. The very notion of 'division' – as indeed with difference – conveys such possibilities of coming apart, such variety of operation, that as an explanatory or ordering concept it exists at the outer edge of intellectual tidiness. It suggests the greatest freedom of manoeuvre and minimum degree of control.

Examples of the direct use are complemented by the implied. One can take the direct pointer as in a remark about *Little Dorrit*: 'the division between a great surface drive and gaiety and an underlying uncertainty of a much more intriguing and revealing kind' (*UD*, p. 102). Or one can see varieties of the idea working through terms that may indicate those gaps, discrepancies, conflicts which condition any reading of complex works – say, the conflict in Dickens between his dependence as a social being writing for an audience and his indifference to it as an artist (*UD*, p. 103), or in the balance of particularity and generality in Keats. The pattern may express a psychological conflict, between the pedagogue and the anarchist in Jane Austen (*UD*, p. 25) or a discrepancy of general qualities, beauty and ugliness in Larkin (*UD*, p. 182), and often the interplay between levels of awareness when the 'statutory front' of a work fits a conventionalised understanding that is itself in conflict with a more subtle form of imagining (*UD*, p. 81, on *The Death of the Heart*). Perhaps one could propose axes of generality and particularity and models that relate psychological content to form, but schematisation would be contrary to both letter and spirit. The ordering principle for varieties of division seems in the placement of these observations in an unschematised tissue of relationships where the sense of relevance draws upon a reservoir of cases of comparison. There are established relationships and differences where the tradition sets the terms of any possible challenge. It contains hidden paths and connections as well as the significant breaks within them.

But what are we to make of the breaks, of the moments of division? Are they part of a tissue of continual readjustment, a flow of shifting relations and revaluations, or do they indicate some fissure in the order of things that a meditation on literature will quietly put in one's way? Perhaps such issues can only be approached through a further perspective which the employment of 'division' does not intend to contemplate. Or perhaps it may open anywhere to a chain of consequences unforeseen.

The treatment of *Measure for Measure* shows the effect of playing several frames of reference subtly against each other. Part derives from the coexistence of two genres, the dramatic form with one convention of expectations in the 'Guarini model' of comedy which imposes its satisfactory closure, and the potential novel hidden within the form in which quite other expectations could be played out. 'The humanity of the play depends upon the comedy ethos. Yet something also stands outside, strong in the protest of its own integrity and its own difference, asserting the division Shakespeare lives, challenging the unity he can always do without' (*UD*, p. 248). It is the difference between *Measure* as a closed world controlled by conventions of comic resolution and an open one where the Duke's authority is flawed, where Isabella may refuse the Duke and suitably arranged marriages may end in hell. Here is the case of one 'language' subverting another, in what is a deconstructive demonstration after its own fashion. But nothing is accomplished by the invention of a new language out of difference and division, rather a use of such ordinary speech to point up the presence of two aspects which are incompatible yet coexist. And beyond the unity that Shakespeare could do without there is yet another which abolishes our own conventional critical language with its talk of genres and forms but exists in that troubling whole which is *Measure for Measure*.

The language of this both suggests its own limits, yet goes beyond them. A certain diffidence or modesty seems to veer away from grandiose claims about one's method, about the implications of 'division', about anything which might point towards general conclusions about the nature of literature or of its study, about anything which might seem theory-laden or theory-informed. The contrast of two senses of genre, one determinate in its pattern and the other disturbingly open, tells us something about the strangeness and imbalance we feel in *Measure* but little or nothing about the nature of genre. The terms are simply taken as tradition has given them, then disturbingly and far-reachingly conjoined. And the contrasts between integrity and difference, unity and division, work within an inherited Aristotelian version of the relation of formal structure to psychological expectation without consciously extending it. Yet there is a strong sense of the wider implications of such limits, an awareness of what is involved in playing the game that way, a game which insists indirectly that indeed it is a way, which can see itself as a form of practice, and demonstrate through its applied and situated activity the existence of something we might as well call 'criticism' as an identifiable version of practical reason.

So is there what we might reasonably call the 'language game' of criticism at work? It would appear that there is such a game; we can see it in action, describe certain of its characteristic moves. But if we look closely the moves seem not to be those limited to that game. They are indistinguishable from those we might use in life itself: the same sorts of similarity and difference, of familiar and unfamiliar comparisons, unities and divisions. As we look closely the game dissolves. Certainly it does not have clearly distinguishable rules, although certain characteristic man-oeuvres are repeatable. And they can be taught and imitated and turned into critical tropes which we can bring together artificially, as in a classroom where they take on a transmitted character. We can show ostensibly the tension, irony, ambiguity, unity, difference, division within the poem, or equivalent features within the narrative, whether this leads to absurdity or to illumination. One is tempted however to say that these transmittable tropes are more like the racquet and balls rather than the game itself. Such vocabulary as useful instrument requires something further in the sense of location to make it part of a larger activity. And of course existence outside the critical game may add both stretch and doubt to the terms of their use.

But does a coherent 'language game' lie beyond that dissolution that I have indicated, beyond the breakdown that appears through close observation? If the game falls into parts can we by stepping back see it in perspective, as the blobs of an impressionist painting become coherent from a little distance? It is perhaps something like this which gives us the valuable illusion of a coherent field. And the very illusion of the game may in a perverse way act to create it. The game is an implied fiction which originates in the focal point of the activity itself. But the illusory game affects the deployment of the elements that feed it, the many kinds of observation – substantive, formal, linguistic, historical, etc. – that one takes for granted as assimilable into literary study. For it gives them a locus where the point of their presence is established in a moment of use. Do we see a Japanese Bridge? No, of course not. It is an arrangement of colours and forms – indistinct and ambiguous forms – by Monet. But from a suitable distance we can infer from those colours and forms what seems to be a representation. And this semblance is enough. The inference can be reached that a representation has taken place, as well as consciously abandoned, and the process of making that inference, of following the imaginative leaps between what we might have expected and what seems to have happened, shows us the presence of a characteristic activity, with a continuity observable in common features which lead from, say, Constable to Braque. The game roughly coheres, although we may see that coherence only with difficulty, with varying refractions and at odd degrees of remove.

Could one go so far as to claim that the very self-consciousness with which Bayley's work turns its back on system or on theory, with a calculated naturalness, might imply that the game has hidden rules, of a kind impossible to state and more difficult than our critical tropes to transmit, but which consist in the kind of awareness of multiple perspectives, or of the shifting alternatives involved in coming to any, however partial and tentative, version of a critical point? On this reading there would be rules of a sort, ways of disciplining one's uses of comparison, of directing one's attention more acutely. But their operation is always qualified by the further awareness that they could be applied otherwise, or altered or varied for the sake of a nuance or contrastive effect. Such awareness is ironising both in terms of the application of whatever rules might govern such a game, and of the notion of rule itself. Can one build a version of their fallibility into their very nature? Lyotard remarks that if there are no rules there is no game. But there might be observable characteristics. 'Cat and mouse' is clearly a game, but without rules. And we might see analogous cases in language.[12]

Are such ironical perspectives part of a strategy of calculated naturalness, enclosable within a general prescription which may suppress the general dimension, which refuses the articulation of its principles, holds the uses of 'division' to the precise occasion of those uses, but which has a quite conscious grasp of its own character? It would assume that the responsibility of saying 'what is really important' is part of an intelligible language-game however indefinite its contours. Or is the very openness to ironising too erosive both of language and of sense of project, too intrinsic to the operative mode to do other than dissolve our sense of the possibility of rules or appropriateness in their application? Bayley in some senses is quite clear about the standing of all of this. One knows the difference between unity and division, what constitutes a 'statutory front' and what might lie behind it. Is a further understanding required? It usually seems not. But there is perhaps in the manner that occasional element of the almost flippantly prescriptive which suggests that playing the game this way is a riposte to other ways of playing. Calculated naturalness can border on the parodic. One watches a skilled player at a stylish move. Yes, the game is there, but we see around it to admire some further quality of style and hence to see beyond the rules.

But does that suggest a simple built-in limitation, or a point at which the game itself vanishes? Consider the analogous effort to define what Kuhn has called a 'disciplinary matrix' in accounting for the 'at least twenty-two different ways' in which he has used 'paradigm'.[13] It suggests a conceptual untidiness on the same scale as 'division'. But Kuhn argues that the many uses represent superficial variants and the essential, important differences are reducible to two. This of course would, if his procedure is correct, indicate a different sense of the functioning of the term from that of 'division'. The effect of the latter was to be found in the strength of its localisations, the way in which its adaptability provided an immediate and particular illumination, not a technical concept whose precise uses are meant to resist such centrifugality. And of course 'division' like 'fool' has a complex natural history in its ordinary language uses. In effect its critical use depends upon this varied natural history, as the use of 'paradigm' might be blurred through such shifting application.

Does this mean that the setting up of criteria for the conditions of critical use would not resemble the criteria that Kuhn gives for the 'disciplinary matrix' in which his notion of paradigm is to be understood? At least at one level there would appear to be some useful resemblance. For he approaches this question of appropriate criteria through the use that a community of scientists makes of its concepts. And the nature of critical concepts, at that outer edge of critical instrumentality that such a notion as 'division' represents, certainly reflects a community activity of at least a distantly analogous kind. And any analogous criteria might throw some light on the solidity or evanescence of the critical language game.

Certain adaptations would of course be required for any comparison. For one thing the concepts themselves would have a different range of implications, as 'symbolic generalisation' has no critical equivalent, and we have seen the artificiality of Empson's attempt to find a notational method of representation. This is not an encouraging point of departure. But if such a notion as a shared paradigm means roughly 'common language' the problem changes its character. And the language in question is not generalisable in the symbolic sense, and therefore not shareable in quite the way of imposing its common ground. Neo-classical criticism may have given more precise conditions for the employment of 'unity' than those in common currency. Bayley's use clearly draws upon it, as the tradition of Shakespeare criticism has re-examined it, but how close his use is to that of a neo-classical 'paradigm' is impossible to say – partly because the distance is continually varied.

When Kuhn moves to shared models we can see some ground for the tightening of our analogy, for among other things they provide the community 'with preferred or permissible analogies and metaphors'. There is something slightly threatening in the prescriptive force of 'preferred or permissible', for this suggests an agreed form of authority, and something restrictive about the use of imagination. The force of such regulative opinion might imply that the progress of science requires a level of agreement about the terms of the *modus operandi*, and while such areas of agreement can well be seen in aspects of literary study it is not the necessary condition of intelligible discourse. That is, the move out of the accepted ground is an accepted move, although there are certain limits. It is difficult to conceive of criticism without the making of comparisons. But it is also hard to conceive of fixed procedures and precise rules which govern such making. And here the idea of 'model' becomes stretched and thin. For even our simplest example of what looks like a model procedure,

'It's like this, isn't it?', can be fitted to every sort of non-literary occasion, and becomes the model of nothing in particular.

Certainly one could argue that the moves are there but are simply difficult to describe. Through our sense of the tradition, of our place in it, of our desire to shed, alter or transform that place, which itself derives from our sense of it, through our cumulative experience of what seem like the relevant, interesting, astute etc., resemblances, connections, affinities, or their opposites, we can situate a critical move in what is a body of practice. But such a description suggests that the cumulative experience dissolves the very contours of the model, making the use of the notion more figurative than not.

A similar pressure can be seen on the notion of shared values. Of course one means not cultural values themselves, but those that are intrinsic to the critical activity itself. The most general value commitments are quite other than that predictive accuracy Kuhn has in mind as the unifying principle of his 'disciplinary matrix'. But if we state our analogous value in such terms as 'further understanding' or 'illumination' we are naming something so imprecise as not to know exactly when those terms are fulfilled. Rather than an intelligible goal it is an almost fortuitous extra step, one which could not itself have been predicted. Stated thus the value is banal, but the form it takes is a surprise – a discovery or reshaping that is the very opposite. And without this element we tend to dismiss, or even to say 'it's not really a critical point', or 'it is subcritical'. But the banality of the value is also the indicator that something further must be done: if not quite a response to 'étonnez-moi' the critical remark must at least cross the 'so what?' threshold. And that exists everywhere and nowhere. The criterion of interest cannot be easily affixed to either the form of a discourse or to precise areas of expectation which might show where that interest would arise.

The final and most important criterion of 'shared examples' might seem the most directly transmittable to the literary case. But one would have to indicate at least two classes of examples. Those that define however roughly the conventional field of operation: literature as the academy understood it. And those that embody the special cases, or those moments of controversy that bring various critical voices into conflict. The former may be comprehensive enough, or focus more narrowly on works that have a canonical status. To talk about the conflict of genres in *Measure for Measure* is to situate oneself at the heart of the field, and of the canon as well. But I shall argue that the canon may subversively control its own violation. Field, canon and crux can of course all be put in question: by those who would dissolve literature into *écriture*, those who would replace traditional canons by others or would deny the value of whatever principles might underlie the formation of a canon, and those who would say that the cruces, either current or traditional, lack the interest which can be found in argument of some other kind. The grounds of various forms of putting in question have been seen in their contexts. What I shall go on to ask is whether or not the rejection that these imply, both of the identity of literature and of the language game of criticism, do not in effect circle back and acknowledge the thing they would deny. I do not mean that the atheist's obsession with God demonstrates that He exists. It is rather that the normative terms of the tradition have a magnetic pull on their denial, and their identity may be reshaped through gestures of rejection, but not diminished. Nor do I mean simply that Eagleton turns from asserting the importance of working-class writing as cultural practice to write a book about Shakespeare. Although it might look as if he needed the centre of the canon to enter into any of the critical procedures that would explore, or even ultimately embody, the very reflective process which seemed necessary to his own project. It is not that Shakespeare is more interesting than the products of the worker writers' movement, but that we can hardly talk usefully about the latter without operations, concepts and faculties that are shaped in the heart of the canon itself. Hence, there is a cluster of activities, something brought into a perspective by the very revolt against it. We see, out of difference itself, the shadowy unity that the neo-classical tradition has tried, however feebly, to represent. If that representation coalesces into a world of stable norms and repeatable rules which the examination of critical concepts cannot sustain, the contrary movement is itself entrapped in the terms it has rejected. So if we write about literary theory to deny its importance or about Shakespeare to show that literature does not exist we are somehow embarked in a contrary sense.

Of course one may ask how far this concern with the nature of the 'game' is necessary or even relevant to the further description one has wished to offer. I have suggested how stepping back is a useful means of grasping something that looks more like a whole from a longer perspective. But one can step back further still and see 'criticism' as it has been practised from, say, Johnson to Empson (the French time-band is narrower, say, Sainte-Beuve to Poulet), as an historically bounded phenomenon, where the cultural establishment of certain models of description and explanation is attached to the literary object as the incarnation of a cultural crossroads, which that object could not fail to represent in a full range of formal, psychological and historical terms. Has that practice faltered in consequence of the crisis seen in and named by Mallarmé, and reflected here through a sequence of commentaries in Richard, de Man, Derrida and Kristeva? Would we say that Richard is among the last to exemplify that game in its 'classic' form, and that his quarrel with Derrida arises from believing that certain descriptions and explanations are still possible? The others are the children of crisis for whom the post-critical reflection must be characterised in another way, one which may dispense, among other things, with such a word. We have seen what a profound ambiguity arises in de Man through denying the assumptions of a tradition of critical practice, yet keeping the word as the very representation of 'crisis'.

But one effect of pointing to the limits and failures of the representation to which 'criticism' once pretended is both a causal and conceptual link. In denying the game one is drawn into it. In marking limits one has extended them. If such further discourse enters into the language game itself, something created as we have seen from the illusion it projects, do we see an older practice refined and extended, or a new form of activity crossing an historical watershed? It may depend on whether we wish to emphasise continuity or difference. It is possible too that the well-marked difference draws its interest from the depth of involvement with what it in other ways rejects. To assess this would be to mark another difference and find another perspective. The question of whether or not our traditional term has that degree of stretch is not a question of how we use a word, but something that depends upon what comes after. For even if we see the end of criticism we may also see its power to reinvent itself and climb craftily, like some curious beast – a new chimera perhaps – out of the abyss. The game will play on, however variable its practices and however curious its flyness in fiddling the rules.

# IX    Pagan perspectives

## 1    Of smaller and grander narratives

If the 'language game' of criticism dissolves under close inspection, if its
'disciplinary matrix' resists the use of intelligible criteria, if its general
concepts work through destructive fragmentation while efforts to give it a
general characterisation fade into useless banality, would it therefore make
sense to abandon our interest in criticism as a form of practical reason and
dismiss its value as a form of discourse? I shall argue the exact opposite and
show the value implicit in its very localisation, the strength in immediacy,
and in evanescence itself.

If we are to follow the consequences of what our cases have shown us,
the attempts to formulate something which one could call a critical theory
cannot be stated from within critical language; the synoptic understanding
lies outside it. Whatever synoptic sense it employs is borrowed. One can see
an effect of this in the later work of Kermode. Dealing with such concepts
as 'attention', 'history' and 'value', he has tried to formulate an approach
to these concepts from the ground in the critical cases that he discusses.
And the critical language appropriate to those cases does not generate the
level of generality to bring those concepts into effective use, or even to
make their larger meaning intelligible. The approach is the opposite of that
of Richards where the generality implicit in harmonious organisation of
the psyche has its obvious if dubious scientific source, and synoptic effect.

This also raises an important issue for the critical concern with value.
Are values to be stated in general terms, or do they arise in such a way from
particular perceptions and choices that they are only intelligible in context?
I shall argue that this issue is partly clarified by the distinction we have
already noted in Barthes between values and the process of valuing. But the
case of Kermode brings out one dimension of this, for the paradox arises
directly from the exempla of Marxist criticism that concern him: how can
one value highly the sort of literary work which contains values that are
contrary to one's own? This is complicated by a double sense of valuing,
for the values that are implicit in the historical circumstantiality of a text

from the past may distance us in another sense than that of our personal convictions. Kermode's handling of this group of problems in terms of what he calls 'discrepancy theory' keeps some useful ambiguities intact. For one can begin to multiply the tracks upon which 'discrepancy' might move. Behind it seems to stand Eliot's distinction in the Dante essay between 'philosophical belief' and 'poetic assent'. The case of Dante is that of a remarkable fusion wherein we can value the work through the thought even if the thought is unacceptable in itself. There are of course many forms of unacceptability, and degrees, so 'discrepancy' stretches to the many modes in which conflicting values coexist. And in doing so it can express the variety of ways in which criteria of value and the effect of the valuing process fail to correspond, or push in the direction of different claims.

I will later consider some aspects of the problem of value. In this context it is simply one form of the awkwardness of fit between general theory and the claims, interests and attractions that particular works may pose. Both the excuse for and the conceptual vehicle for adjusting the former to the latter haunt even the most rigidly ideological programme with the sense of unfinished business. It is not a question of satisfying an artificially constructed criterion for the completeness of account but, say, to recognise that however exhaustively one accounts for the economic and social pressures within the Elizabethan age – for property, marriage customs, gender conventions, the revelation of psychic strains beneath the surface of language – to give an intelligible account of *Twelfth Night* demands something more and different. This is not to privilege the 'mystique' of literature, but simply to admit the complexity of the demands which the work makes upon us. Even when Kristeva situates the historical crisis in the nature of the language of poetry the explanatory frames both multiply to accommodate the complexity, and inevitably in terms of their source move us outward into forms of explanation that are both justified in terms of their own external *raison d'être*, legitimated from without, yet are shifted, remodelled, transformed in their application. This suggests in effect two alien kinds of legitimation. And, what begins in the grandiosity of *soi-disant* universal laws ends in the bits and pieces which we find limitedly and contingently useful.

However, the transformation that critical use imposes on general theory also indicates the conceptual dependency of critical thought itself. For if there is no synoptic understanding that can be generated within the practice of criticism – hence the limitation of the case-by-case method – then there is no critical synthesis, indeed, no generality beyond further description. Yet these further descriptions are themselves acts of accommodation and derive from the languages and concepts that feed them.

So it is the limitation and partiality of critical activity that draws upon the explanatory force of the concepts it employs, yet in doing so confines their power. Such descriptions are partly explanatory, yet interrupt or break off the process by which such explanatory systems are fully deployed. A necessary dependence is balanced by a resistance to assimilation. Theory is used instrumentally, as we have seen in some of the versions of it in Derrida and de Man, to accentuate this very failure to assimilate critical discourse to a conceptually ordered world.

One way of describing this is to look at the critical enterprise through the distinction made by Lyotard between 'grands récits' and 'petits récits'. While this distinction is made with respect to political beliefs (*Lessons in Paganism*) or the legitimation of scientific accounts (*The Postmodern Condition*) the common factor is the loss of faith in the possibility of the 'grands récits' – grand narratives. It is both a loss of faith in the content of the grand narratives themselves – the perfectability of man, the spirit as absolute idea, the Marxist millennium, etc. – and also in the possibility of constructing accounts of that kind. The reasons for this are of various kinds, some to do with the fallibility of the required arguments, disillusionment with the conceivable circumstantiality in which the 'grands récits' would be realised, and with changes of historical perspective.

With criticism there have never been such illusions to lose. But the process we have observed in critical discourse is one of turning 'grands récits' into 'petits'. The larger theoretical claims have become when applied something more fragmentary, and instrumental in a localised way. The critical intelligibility is local. At least in the first instance, for comparison may produce that tissue of connections which creates the longer view without validating the method of any larger one. One aspect of Lyotard's 'pagan instructions' is an analogous localisation of validity – the instructions hold only for the single move. And while I would hesitate to use the notion of validity for critical moves, the level of conviction that seeing any complex series of relations requires is built up out of the convincing strength of the discrete perception. Lyotard's attachment to the word 'instruction' seems largely because of its precise limitation to the 'pragmatic context'. An instruction holds for just this state of affairs and for now. The aim seems partly to be a sharpening of one's sense of immediacy. And there is a similarity to what is the instruction implicit in critical language: 'look at this'. The notion of an ensemble of such instructions is brought together – if not united – by what he calls 'paganism'.

This has its clear resemblance to the case-by-case method that we have considered. It is expressed in much the same language: 'And so one works almost "case by case", move by move, and instructions are a move by move process'.[1] Yet it is clear that the narrative, the 'récit', cannot be limited to a single move. The image that unites them is that of a society in which diverse elements participate, although this notion of society is couched in the Kantian terms of an idea. 'It is simply the idea of a society, that is, ultimately, of a set of diverse pragmatics (a set that is neither totalisable nor countable, actually). The specific feature of this set would be that the different language games that are caught up in this pagan universe are incommunicable to each other. They cannot be synthesised into a unifying metadiscourse' (*JC*, p. 58). And this term, 'paganism', is to stand for, or name, a social universe, one which 'is formed by a plurality of games without any of them being able to claim that it can say all the others' (*JG*, p. 58).

The relation between the notion of paganism and that of society seems sufficiently figurative that it is hard to know what force to give to 'incommunicable'. The various language games within this society cannot exist as windowless monads in total isolation. But they will certainly resist the reductive procedure which would make them into a single kind, and the organisation into a meta-narrative, which would be the model of a systematic totalising. And of course this society is one of language games which might operate with similar vocabularies, overlapping frames of reference, common points of focus, yet retain in each move certain distinctive characteristics. Perhaps the distinguishing feature would be difficult to state except in the 'pragmatic context' which is 'the effect produced by a text, that exists only in a given text for the one who reads it ... ' (*JG*, p. 56). Hence an immediacy and particularity – the game can be identified in the moment of its use.

Paganism – for my purposes at least, stripped of its Kantian aura – becomes a representation of critical reasoning and the relations which varieties of criticism may be seen to have with each other. Rather than the single language game there may be a substantial plurality which shares the common characteristic that the speculative instrument has only the force of the single move – to which another may be added, and then others, in the process of exploring the 'pragmatic context', the moment. Indeed the succession of them is localised in the text, where each move becomes the intersection point of the operative language games. 'What is pagan is the acceptance that one can play several ... ' (*JG*, p. 61)

Of course the coexistence of such multiple games does not mean an equality among them, or at least not a permanent one, nor does it mean that a precise and permanent hierarchy of relations can be established. It is rather that some become dominant because of the shifting urgencies with which the text is questioned. And positions of dominance may be shifted or interchanged. This is the normal state of our critical processes, with an awareness that many things, and kinds of thing, are important and that these take on varying degrees of dominance without excluding or effacing each other. And the process of decision making about the relational interplay is essential both to consideration of value and to the connections that any one game may have with the synoptic sense that comes from without.

For without seriously qualifying the primacy of the 'petit récit', the role of a larger narrative is like the window examples can open to 'theory'. It provides the framework of external reference as part of the contexting that the case implies – a pointer to the horizon beyond the case itself. And it acts instrumentally to give a focal point to a local perception. Or, and this is certainly consonant with an adaptation which we can call critical paganism, it acts as a unifying myth, a way of giving the further description which is an imaginative vehicle for our understanding, and which provides not a totalisation but a perspective – even though this perspective is only uncertainly related to the legitimation the larger story would require. Consider the kind of imaginative overview provided by Frye's theory of archetypes. Literary works enact certain movements of thought in variants of fundamental motifs. These can be seen as representations of archetypes which make a repertoire for the imagination's activity, and basis for the proliferation of literary forms. Of course, the myth does not exist except in its exemplification. Yet the understanding of literary form is implied through the hypothesis.

Frye's is a larger story certainly, but one which can only be reached through the fragments of its incarnation. And the large story acts almost as an edifying tale providing a perspective on the critical examples, as if the meta-game drew the fragments of the primary game into a contingent order, many orders, and certainly, a plurality of perspectives. Yet it is not quite a 'grand récit' in Lyotard's sense of giving an understanding of our situation as a whole. It evokes the synopsis that it fails to be. And it may be as false as other 'grands récits' even if it avoids the most falsifiable claims. In fact it precisely breaks off from the further explanation of saying what sort of thing the repertoire of myths might be. Jung or Plato may beckon yet not be fully installed. The story breaks off and accepts its limit. And the limit on the critical fiction fixes the limit of the perspective, as in a painting. Larger could be invented, of course, with such attendant problems as Kermode's example shows.

A similar sense of limit is also built into the critical use of structuralism. We have seen the analogic source providing relational models which turn out in practice to be the borrowing of descriptive vocabulary, which in turn represents the enchantment with a 'scientific' method. But the failure of the method to attain to a general explanatory dimension has not deprived it of a localised interest. If the 'petit récit' sometimes masquerades as 'grand' the illusion is encompassed again as a working fiction that gives point to certain analogies and resemblances. Todorov's problem with James is but one sort of example. And if Graham Hough's comment that it causes one to talk of Tolstoy as if it were a matter of Russian folk-tales contains an innocent touch of send-up, it is one of a kind that arises naturally enough from the method.

The enchantment induced by deconstruction is of a quite different order, for if the method is followed through – or some plausible version of it – there seems to be a 'grand récit' implied in the working of the method itself, while its product is to demolish the possibility of any such thing. Look at Gasché's formulation of it:

At its first step, deconstruction thus presupposes a concretely developed demonstration of the fact that concepts and discursive totalities are already cracked and fissured by necessary contradictions and heterogeneities that the discourse of philosophy fails to take into account, either because they are not, rigorously speaking, logical contradictions, or because a regulated (conceptual) economy must avoid them in order to safeguard the ethico-theoretical decisions that orient its discourse. These fissures become apparent when we follow to its logical end that which in the process of conceptualization or argumentation is only in a certain manner said. Deconstruction thus begins by taking up broached but discontinued implications – discontinued because they would have contradicted the intentions of philosophy.[2]

All about one are fissures, but one may follow through logically to the end. Of course what is in question is the discursive practice of philosophy itself. And following through with the critical example may involve – as the relation of text and commentary in the case of Mallarmé, Richard and Derrida suggests – a different sense of the acceptable end. One may well agree with Gasché that the working through of the philosophical implications of Derrida's method is a very different matter from the application of it – partially and haphazardly understood – to literary criticism. And I certainly agree that much that passes for deconstructive criticism is a direct descendent of the new criticism and may not use its 'deconstructive' passport with suitable authority. It is unclear here whether he is concerned with critical practice or only with the ontological status of literature, its relation to truth, its metaphoricity, etc. But the failure to value the magpie effect, the way in which unsystematic borrowing feeds understanding at the level of the 'petit récit', and his dismissive attitude towards appropriation and use indicates little engagement with criticism or interest in its characteristic working.

I have speculated that Derrida would be in accord – as indeed would Leavis – with what has looked like the radical incompleteness of any

imaginable critical practice. Except that Leavis does not see the consequence of the 'buts' going on and on. And Derrida seems to imply, in one
case at least, that such incompleteness undermines the possibility of any
satisfactory notion of a critical account. I have argued the opposite, that
this constitutive incompleteness is essential to its use, an essential feature of
criticism as a form of practical reason. Is this incompleteness a great
feature or small? It can be seen both ways, but it indicates the cut-off points
intrinsic to a form of discourse, even if they are plural. Their positioning
and effect is only seen when so deployed as to see how far a sequence of
'petits récits' will take one towards a larger, if always and necessarily
incomplete, story.

Another form of the movement from the particularised small story to a
larger perspective is in the creation, maintenance and revision of the
literary canons which convey values of cultural importance. The effect of
the contradictory demands in canon formation is obvious in the strain
engendered by the dual positioning of texts in the canon. They must both
be the incarnation of some intrinsic excellence, and yet admit of that larger
role in which value is a function of a 'form of life'. That is, Homer is both
in some mysterious yet describable way excellent in himself and 'the
education of Hellas'. To accept the ultimate contingency of value, and
hence that the critic is not embarked on a 'foundationalist' enterprise ('no
ontology' as I shall later argue), still leaves the description of valued
characteristics to find the consonant critical terms. And those terms point
outward to that larger set of choices and commitments which are involved
in the shaping of a form of life. So canon formation exhibits the need for
the larger story, at the same time that the synoptic version of the larger
story is not contained within criticism itself, that group of particular
choices through which the canon is shaped.

Critical activity becomes a mediation between the perceptions and
decisions of the 'small narrative' and the demands of something further.
This can take the form of discrepancy management as in the type of case
that bothered Kermode. And it can take the form of revising and reshaping
the canon in terms of the claims of individual components, bringing out the
full effect of the smaller and more localised. In this the canon may give way
in terms of any concern with its total architecture to the force of the 'petit
récit'. The extreme version of this would be the collecting of cultural icons,
of Arnoldian touchstones – 'the best that has been said and thought' –
masterpieces that exist in themselves without regard for further criteria,
suggesting through their very being a world of value. This may not be
abstractly statable, but characteristics and affinities can be described.
'Great books' are of all sorts. They have value but their values are not the
same. Denial is also an assertion of value, so even the alternative canon

which is set up against *bien-pensant* values may paradoxically carry in its wake the Arnoldian shadow.

The principles of their formation may be quite different. The social and cultural pressures behind them may be obvious both for exemplary canons, and what one might call canons of resistance. The principle in question becomes quite transparent: one may accommodate to ideology, accept and manipulate one's historicised identity, make gestures of refusal. Derrida presents what constitutes a little canon of his own which puts in question the nature of 'texts classed as "literary" for they operate 'breaches or infractions' of such an idea: Artaud, Bataille, Mallarmé, Sollers. 'These texts operate, in their very movement, the demonstration and practical deconstruction of the *representation* of what was done with literature ... ' They 'mark out and organise a structure of resistance to the philosophical conceptuality that allegedly dominated or comprehended them ... ' The force of this canon is directed against 'the categories of esthetics [*sic*], rhetoric, or traditional criticism'.[3] And hence it is directed against the notion of the traditional canon, and against Kermode's notion that the canonical text is the timeless text, that its perpetual modernity is ahistorical – unless the organising of resistance is the timeless business of all texts.

But of course the refusal of canonicity can create another version of it. One wonders about the effect of the word 'organise' for a 'structure of resistance'. What is the organisation of such a structure if not another 'conceptuality' which is different from its predecessor? He is merely denying the existence of the grand narrative while creating one in another form. One may operate with distinctions which indicate that such a 'conceptuality' is markedly different, as such a canon represented the breaks and discontinuities within the cultural tradition rather than a substantive aspect of it. But the cumulative effect of resemblance is such that it is difficult to avoid the impression of a kind of tradition. The moment of 'dérèglement des sens' – derangement of the senses – which begins as a startling discovery becomes a practice with its understood procedures. And the conceptual language will grow to meet the consequent needs of transmission, explanation, further use.

One necessary condition of the structuring of resistance is its historical siting. The obvious use of a shifting canon as an historical weapon is an acknowledgement of the variable rhetorics that canon formation can deploy. Bloom's canon uses such variables to effect its forced assimilations. And the historical relation is an extended narrative in which the cultural role of the canon may be as the full expression of the relevant moment, or as its qualifying feature, or as a cultural *gestalt* that cuts across it. The variety of these uses makes the canon a substitute for the grander explanation itself, possibly as the most dramatic cultural evidence of its character, the fullest picture of the 'present age', the capturing of an aspect, or of an act of resistance. And beyond the question of whether or not acts of rebellion become parts of a curious order of their own there is another possibility: what looks at one level contradictory is at another a recognition that texts taken together say something that their individual roles do not.

Beyond Derrida's polemical point that there are some few texts whose character puts in question the margins of the class to which they would normally be taken to belong, there is the further implication that the very way in which texts work is not to be fully encompassed in general explanation. The very taking together of certain texts (although in making this point, he in fact mentions persons) creates an ostensive presence which is not reducible or explainable by the sorts of 'grand narratives' which have normally been devised for this purpose. The canon therefore may stand outside explanation and substitute for it. And there is no reason that this should not apply to canons of all sorts: those that include King Lear as well as Artaud. We can therefore envisage a function that is more far-reaching. The group taken together is itself a mediating device which stands between the value perceived in particular works, and the incorporation of that perception into the kind of larger explanatory commitments in the synoptic version of the 'grand narrative'. And if we have, as Lyotard claims, lost confidence in our capacity to legitimate a greater story of that kind, the canon which one can ostensively point to becomes a substitute for it. When the legitimation of any larger world picture fails us we can at least point to those cultural icons that may stand for congeries of understanding and belief, a representation of a pattern of commitments, values – in the end of 'forms of life'.

There are at least three effects of this substitution. One is that the canon may in itself carry the weight of a rhetorical strategy and be a primary vehicle for persuasion. Secondly its ostensive nature stands in for argument and often represents the moment where argument has broken off and takes a more concrete form of demonstration. And thirdly it avoids the unacceptable requirements of foundationalism, that ultimate defence of criteria which it is impossible to state.

The first is often merely the instrument of another persuasion, and stands for the other, ideology or otherwise, as illustration, or masque, or device. This may be wholly open and benign, or may reveal a further difficulty, as when one asks whether Leavis's use of this type of argument rests upon concealed premises – when a moral position might be ridiculous if directly stated, but made tolerable in its example. And further, claiming 'centrality' within a canon which is already highly selective may beg the question it sets out to answer.

The second effect points to the opposite, to the uncertain relation between canons and reasons. This is something Rorty has remarked in commenting on the way in which cultural values are not shaped by the rational procedures of philosophers. Philosophy universalises at the expense of value. The great philosophical texts are anti-social; they appeal to a reflective process exercised in isolation, not to shared processes which appeal to human solidarity. Value is created (discovered?) outside philosophy. Hence literary models provide our values, especially those values that give a sense of direction and community. He has in mind the kind of exemplary canon which informs a sense of social justice and decency, one which would include *Bleak House, Uncle Tom's Cabin* and *The Gulag Archipelago*. These create our knowledge of justice by showing us injustice in its palpable forms. How is such a canon made up? Rorty replies, 'I don't know, it just happens'.[4] Perhaps it is like metaphors that 'catch on'. One could certainly invoke theories of moral sentiment or intuition. But the implied conclusion seems to be that such models establish themselves by pure attraction, and that the establishment of value, such as it may be, is irrational. Or at least the reasons cannot be substantially given.

The problem of the moral responsibility of 'textualism' gives Rorty a context for stating the problem of incommensurable views of 'man' expressed in Bloom's commitment to person and voice and Foucault's elimination of both author and the very idea of man. 'I have no wish to defend Foucault's inhumanism, and every wish to praise Bloom's sense of our common human lot. But I do not know how to back up this preference with argument, or even with a precise account of the relevant differences.'[5] Again, the ground of value cannot be stated. But the example has the kind of force that seems not to require a precise account. Some sense of the difference between the edifying and the horrifying frames a much more nuanced sequence of distinctions. But does it allow for a mixed canon? Certainly the mixing of the edifying and the disturbing could be seen as having some kind of critical point which had little to do with moral example. But the kind of example embodied in shaping a canon moves us away from generalised criteria and towards a tissue of concrete relationships. For these there may be reasons that are partial, indecisive, but which carry some weight.

It is the awareness that we can give reasons for choices, but that these reasons are worryingly diverse and do not reflect the ground of value so much as the complex conditions of our lives, which suggests both the vulnerability of the canon and the contingency of the values which lie behind it. It acts as the best substitute we can devise for the rationale which we can only reach through an appeal to a transcendental we cannot verify, or one of those grandest of 'récits', like the Enlightenment myth of the perfectibility of man, which may itself serve as a cultural icon but which has, as Lyotard says lost its power to command belief. The paradox of criticism is that it is immersed in value, can persuasively show us particular value distinctions, but cannot establish values in a general way. The pagan imagination may illuminate the contingent world of our culture but not enter it into the Kingdom of Ends.

The difficulty of this is powerfully represented by Roger Scruton in characterising the role of aesthetics in modern philosophy.[6] It is the reverse of Rorty in that philosophy must take the *lebenswelt* as a primary concern, and resume 'its place as the foundation of the humanities'. Otherwise 'those disciplines which have the human world as their subject matter will be exposed to intellectual corruption'. Such corruption is attributable to a nihilism which denies the union of thought and feeling, and presumably denies the difference between good and bad reasons. The foundational role of philosophy seems to be that of a conceptual guide which shows the way to other disciplines by the rational instrument of conceptual analysis. However, concepts do not belong to a pure world of science or logic but involve our emotional lives in a 'vital connection which links our response to the world'. And,

The concepts which inform our emotions bear the stamp of a shared human interest, and of a constantly developing form of life. Whence do they come? The answer is implicit in Leavis's attack on Snow: these concepts are the gift of a culture, being neither consciously made nor deliberately chosen but inherited. It is by the use of such concepts that the moral reality of our world is described: concepts of good and evil, sacred and profane, tragic and comic, just and unjust – all of them rooted in that one vital idea which, I would contend, denotes no natural kind, and conveys a classification that could feature in no true scientific theory of man: the concept of a person. The concepts of a culture classify the world in terms of the appropriate action and the appropriate response. A rational being has need of such concepts, which bring his emotions together in the object, so enabling him – as the Hegelians would say – to find his identity in the world and not in opposition to it.

Sympathetic as much of this is there seem areas of uncertainty. Our concepts may derive from our culture but we may do many things with them. And to deify culture with its implication of wholeness is to evade the complexity which contains an uncomfortable coexistence among its elements. The Leavis concept of culture is based on ruthless simplification by excision and purification. And this is done through the intentional narrowing of the acceptable canon of cultural works, and in a conscious and deliberate exercise of choice. The rationality of much in this choice would be difficult to establish. Scruton acknowledges that there is something mysterious about our relation to our culture. 'It is to possess a sensibility, a response, a way of seeing things which is in some way redemptive. Culture is not a matter of academic knowledge but of participation. And participation changes not merely your thoughts and beliefs but your perceptions and emotions.' But to which of our cultural voices shall we submit? If it is 'in the works of the prophets that a language strives to its utmost towards the perception of a justifying sense ... ' why should the voice of England's provincial prophet Lawrence have a justification that is denied to the great masters of modernism, Proust and Joyce? Words like 'redemptive' and 'justifying' do not quite stand on their own. Are we Birkin, Uncle Tom or des Esseintes? Somehow, not a rewarding game.

Yet both Scruton and Rorty imply that it is one of the few ways that we can convincingly approach the problem of value, or establish the force of any moral commitment. Without the key role of exemplarity our reasoning thins to emptiness. And the examination of those particular aspects of language which have become a form of moral philosophy is only marginal to decisions about value. Through the example we can see the ground of choice; the form of life and its implications are revealed. But the rationale may elude us. Being 'like that' evokes a description which, as in aretaic ethics, relies on the allure of the model, that impalpable mixture of reason, admiration and desire.

Nor can the ground of good and bad choices be reasonably determined through our identification with our cultural tradition, for our 'participation' in it may be on a cosmopolitan scale, or that of a Leavisite *campanilismo*, or may be an eclectic mixture revealed in the range of canonical touchstones. Many of the most interesting of rediscoveries of things which once lay outside the acceptable canon have seemed difficult or exotic: metaphysical poetry, archaic Greek art, the Baroque. Yet all have become assimilated, and achieved some degree of 'centrality'. But the detailed sequence of recognitions which has produced this kind of change in cultural perspective derives from an accumulation of 'small, even fragmentary, narratives', individual moments of awareness exerting through many examples their cumulative power. Good reasons in such a process consist largely in seeing the interesting detail, and the way in which such interest illuminates other works which a tradition had taken fully to heart, and does so by moving out from any assumption of centrality, by the exploratory move that a particular perception or comparison makes possible. In so doing one may find in Scruton's account a constriction which might be awkward for the working of the valuing process itself, above all insofar as that process tries on the unforeseen in the open-endedness which 'revaluation' may require. For that may turn one's sense of tradition towards something it substantially contains but has not yet become, towards what Lyotard calls 'the exploration of the possible' (*JG*, p. 59).

Lyotard marks the turn from the knowledge of the given to the exploration of the possible by the 'transit point' of the prescriptive. It is almost a moment of necessity which moves us on from one language game to another, from the terms of an accepted game to the new invention, which follows up the invention of new rules, or simply the introduction of new forms of enquiry. He gives Parmenides and Freud as examples, and indeed 'it is the artists that always establish the rules of a language game that did not exist before'. And he contrasts the value of paganism with those who 'believe in the signified of what they are saying ... (and) stick to this signified ... That is where paganism stops and something like doctrine, let us say, gets back in' (*JG*, p. 62). Is it the 'postmodern' condition that we cannot believe in the authority of one 'signified', of a primary doctrine, that our prescriptive transit point is the one that moves into the succeeding game? Not even Scruton's cultural philosopher has the authority to deny the value in plurality. He seems caught between the modern fate of plurality and a 'doctrine' that one cannot assert, as its own 'legitimation' eludes him. What one can assert instead is the adherence to the tradition to which such doctrines belong.

But suppose that the Marxist language game, or the Freudian, is held in the spirit of doctrine, the true believers might wish to obliterate all alternative games, or as with Kermode's 'discrepancy' indulge in the necessary double-think to slip some measure of plurality into a prescriptive ideology. Alternatively, in the pagan world the doctrines may themselves be false – the dialectical vision of history, or Freud's map of the mind – but the very introduction of these games has enabled us to re-examine and retraverse important and complicated ground. Such a form of reseeing in effect reduces the 'grandest of narratives' in all of its fallibility to those angles of perception that have their essential if imprecise model in 'criticism' where the very evasion of the doctrinal is an insidious form of strength.

## 2     The truth of example

The way in which the contrasting commitments of Rorty and Scruton have turned to the importance of critical reasoning lies in its dependence on the particular occasion, on literary examples, vision, cases – on showing rather than arguing as an essential means of understanding our world. The heart of any critical reasoning is of course the example. That is the necessary means through which the critic's multiple discourses work, and however far he may stretch beyond it there is necessarily a link with this beginning point, with a certain perceived given. This involves the double sense of primary subject and of subsequent comment. We have seen that there are difficulties in case law standing wholly on its own, but without the case, criticism in whatever possible mode is inconceivable. One states the obvious simply to isolate for a moment some aspects of how exemplarity works – although in practice it has been the substance of my examination of critical language. In a sense both Rorty and Scruton point beyond any precisely critical purpose in the understanding of literature to the use such understanding may have in establishing those values that, as cultural liberal and cultural conservative, they may wish to give substance to general claims about a 'form of life'. In this section I want to point to three features of the working of exemplarity, and in the final chapter draw some further consequences from them.

The first feature is of the example as model. In one version of this the example may be simply illustrative: the illustration of a general point is meant as the end point of an explanation rather than something which points further. Something like this seems to be Hegel's use of the *Antigone* in section VI of *The Phenomenology*. In a general picture of human relations and duties the presence of the Antigone story both establishes the form of a certain pattern of relationship but also makes it intelligible. Is something like this also true of Kierkegaard's use of the Don Giovanni story in 'The Diary of a Seducer'? If one says both 'yes' and 'no' it is because Kierkegaard clearly intended one story to illuminate another, but a more complex relation of reciprocity develops. We are not meant to say, 'Ah yes, I see, it is like that' in quite the reductive sense in which the model seems to be used in Hegel, but one story enters into another with mutually transforming effect.

Now, what kind of effect of example would Rorty wish in indicating its persuasive force? Certainly we have the suggestion of a rather simplified entry into the ethical, a transition from the troubling density of so many major literary works to the clarity of an ethical stance – unstated because, perhaps, unstatable, but clear in its ostensive presence, and without any overwhelming ambiguity about its message. Yet this poses an odd contrast with critical procedure where the force of the example seldom clears, but complicates – even thickens. The transition to the ethical leads us away from that richness in literature which seems to be its intellectual challenge and where its critical interest is found. And this is more than the simple paradox of using criticism in an uncritical way, but an implicit rejection of critical enquiry.

It is true that Rorty describes the 'placing' of works among others in a manner reminiscent of Leavis, a revision like any placing of new friends among old. But as described this seems to involve no reasoning process at all, as we noted with respect to canon formation. Having already rejected the abstraction of philosophical reasoning, this abandoning of the critical is to leave the example looking like an icon which points its moral with cartoon-strip simplicity. It is to evoke a contrast that resembles the Leavisite dichotomy that we have already seen in its insistence on the separation of the philosophical and critical, while not engaging with the methods of either. To produce a 'reflective equilibrium' between the proper names of writers is to let allusion stand in for a variety of feelings and commitments, while the observable 'stretch' by which criticism has reached into our moral and cultural lives seems not to require any further sense of how it works. There is only the equally observable feature of the fading of the 'literary'. The image of knowing persons rather than texts helps emphasise the literature of the ever-expanding canon, with its suggestion that there is no one with whom we would not sit down to dinner.

It would seem, however, that in this process the example as model takes on a kind of transparency which allows it to register a directness of appeal. This is the opposite of the fascination we have seen in Derrida or de Man with the opacity and difficulty found in literary texts, something which requires an elaborate, if always inadequate and incomplete, working out. This is the text's own problematic, rather than that of the use to which it is put. Does the transition to the ethical require such simplification, models which give us a clear ground for a determinate moral intuition?

Martha Nussbaum is equally concerned with such a transition which she represents in at least two different ways. (There is the cost here of a certain simplification.) One is described as a 'project' of a 'dialogue between philosophy and literary analysis' in which truth about the human condition is expressed in narrative form, and is based on the claim that literary form and human content are inseparable. Such a programme has many dimensions, and it is in fact the working hypothesis for multiple kinds of analysis. Here is a far-reaching equilibrium between text and use, but equilibrium in many sets of terms. And there is an interesting uncertainty about the way in which this rapprochement is to be carried out. Is this a critical operation or a form of philosophical analysis? Need we make a clear distinction? In her book it is not a clean-cut dialogue between different voices, but a working fusion where the elements are indistinguishable. Perhaps the effect is simply: yes, that is one of the things criticism is, and philosophy is one of its modes. The project itself suggests the innate instability of a mixed genre, and its attraction.

It is her second 'transit point' that comes closer to our sense of the working of the example, in the process of deliberation in the consciousness of Strether in *The Ambassadors*. If only the precision, refinement, well-tuned awareness of James's representation of Strether could be a model for the assessment of public affairs.[7] The example here works more as representation of a method, a process of assessment which is shown as Strether's own. It is of course neither philosophical nor critical, but is the kind of practical reflection on experience which at one level is indistinguishable from prudential or calculative reasoning: what sort of situation is one in, what is one to do and how is one to do it? This group of questions is constantly reinterpreted in a reflection which opens in other ways: what are they really like, and indeed, what am I, and how do the events now transpiring effect a transformation of my whole understanding? In such a doubling of levels the interpretative process may to some extent resemble the usual critical reading of a novel, in which a major aspect of the rhetoric of the novel relies on our understanding of Strether's deliberative processes. When, however, it is transposed from the novel into a model of the operation of practical reason, does it cease to be such a rhetorical structure and become an example of something else, with what Habermas would call 'the discipline of a *distinct* form of argumentation'?[8] But such a distinctness of form would appear only as a change of function. The words would be the same. Or words very like them.

Does this strange mixture of sameness and difference transform the analysis of particulars in a way that moves from private to public and in doing so turns perception into a cryptic form of moral principle? Yes, we could live it like that, think through it like that, imagine it like that. Strether's way would be marked out for us, although the various contexts through which it might take us might be a sequence of analogies, and hence of reinventions. But one thing we might find it very difficult to do would be to say whether or not we were applying it correctly, whether or not any specifications could be drawn up for a Stretherish method for any other set of circumstances, so we could say with some degree of confidence that that was how it was done. One might simply have to say that one must go back and read James, get the sense and feel of it in all its immediacy; and here, as in other critical cases we have seen, criteria cannot be given. This might exclude the possibilities of generality and suggest that Strether's way belonged to its own rhetorical structure and circumstance and that the truth of example was wholly singular. There is in it no 'example of'. The reason for this would lie in the very complexity of that structure, and if we tried to draw some general force of example from it the result might be reduced to banality: be fully aware. Oddly, it is hard to think of Strether in anything resembling Rorty's paradigmatic use of the example. The notion of drawing one in so that there is a prescriptive 'that's how it's done' which might be embodied in a person runs counter to the Jamesian effect, in which we are more conscious of the process than the person. Important as that person may be. Strether's subversion of self in the process of discovering it, or even Maggie's highly successful stratagems in the exercise of power in *The Golden Bowl*, are perhaps more distancing than involving.

What kind of truth, then, can we see in Strether as example? Our interest certainly lies in the convergence of three forms of reasoning: the sorting out of circumstances, impressions, and their further implications on Strether's own part, itself a mixture of practical calculation and subtle assessment; a critical account which selects, describes and evaluates particular moments in or aspects of that reflection; and an argument relating it to more general versions of ethical problems. The example never operates through any one of these exclusively, and it is hard to see how it could. And it is here that the generality of what might be shown through it has its presence marked. The further exercise of looking at these overlapping language games and their relations with each other is either a meta-critical or further form of philosophical undertaking – as one will. In all of this it is hard to isolate the example, to see it as separate from the various modes of thought that play upon it, or to see it as peculiarly the property of any one of them in a substantial degree of separateness.

One thing that has clearly happened here is that process and method have become the important feature of what the novel shows. It is the example of Strether's reflective process that we wish to catch and analyse in our critical account. Then we wish to explore its further working, and to see its analogous applications. The steps may not be specified, but we can get a feel, a perception, to satisfy ourselves that we know what kind of thing is going on – roughly speaking, how it is done. On the other hand, how do we know that it rings true, that outside the rhetorical structure of the novel such a thing can really be convincing? The danger is that in pointing out a version of the method we are only gesturing towards such a type, and dependent on a naive mimeticism.

And other difficulties arise. The curious evanescence in Strether's reasoning process, the final exclusion of himself from possibilities his perceptions open to him, a certain capacity for withdrawal, perhaps a touch of fatalism, all of these might so complicate the picture of that process as to leave the use of exemplarity in doubt. The more closely regarded, the example 'turns'.[9] And the turn lies not so much in the problems in a transition to the ethical, but in trying to establish the critical picture. The critical reflection goes on giving us further aspects, hidden dimensions, returns us to the context to send us back with an altered understanding. Does it then destroy the case? De Man once remarked 'whenever you give an example you, as you know, lose what you want to say'.[10]

As for critical language itself, insofar as it can be identified as a distinct thread in this fabric of language games it is treated, reasonably enough, in terms of pure instrumentality. For Rorty it is a vehicle for making claims about life and how it should be lived that philosophers are too fastidious or crippled by abstraction to make. We have seen how he evokes this path from Trilling to Bloom. For Nussbaum the language of criticism seems quite transparent, perhaps little different from the other languages in which we discuss human affairs and their consequences, except for a certain attention to form. If one considers a formulation like that of Habermas, in which 'criticism performs a translating activity of a unique kind. It brings the experiential content of the work of art into normal language ... '[11], the necessity of translation is minimal. Yet even at that minimal level something happens which may be unique in another way. The representation of the case through which any such translation is accomplished is so substantially qualified that the example both fits and does not fit.

At the heart of the variety of discourses about literature that 'criticism' brings together there is this problem: criteria for the success or failure of the example cannot be given, any more than the criteria for what would be the next illuminating move. Hence what we have seen as an underlying instability, one which seems to follow from the primacy of the particular. The example is never wholly right. In the end it is impossible to conceive of the example as other than 'relatively right', or whatever conclusions are drawn from it as other than 'relatively valid'. The example always places itself in a context of further possible uses. It makes, to mimic Derrida, part of its case and a little more than its case. If we look back to Eliot's treatment of 'wit' we saw the sequence of relational placings in which the allusions both complement and qualify each other. We can only grasp some sense of Marvell's wit through the wit of others, the contrasts and affinities which play upon each other. The successive 'not ... not ... not' imply 'and ... and ... and'. Even if the depths of contempt, hatred and disgust – as well, perhaps, as frivolity – are left behind, the notion of 'wit' never entirely excludes them. All belong with the accumulated echoes that form part of that 'scale of great imaginative power'. Such description, one has said, thickens when it pretends to exclude, accepts in practice that the examples cut more than one way.

The examples may have been part of a cumulative movement, but each has that capacity to divagate, or turn, to give signals that point in another direction. One consequence is that the movement of examples cannot be knowingly pre-empted, nor seen as a determinate pattern in which we know how the continuity of the sequence would work out for us. The steps may assert their independent life, or confront us with the unacceptable, or make their awkwardness of fit into a revealing and fruitful disturbance. But the individual step cannot be so tracked that its further implications vanish. They will be there for anyone to see, open to whatever alien use they may be put to. Such attempts to limit and direct the force of example will always fail us in part. And that part will put in question the direction of the whole. The rule of example is both in one sense absolute, as an irreducible point of reference, yet indifferent to the extended use. It is as if we were given the materials of a general theory of the concrete, while denied the capacity to state it. Critical method then becomes the instance and not the expositor.

Of course one has considered the truth of example in two quite different senses. One is that paradigmatic use which makes a claim lying within the traditional scope of practical reason. But clearly both Rorty and Nussbaum in elaborating the use of literature as a form of moral philosophy, and in Rorty's case as a stand-in for much of what traditional philosophising undertook with respect to human action and its responsibilities, have made ostensive use of that concreteness literature can provide. Both critical method and moral reasoning are dependent on the whole process of depicting and inventing of which literature is capable.

One may however hold that moral reasoning is doubtfully intelligible without the close analysis of cases of behaviour, feeling and intention, while finding difficulty in Rorty's particular adaptation of a critical model for it. I have already mentioned two of these problems: the inability to give good reasons for the canonical status of one work as opposed to another, secondly, the entropic effect of this levelling out of values in the liberal conception of the canon, an expansion without governing principle, where every imaginable sort of example becomes a competitor among moral paradigms. And there is a third: the ironic effect of the 'placing' and the subsequent process of revision as each placing alters the relationships of the other works held in one's 'imaginary museum' is an effective representation of the critical procedure. But is the ironising in conflict with the paradigmatic use, and hence of the moral intention of the enterprise? The relational placing must qualify the magnetism, the initial drawing power which suggested the claims of an observation, character, or extended picture of a form of life. Of course, if for 'ironists' there is no 'final vocabulary', that is no final 'placing', at least some degree of the implicit relativism must be acceptable, and the conflict of process and paradigm continually renewed.

For Nussbaum the direct use of the literary embodiment of moral characteristics and dilemmas, in an acceptance of this immediacy of the example, seems to slip past what Habermas calls 'translation' and hence past anything problematic attached to the critical operation which it subsumes. The enactment in Proust and James would then lack any need for mediation. The difficulty then arises with alternative interpretations. Should that change the story, what happens to the moral force of what the story was thought to enact? The Maggie who is the sublime incarnation of the principle of Love is also the Foucauldian operator of the levers to power. If the moral use lies on the far side of a possible mediation, where the capacity of the example to turn, to indicate something other, to show either more or less, is intrinsic to the nature of stories and hence to the ways of making use of them, how then is exemplary force to be established? These applications of narrative, or of the appeal to character, to illuminating fragments or to long perspectives may make of their own reasonings a meta-narrative, a dependent form of practical reasoning which would see its own truth in the concrete and immediate terms that such narrative employs, even if the status of such claims may itself need further description.

Our third aspect of the truth of example, which we can consider more narrowly critical, may suggest a distinctive relationship of process to tradition. If, as we have seen, the example always cuts (at least) two ways, and carries its alternative message with it, it may become part of a sequence without losing that disruptive character. So it both extends an argument yet punctuates it at the same time, and we may see continuity and the alternative simultaneously. We have become habituated to this form of doubleness: the intellectual movement of critical argument and the divergence of further openings can be taken together. So the radical disturbance possible to the example is uneasily consonant with a larger construction, one which embodies ideas of order, of appropriate placings. Hence, as I shall show in the next section, even a neo-classical view can be expressed in terms which assimilate this doubleness, integrating relativism into the tradition.

But critical truth above all lies in the irreducibility of the example to the purpose to which it may be put, as literature itself is irreducible to the languages that play upon it. Hence exemplarity is a defence against banality, and preserves the most powerful of critical effects, the dislocation of surprise, and the discovery of the new and further relations.

# X    The Tao of criticism

## 1    A structure of fragments

If one has tried to place the intensity of the particular perception, the
localisation of its operation, in that single move at the heart of critical
reasoning, this is not to lose one's sense that the critic does inevitably
operate in a larger perspective and see those individual moves as part of a
tissue of relationships, a cumulative process that calls for a further
description. One has seen how theory acts as a purveyor of such
descriptions as a way of placing coordinates through which the larger view
takes shape. But this now requires me to take further the connections
between such coordinates and the effective operation of the particular
'move' or sequence of them. For the abandonment of the 'grand
explanation' in the sense that Kristeva wished to employ it, indeed to
employ a sequence of them to place the revolution in a comprehensive view
of the world, does not mean that we cease to see the world in larger ways,
only that the determinate role in such an overview has vanished. The legacy
is a series of fragments which to varying degrees imply something larger of
which it actually appropriates only that corner where an impingement has
its vivid presence.

We can find some measure of the effect of this if we return to one of our
earlier cases, to reconsider the placing of 'the romantic view of the world'
in the concept-free mode of reasoning that Leavis evokes to define the
critical operation, and in the more precisely formulated conceptual
structures of a Kristeva or a Bloom. Of course 'the romantic view of the
world' implies distance, the vaguely or pervasively cohering sense of
attitudes and stances, of an almost unanalysable body of feeling. It is a
kind of shorthand, from which we might either go further in our
expatiations or simply allow our shorthand to stand as an elliptical step on
our way to something else. But whether an invitation or a convenient tag
one can see the reductive effect of a cliché, as if something quite mind-
numbing were on offer and the irritation of Leavis in resisting the cliché
implies that such generalised talk is miserable stuff.

M. H. Abrams has written with an eloquent diffidence of the problem of using such expressions as 'the Romantic ethos' when one knows that it suggests a grandiose general picture.[1] And of course he is fastidiously aware of the limitations all such general notions involve in context, especially of the oscillation of such terms as 'Romanticism' between the suggestion of a Platonic essence and a more modestly nominalist claim about accumulated meanings and uses, between the global sense of the conspectus and the contextual attribution of a quality. It is all too familiar to most of us to see the invisible slipping of inverted commas around terms upon which we depend, but where we have no intention of accepting responsibility for the full range of meanings and their multiple debasements. But Leavis's elaborate posturing before Wellek's unexceptional phrase both exploits the common embarrassment and denies critical value to such generality as to also deny us the means of placing in an historical perspective.

No such self-limiting reduction applies to the 'paganism' of the small story simply because the particular critical observation, the comparison, the new insight or revision of awareness, may be expressed in theory-loaded language, or may find its immediate sense in terms of theoretical implications, without reaching for a global use of theory as a form of explanation. There is an acceptance that one's language has multiple dimensions at its most immediate level, where general implications are inseparable from the concrete perception of the moment. That there never can be an absolutely pure, a raw empiricism, or Poulet's pure flash of consciousness, need not deflect from the centrality of that moment. Equally the sense that our language is saturated with concepts of every imaginable order does not mean that the use of these concepts entails the commitment to all of the theoretical claims their sources may have intended for them. Out of the language in which we discuss philosophical, social, linguistic, psychological and economic issues is constructed the filtering and refracting process which enters any critical perspective, any process of critical reflection. That they should carry with them the explanatory systems of Hegel, Weber, Saussure, Freud, Marx, etc., is to suggest the coexistence of multiple coordinates where the accommodation involves complementarity, as we have seen in Kristeva, but also excess baggage. It is the fragments of system that move in the critical discrimination. And this is partly because critical use promotes some measure of fragmentation.

This is to say more generally what we have observed in practice of the fracturing effect of critical use. The implication we have also seen, that critical practice is resistant to ideology, even in the loose sense that we have used of any systematic structure of ideas. Is the crypto-ideology of the canon a more acceptable form of the process of valuing than those that our ideological or other persuasions provide for us? Whether we wish to substitute them or not is not exactly a critical issue. But if the synoptic sense lies outside criticism itself, and the effect of the critical activity is to morselise the ideologies on which it feeds, the operation of a particular choice is both commitment and indication. When Werther was sane he read Homer, and when mad, Ossian. And the alterations in ourselves, of what was once called taste and now perhaps a structure of ideologemes, run deeper than what is usually called 'reader response' in assuming the transitivity of the reading process. As one accepts that all educational practice must.

Choices make the tradition, as they also revise it. We are adapted to an increasing rapidity of reassessment, and an increasing fluidity of the relation of the fragment to a however fleeting and fictional sense of the whole. For the moment the canon is a picture, the effective representation of a mental set, an aspect of a tradition. We grasp it partially, and then our focus changes. If these relationships are never permanent or exact this is what we would quite naturally expect of them. The irony implicit in the use of example both pervades the process yet does not undermine the importance of what the next move may imply. For the critic's next move is free, whether the freedom to exhilarate, to bore or to alarm. The very changes which lie in the process of revaluation, in what Lyotard called the 'transit point', imply that whatever choice is made the critical perspective will alter, in however grand or minute degree. And there is something in that choice which is absolute, which is never totally determined by its precedents. The critic is someone who is by necessity free. However gripped in his historical tracks, or caught in the claims of a self-limiting jargon, he cannot escape the sense that his next word has alternatives of whose temptations he is aware.

Historically, of course, an institutional dialectic has come to govern the permutations of the critical game. In that degree conservative and radical movements of mind are part of the same interplay. Whether we regard history as that series of continuities and interdependencies (intertexualities even) which constitute a 'tradition', or that series of breaks, gaps, Barthian *ruptures*, discontinuities, that point their way to the avant garde, the critic has found his own freedom in adherence and loyalty, smashing it up, or whatever his individual mixture of the two. But one can see from someone who passes as the pillar of critical conservatism how deeply such a dialectic, or should one call it an ambiguity, is built into critical reflection. Consider Eliot's formulation of the process of revaluation:

From time to time, every hundred years or so, it is desirable that some critic shall appear to review the past of our literature, and set the poets and the poems in a new order. This task is not one of revolution but of readjustment. What we observe is partly the same scene, but in a different and more distant perspective; there are new and strange objects in the foreground, to be drawn accurately in proportion to the more familiar ones which now approach the horizon, where all but the most eminent become invisible to the naked eye. The exhaustive critic, armed with a powerful glass, will be able to sweep the distance and gain an acquaintance with minute objects in the landscape with which to compare minute objects close at hand; he will be able to gauge nicely the position and proportion of the objects surrounding us, in the whole of the vast panorama. This metaphorical fancy only represents the ideal; but Dryden, Johnson, and Arnold have each performed the task as well as human frailty will allow. The majority of critics can be expected only to parrot the opinions of the last master of criticism; among more independent minds a period of destruction, of preposterous over-estimation, and of successive fashions takes place, until a new authority comes to introduce some order. And it is not merely the passage of time and accumulation of new artistic experience, nor the ineradicable tendency of the great majority of men to repeat the opinions of those few who have taken the trouble to think, nor the tendency of a nimble but myopic minority to progenerate heterodoxies, that makes new assessments necessary. It is that no generation is interested in Art in quite the same way as any other; each generation, like each individual, brings to the contemplation of art its own categories of appreciation, makes its own demands upon art, and has its own uses for art. 'Pure' artistic appreciation is to my thinking only an ideal, when not merely a figment, and must be, so long as the appreciation of art is an affair of limited and transient human beings existing in space and time. Both artist and audience are limited. There is for each time, for each artist, a kind of alloy required to make the metal workable into art; and each generation prefers its own alloy to any other. Hence each new master of criticism performs a useful service merely by the fact that his errors are of a different kind from the last; and the longer the sequence of critics we have, the greater amount of correction is possible.[2]

The tone is very flat, and Eliot's use of the distant perspective makes the process seem as undramatic as possible. Of course the aim is 'readjustment' rather than 'revolution'; the time scheme is almost startlingly leisurely; we are warned about the dangers of the optical figure as a 'metaphorical fancy'; and the corrective to fashion's whirlings in the order to be introduced by some new authority is predictably consonant with Eliot's conservatism. Yet even if the optical figure seems more obvious and less dashing than Barthes's anamorphism we must ask once again where the metaphor takes us and where its implications stop. For however fixed in a sense of tradition, and affixed to necessity of authority, the open-endedness of perspective is fully accepted. What could be more vertiginously clear than the awareness that this far-reaching freedom is built into our situation as historical beings, and is inseparable from the fact of our existence in time?

The deployment of the long perspective may seem contrary to a more characteristically contemporary sense of urgency, which de Man's view of critical language as the vehicle of crisis may dramatise with a certain air of inflation, but which I have taken as that necessary struggle and invention, that working through of difficulty by which we situate literature in our world and in our lives. Eliot's circumspection limits the terms of play by its very diffidence before time's movement, and a general aloofness with respect to the quality of most critical utterance. But the long perspective does not so much indicate absence of urgency as the realisation that whatever element of urgency there has been, some critical marks stick with us and others do not.

Perhaps de Man was closer to seeing any such large-scale critical reassessment more as 'revolution' than as 'readjustment' and this may reflect wide changes in historical circumstances. But the difference between them is, as Eliot would be quite aware, only a matter of degree. The same process is at work, the same reasoning, the same revaluative aim in view. The optical 'metaphorical fancy' opens to all of the language of perspective and horizon with which later critics have described the terms of their shifting assessments. And we may discern even in the cool and measured handling a certain trembling on the edge of the precipice. The passage is flagged with warning signals with respect to paths not taken which indicate a full awareness of their presence. And even if we would be overly fanciful in seeing the faint outline of a deconstructionist's charter we can see the implications of historicism clearly marked. The contemplation of the present is the past of the future. It is not only that different generations bring different interests to that contemplation, but that they could not do otherwise. Such an argument underlies the whole of 'Tradition and the Individual Talent'. Certainly others will see us in ways that we could not possibly conceive, a seeing which will not necessarily be a rejection of our own terms of understanding, but will necessarily be different because ours has gone before.

The word 'correction' of course suggests the rule of a standard by which our errors can be measured. But the frank admission that our corrections will be further errors places the corrective process in a difficult light. All judgements, all corrections are relative. If only because we will continue to see new aspects of literature that were not seen before the authority of whatever moment will be qualified. All corrections are indeed errors which await further corrections and we make our own adjustments and revisions in the full awareness of this, awareness that the final order of corrections can never be fixed. The forms of order suggested by the great critics of the past do not even seem to be in competition: Dryden, Johnson, Arnold made forms of order which were appropriate to their time. We could hardly expect the authority of those voices to project a timeless universality which would imply the exclusive nature of any choice between them. And if we wish to point to the limitations of, say, neo-classical ways of making corrections we may see those too as qualified by context. The value of neo-classical criticism need not come from taking it *au pied de la lettre*.

What is clear in Eliot's perspective is how deeply these historicist and even relativist elements are embedded in any reflection on the tradition itself. All solutions are themselves problems, and while the recognition of this may take different forms in Eliot and in Derrida something underlying is the same: the contingency of one's situation before the text means that self, text, commentary cannot be placed so that the relations between them are fixed and constant. Yet whatever relativism is implicit in the correction which is necessarily an error is surely benign, and in no way inhibits a commitment to those values whose form may shift and recede as critical language struggles to give them shape. For Eliot this struggle is not only present in the heart of the tradition, but is a condition of its continuance, a part of the ever volatile process of tradition making.

Thus the critic is doubly an ironist and inescapably so. We have seen how the example turns, showing its double edge. And in the construction of our longer view our fragments do not fix. Rather than shored against our ruins or sticking together our substitute for a world view they are in movement, their relations subject to a continuous process of revision, the perspectives which form them into a reasonably intelligible whole subject to that blur and refocus which turns them into something different. And if this is a more heated and unstable account than Eliot has given us it is not different in kind. Yet surely this is not only the necessary condition of critical thought, but a representation of its value and essential interest. And in its language the management and exploration of this relational world is undertaken.

The question then arises as to how far the process Eliot has described and I have in small ways extended commits us to what has been called 'relativism'. For obvious reasons I shall want to restrict my discussion of this notion to its critical use. The general philosophical consideration of this issue is far reaching, the literature enormous and its entry into critical discussion a muddying of waters. For the sake of what I hope is only slightly misleading simplicity I shall indicate three types of concern with relativism, or three groupings of such interest. The first has to do with issues concerning language (the arbitrary nature of the sign, etc.) or epistemology, many of which are versions of traditional problems concerning philosophical scepticism. Is Derrida a philosophical sceptic, and if so to what end? An interesting and amusing question with which I am not concerned here, as one is not with a variety of problems in philosophical and epistemological scepticism. A certain 'given' has seemed necessary.

The second group is concerned with historicism, and it is clear from the preceding that historicism in at least one of its major senses is built into the critical operation. Of course this is consequential in a variety of ways, above all that one's understanding and valuing are the product of one's own position in history and culture, something which sets one apart from readers of other times and cultures. So one's view is relative by an absolute necessity of one's circumstances. All critical language, tacitly or otherwise, accepts the mediating activity which such circumstance forces upon it. Efforts to establish a suprahistorical ground of meaning, as E. D. Hirsch's claim to establish the author's authentic intention through the hypothesis of an Husserlian mental phenomenon, must face the recognition that the recovery of that intention is pursued by those who are time and culture bound. The abstract hypothesis is a pole-star rather than a crate of mental documents which can be unpacked without mediating the space between the contents and the reader. And Hirsch's distinction between 'meaning' and 'significance' (which latter admits of this mediating process) seems to founder on the fact that the same positioning and same process are involved in the establishment of either. One's moral obligation to the pole-star's existence does not translate into a scientifically acceptable analysis of its precise components.

Within this group of problems the notion of cultural relativism has developed an importance heightened by its political use. The valuations that have composed a traditional canon have become seen as partial, culturally loaded, and representative of an elite minority. Even if one has wished to place the all too real worlds of politics and pedagogy within one's own version of Husserlian brackets, one must reply that of course literature is limited by its cultural origins. And certain pressures from the cultural conflicts they represent may enter into exactly such a revision process as Eliot described, even if we might discover that some of the elements in such a conflict were of other than critical interest. But however far its social and political consequences may stray from literary matters they are something which enters into the process of critical revision. To what extent does such a participation suggest a dependency that would imply the relative value of different works for different cultures? In a sense we take this for granted. The great novels of Tsao Hsueh Chin or Murasaki Shikibu have a 'centrality' in their own cultures which even the presence of excellent translations does not create for them in ours. The political issues are of course hardly put in this way, but the versions of relativism that enter into such controversies are largely attached to issues of equality, fairness and other social and moral concerns that require their own exposition. Yet the impingement of critical reasoning upon these issues has the curious effect of seeing the relative placing of works in terms of their cultural 'specificity' and nevertheless exploring interest and value that goes beyond the special features of a particular culture. The rationale of Rorty's widening of the canon would no doubt try to relate these localised values to the more general, and political, features of his own version of liberalism.

The critical anxieties that have circled around the notion of relativism largely derive from the possibility of alternative readings or interpretative principles. But few critical disagreements are concerned with totally incompatible presuppositions. In the most scrupulous and comprehensive of studies Wayne Booth has elaborated a 'pluralism' which accepts the necessary coexistence of the multiple strands that enter into critical thought: criticism is at some points cognitive, at others not; a poem in some senses has its independent ontological status while in others it is a construct of the reader or of the interpretative community; the enormously varied input of other intellectual disciplines both has its value and its limitations, etc.[3] Yet there seems to be a spectrum that moves from such sensible pluralism, through eclecticism to 'relativism'. In all of this I wish to touch only on a single thread. When the ironic critic looks to his next move, in the awareness that this step will only be partial – its 'rightness' or 'validity' will be qualified in relation to other aspects – he cannot but reflect on the many forms of relativity that are built into the enterprise.

But is this the 'relativism' which traditional critics have feared when they hoped to establish a solid and reliable understanding of a text? The notion of a cognitive criticism, built on an accumulation of evidence, suggests partly a more historical model of literary study. Yet even this involves the 'placing', the seeking of the revealing comparison, that dissolves an historical model into critical perceptions. The categories and dependably delineated terms upon which the institutional needs of the teaching profession have depended are of course the product of a working agreement, the consensus that even the most nominalist approach to meaning requires. And the historical frame of enquiry works with accepted coordinates. To what extent is a roughly intelligible field of study destabilised by such a form of relativism?

I have argued that while a general position called 'relativism' may be impossible to state – it is at least in some senses self-refuting, like a version of the liar paradox – the continuous repositioning that critical argument employs is relational to the point that a form of relativism pervades one's practice. Now to what degree would Booth's 'pluralism' provide an adequate description of critical practice without involvement in the uncertainties that the notion of relativism seems to imply? Certainly the logical character of the terms is different to this degree: one can state a notion of pluralism without the implied reflexivity. It is a statement of 'live and let live' that seems to admit of the many ways of going about the practice of criticism, without an underlying scepticism implied by the possibility that any of the many might undercut each other. Booth gives a test (*CU*, p. 33) for a pluralism that is not 'to be dissolved into scepticism', in terms of two rival truths, employing two valid reasoning processes, yielding two different claims about 'what makes an adequate picture'. Booth realises that the abstract criterion is impossible to apply. And for more reasons than he gives. It is both too exacting and too vague. The problems implicit in 'adequate' alone render the variables quite daunting.

Booth characteristically puts most things in the plural including 'pluralisms', 'relativisms', and 'modes' of both of them. Such plurality seems to be the condition of the subject, and does not admit of precise distinctions. The implicit accommodations lend themselves to what Pepper called 'reasonable eclecticism' in the partial convergence of his 'world hypotheses' (*CU*, pp. 376–7), and the built-in elasticity indicates a space for the plurality of modes of pluralism. And if the general model tends to disappear in the profusion, so the distinction intended becomes overlaid with qualifications and its application progressively uneven. Booth is of course quite aware of the difficulties, that the distinction between 'relativism' and 'pluralism' is uncertain in some contexts and quite untenable in others. But he believes in its instrumental use, as he believes in the value of pluralism in the face of the thinning of the concept itself in a potential regress:

Finally, can we imagine a genuine pluralist of pluralisms, one who can accept and use many different umbrellas – a plurimodist of plurimodes, a metalinguist of metalanguages? But how could such a one, praising and relating many ways of praising and relating but encountering other pluralists of pluralisms who insist on different ways – how could he avoid an infinite regress of ever more vacuous pluralisms? (*CU*, p. 34)

Here the honest critic turns to engage with the arguments of others, and what may not be determined may be to some degree seen through.

An analogous difficulty exists for Isaiah Berlin's many reformulations of the difference between cultural relativism and the civilised pluralism of democratic societies. Relativism is posited as an incompatibility which cannot be discussed or the epistemic gap between cultures so distant as to prevent understanding. Pluralism is the acceptance that 'there are many ends men may seek and be fully rational'. 'Forms of life differ. Ends, moral principles are many.' There is a plurality of values, equally genuine, equally ultimate, above all equally objective, incapable therefore of being ordered in a timeless hierarchy, or judged in terms of one absolute standard.[4] On the other hand, relativism seems to hold that there are no objective values. But does 'objective' consist simply in the existence of someone who holds that value for its own sake? Would this be a sufficient condition for the entry of a particular value into a liberal plurality? The holder of this plurality may grant that there are those who have such values, but it is possible oneself to attribute a relational series of claims to a variety of them. In effect is some form of relativist thinking forced upon one by the acceptance of pluralism? If so, of course, the distinction would be impossible to maintain.

Another aspect of Berlin's identification of relativism with the lack of any objective values is to define through such relativism a cultural nihilism. Certainly there can be critical nihilists as there can be moral or political ones. Yet in describing the relational working of critical language one has not felt the absence of value but the impossibility of positioning oneself unambiguously with respect to any of its instances. It is both that the further, synoptic sense lies outside criticism itself, and that in the consideration of those essential particulars with which the critic works, the revisionary process which is part of his operative vocabulary suggests that 'relative rightness' and 'relative validity' are the stuff of which the great family of critical discourses is made. For if the most traditional of critics sees the innate error in his most measured correction this acceptance of relativism is built into the enterprise. This may mark the difference from the political commitment of which Berlin is speaking, the kind of commitment which demands choice, consequential choice between incommensurables, and where the choice may involve sacrifice, in extreme cases of tragic proportion.

My question concerns the extent to which these two relativisms are different, which involves the further question of whether or not they are ultimately separable. Hampshire has described one view of the way in which aesthetic judgement slips over into moral when the showing of particular features of aesthetic arrangement becomes one of 'larger comparisons of scale' and turns into the 'practical advice that certain things ought to be read, seen, and heard, and the advice must involve some reference to the whole economy of human needs and purposes ... '[5] At this point one language seems transformed into another. The example 'turns', beginning to carry its moral injunction. An intention to separate indicates a natural path of transition. And Rorty has described a complementary movement, a drawing from the literary example of its force as moral paradigm where the activity of showing the nature and claim of the paradigm is more akin to criticism than to more usual models of philosophical reasoning. To what extent does this element of critical language, with that implied relativism we have seen embodied in it, somehow infiltrate this world of choices, a version, to adopt Rorty's language, of redescription rather than inference? This of course is not a precise set of alternatives. Hampshire's essay is not so much a chain of inferences as a set of recommendations about how the operations of quite different, or supposedly different, concepts involve us. And it is not concerned with descriptions of any kind, or indeed with examples. The latter is also the case with Berlin where the gesture towards examples is so often off-hand. Take the cases of what would constitute relativism: 'I like mountains, you do not', or the comparisons concerned with progress in the arts. Or again, 'I prefer coffee, you prefer champagne. We have different tastes. There is no more to be said.' But alas, there is. The very time of day, the nature of occasions, the company we keep, extend the most simplistic example into qualifications and complications.

This dismissive use, as if the cut and dried case must be tersely disposed of, almost suggests some unease or even embarrassment. The presence of examples, with their capacity to generate alternative readings and divergent narratives, seems like the presence of the moneychangers in The Temple, muddling the truth with shady and unworthy transactions. We have seen some of Rorty's difficulty in turning example into paradigm. And Berlin's perfunctory use suggests that the more we sought an understanding of relativism and pluralism in practice the more difficult it would be to determine securely their character and implications. There is greater safety in what is effectively definition.

But I wish to argue that the relativism embodied in critical practice is essentially benign. The continuous revision of our understanding of the relations of texts, their worlds and our own, does not undermine the possibility of value but refines and sharpens our awareness of it. Needless to say, this process of valuing, as Barthes would have it, or of redescribing, does not create an adherence to a value-system, but makes our understanding of those commitments something that can be realised in all of its immediacy and complexity. The critical procedure means that the existential choice is not, as it sometimes seems with Berlin, a mystical absolute, like the preference for coffee, which is indeed the logic of The Temple. It is rather the examined world of multiple perceptions, where awareness is of many overlapping, mutually qualifying things. To make sense of our personal choices one must try to see what the consequences would look like, and then look further, for what I am choosing in the particular case involves a full sense of 'forms of life' and does not require Hampshire's quantum leap from pointing out the 'originality of arrangement' to 'the whole economy of human needs and purposes'. And at every step the ambiguity of the relation hangs upon it. Should it desert us, so does criticism.

We have, however, seen certain of the difficulties that arise in Rorty's wish to establish the example as the argument, and to commit the use of the canon to the reductive paradigm of a desirable form of life. In such a project the directive effect of the paradigm is as we have seen qualified by the critical process, something which Rorty calls the recognition of contingency. But the very project raises the question of how we construct the form of life to which we might possibly adhere. And the effect of contingency is put in terms, borrowed from Joseph Schumpeter, of recognising the civilised necessity of acting on the basis of 'relative validity'.[6] The role of such a 'relative validity' may enter in quite different ways into practical calculation or assessing the claims of competing principles of conduct while only indirectly employing anything that resembles a critical method – the sequence of comparisons by which the essential interest and value of literary works is thought through. Examples here too may increase our uncertainty. We have said that Hegel's use of the *Antigone* in section VI of *The Phenomenology* has a simply illustrative and reductive effect. Yet here too, if one looks more closely at the *Antigone*, one might see the example beginning to turn, to make out of the conflicts and ambiguities of the play itself something which failed to serve a schematism of the ethical life, where a critical reflection might naturally intervene to put aspects of that schematism in doubt. It is of course not my aim to recast the 'relative validity', for what it is worth, of the basis of moral choices and actions in terms of the 'relative rightness' which has seemed a persistent feature of critical discourse. That Rorty has found difficulty in saying how the process of working out the canon of literary models relates to the establishment of the moral awareness that those works embody leaves a quite palpable area of uncertainty.

Another way of expressing the benign character of the relativism which attaches to critical language is to look once more at what our own case studies have shown us, at the power of critical activity to break down the pretensions of the grand story, to fragment the claims of ideologies and theories. It is to turn the apodeictic force of these grand structures into myth. The structure of fragments can then coalesce according to principles which then may inform but not determine. As the picture complicates, as the myths into which theory is transformed accomplish their rearrangements, our thickening descriptions supplement each other, so the tradition is formed and dismantled and revised. This may seem like only a manner of speaking, a way of indicating a further characterisation which will yield an accommodation between the longer perspective and the fragments that compose them, without entering into the conceptual contract that theories and ideologies propose. Myth here no more than indicates the quality of a narrative – yes, perhaps a resemblance to the *grand récit*, but with that difference which critical use has forced upon it.

It is another version of relativism that is consequent on those varieties of reader response theory that make the reader the ultimate arbiter of meaning. In their weakest forms such theories need only hold that the very existence of literature is unintelligible without a world of readers and that the interaction of text and reader is the necessary condition of critical understanding. Understanding is necessarily on the part of someone. Even to such weak forms, the notion of Hirsch that a 'meaning' fixed at the moment of creation can be recaptured through historical reconstruction is an illusion. The original moment of intention, as Wimsatt and Beardsley argued, is inaccessible to us. We cannot get out of our skins or our own historical moment, as Eliot's implied historicism takes much for granted. And this emphasis on response has not depended on the theoretical work of Jaus, Iser and Fish. It is also prominent in Richards, much of the new criticism, and especially in Leavis for whom the fullness and adequacy of response were measures of one's critical achievement. But the assumption of the latter was still that there was a text whose formal features could be given. This implied a double transitivity by which our skill, discipline and feeling reached out to the text which in turn is an 'invitation' to our response.

Varying claims of strength for the theoretical account of the reader's role involve those 'schemata', 'codes', 'repertoires', 'strategies' which are built into the cultural situation of the reader and which construct his path. We can say with varying degrees of comfort that all texts are only understood as interpretations. To extend this to the radical move of Stanley Fish and hold that texts only exist in their interpretations constitutes not so much a metaphysical claim (as such it is unintelligible) as a placing of intellectual responsibility in the reader's own world. In conveying an experience the text conveys its meaning. The direction pointed is not that of the subjectivism of the casual and undisciplined reader, although the dissolution of any intelligible understanding into multiple subjectivities seems a speculative possibility. But Fish intends a series of controls. His essay 'Interpreting the *Variorum*' gives us at least two contexts in which these operate.[7] In Milton's twentieth sonnet a clue to conflicting interpretations is found in the invitation which the text proposes to the reader's own judgement. The strength of judgement lies in the experience conveyed, and 'the configurations of that experience' are a check on the inconclusiveness of formalist analysis. And the responsibility involved in that experience is established through at least two procedures. One is the careful analysis of the activity of response itself: 'the making and revising of assumptions', the features of our own reflective process, the ways in which an 'experiential' meaning is established.

The second measure of that responsibility lies in a further consideration of ourselves and our situation. We cannot conceive of ourselves reading without being certain sorts of persons, with a distinctive education and training, characteristic mental horizons, personal and literary connections, and purposes which are shared by others in what Fish calls an 'interpretative community'. Such a community will have its shared strategies, areas of agreement about issues and methods – its formal and informal rules of play. Such communities give, within themselves, a degree of stability in shared assumptions 'which enable us to talk to each other'. But communities, like ourselves, are contingent and transitory; they also 'grow and decline'. And our ways of forming our critical opinions are less fragile only than those opinions themselves. The recent history of critical fashion would show as much.

This seems in many ways a reasonable and astute account of the ways in which our critical institution has been shaped and how it operates. However as a theoretical model it has three distinct limits. One lies in the shadow of the text itself. How can the most careful consideration of one's critical procedures, the fullest exercise of one's responsibilities, be decisive when the presence of the text, both impalpable and real, will inevitably generate further procedures and exercises? That towards which any responsibility is directed may be pushed off stage but not eliminated. The real force of Fish's argument is a change in our mode of attention – 'reader-oriented analysis' as he says. It may check the futilities of formalism, but the object of attention may yet outflank it. A second problem lies at the outer margin of the community. There seems a tendency to see communities as self-contained, and contacts with others an uneasy incommensurance. And as far as anxiety over irresponsible relativism may arise the notion of community has merely shifted us from individual to cultural relativism.

However, even within the community in its narrowest sense certain conflicts seem irresolvable. I shall narrow it to the case of a single person in what might pass for another example of Eliot's radicalism. It comes from a conversation recorded by Neville Coghill about a production by Rupert Doone of 'Sweeny Agonistes':

*Myself* [*Coghill*]: I had no idea the play meant what he made of it ... that everyone is a Crippen. I was astonished. *Mr. Eliot*: So was I. *Myself*: Then you had meant something very different when you wrote it? *Mr Eliot*: Very different indeed. *Myself*: Yet you accept Mr Doone's production? *Mr Eliot*: Certainly. *Myself*: But ... but ... can a play mean something you didn't intend it to mean, you didn't know it meant? *Mr. Eliot*: I hope so ... yes, I think so. *Myself*: But if the two meanings are contradictory, is not one right and the other wrong? Must not the author be right? *Mr. Eliot*: Not necessarily, do you think? Why is either wrong?[8]

Part of the shock of this comes from the lack of reasons. A crevasse within the community, within Eliot himself is simply taken for granted.

What matters is how something was imagined, rather than pointing to any formal features. It would be in the vivid primacy of experience that the perspective of Fish would have a useful claim. For Eliot as reader/spectator experienced his own text in a wholly unexpected way. He does not give the detailed and considered report on that experiencing that Fish might see as appropriate to a community. It is rather a small Barthian earthquake which pushes the limit of credibility.

## 2    A strange serendipity

The history of modern criticism is that of a continuous ingestion, an absorption from other orders of thought: versions of history, psychology, sociology and anthropology, as well as the preoccupations that come with moral, metaphysical and theological commitments. The survey in Stanley Hyman's *The Armed Vision* differs from those of the structuralist/post-structuralist 'revolution' or the current preoccupation with gender and with cultural production in its content but not its kind. The critical institution has been formed of such diverse elements. For this omnivorous institution has a strange serendipity which leads one to ask why so many of the controversies that animate one's culture take place on critical ground more actively than in their place of origin, turning critics into amateur philosophers, psychoanalysts, sociologists, etc. Is it that criticism has accepted the influx that more rigorous disciplines would refuse? Yet we take this exogenous flow as natural to the operation of critical activity.

While the sources of this input may not be different in kind from those of the not too distant past, their presence may suggest a different use. For there has been an indistinct but effective watershed. The sources of intellectual energy described in Hyman's book were devoted to critical explanation. How did a particular perspective come to provide a useful dimension for critical method? And this encompassed such projects as imagery studies with their psychoanalytic derivation and the great vogue of myth criticism which culminated in the work of Northrop Frye. Such work used its anthropological sources for a highly developed series of imaginative structures whose forms were linked to the understanding of literary texts. With more recent uses of theory the opposite has been true. The growth of substantial subliteratures within the critical enterprise indicates a break from traditional explanation and the establishment of a loosely defined independence within the host institution.

Perhaps gender studies creates the most vivid examples, in the curious indeterminacy of the relation of its textual base to its further purposes and intellectual structures. Certainly Mary Ellman's *Thinking about Women*, for all of the sharpness and clarity of its examples and arguments, is difficult to locate.[9] Its methods are those of a literary critic; its substance is literature; but its subject matter is not. The brilliant account of stereotypes and modes of thought, of social coding and the special pleading involved in it, is drawn almost entirely from literary sources. The method is one which training in practical criticism might well perfect, a careful attention to similarity and difference, with a high sense of the attendant incongruities. But the real subject matter lies the other side of the literary cases, in the social order and tradition that have shaped literature itself and the forms of consciousness which it represents. And for those forms of consciousness literature is simply a repertoire of evidence. It is the appropriate mirror where the image can be caught, and society's most honed and concentrated recording angel. The examples – unlike whatever empirical evidence a social scientist might provide – are common property and there for all to see, and the pleasure of the irony is cumulative in the extended sequence of comparisons. A culture is on trial, not in a systematic way but through insights deployed like literature itself. 'System' consists only in a rough sequence of categories, and the absence of a theoretical focus may suggest that there is a tension between the project and its means.

The project points to a picture of the order of things. Yet the terms of that order cannot be mapped in their relational features. Nor can an account be given of the causal patterns behind an observed mode of thought. There are neither scientific nor social nor other psychological explanatory schemes. A nexus of stereotype and convention is simply the given which is reflected in the written record of our consciousness, selected and intensified no doubt for its direct presentational effect. And that effect is measured by the conviction that follows without assimilating it to a general hypothesis. But what kind of hypothesis would provide a unifying ground? There is no doubt that literature is used as evidence for some pervasive features of our culture and that the method of deployment is a critical method. Its moral force operates in the traditional antithetical manner of satire, not through the creation of a conceptually coherent order of its own, but in showing the indignities and follies of the state of things as they are. Correcting through 'piecemeal engineering' might address some of that conventional order without imagining the total construction of its alternative. The move from the satirist's presentation to the systematic construction of alterneity would require some mode of its own formulation, and such notions as difference (Derrida) or otherness (Lacan) can become the pivot around which alternative observations may cluster in the search for a new and appropriate idiom. Perhaps implicit in Ellman, as in writers attached to a traditional feminism, is an underlying concept of justice or fairness which can be actualised through an egalitarianism which even piecemeal modification would substantially effect. Or one could perhaps conceive, as in Simone de Beauvoir, a revision of the social order according to some larger principle in which the feminine will find its authentic voice. But even this larger step is towards a world of general equitability which is shaped in wider moral or political terms not principally endogenous to feminism.

The project of converting difference into generality, or otherness into totality or anti-theory, into theory characterises those later feminisms that have chosen to isolate feminine consciousness yet construct a world picture by way of it. The claims of the autonomy of feminism balance uneasily with larger political totalisations. The commitment to the other may extend, as it does for Cixous, to the point of considering all forms of general theory a masculine imposition, with the law of logical contradiction a form of tyranny. Hence to evolve a discontinuous mode of writing where the 'Imaginary' exists as a seemingly limitless and undefinable form of self-creation is to posit criteria of intelligibility, understanding and expression which lie outside the categories of explanation which both philosophical argument and criticism normally employ. Its enactment would take it beyond Barthes's versions of rupture and discontinuity, in its refusal of something like Barthes's explanatory process. The question of what the imaginary would exclude and where it would situate itself in any 'imagining' of human activity as a whole leaves its character, surely intentionally, indeterminate. Whatever relation it might have to critical theory is proposed through forms that theory does not take.

If we are seeing the articulation of different forms of consciousness, of perspectives that do not belong to recognisable traditions, the development of language is a necessary condition of its accomplishment. This mixture of experiment with more conventional verbal means in Kristeva's 'chora' was a point of departure for her reading of Mallarmé. The term operates to suggest an opening which directs to the 'unfolding and gap' by which Mallarmé is taken, through the person of Lady and Patron, to represent the feminine. In the strong sense of 'use' it is hard to see the schematic working of a concept. Yet an area of suggestion, of implied meaning, is active as part of a broad understanding rather than as an analysis. If we recognise its centrality in Kristeva's conception of poetic language, in its evocation even of the music beneath symbolisation, the refusal of symbolic form, the discontinuity and disturbance which lie in the substructure of Mallarmé's language, its indication is nevertheless given through in-direction or conveyed through analogy with discontinuities of other kinds, in the psyche or the social order. The non-linear polymorphism can be identified, shown, related back to the 'chora'. But this focal point is indicated with an indeterminacy which either unsettles the very attempt to spell it out or makes of the resistance to theory an element of its justification. As with the 'Imaginary' there is something which lies beyond our normal mode of conceptualisation yet indicates an area of feminine consciousness which may both suggest the presence of the 'other' while putting the possibility of its own enterprise in question.

The problem of centring the decentred, of giving a necessary degree of intelligibility to what lies outside the area of rational and structured argument, has its protean aspect. In Kristeva's highly structured, actively theorised, closely argued work the paradoxical character of the feminist dimension, in its articulation through Mallarmé, may make it an ambiguous case. Yet the 'chora' seems intended, like the imaginary, as the vehicle of a poetics. That element of otherness or difference both sets the touchstone of a feminist poetics and blocks its development. A feminist poetics seems innately problematic. Elaine Showalter asserts the existence of such a poetics largely by simply marking out two areas for the direction of critical attention.[10] One is in finding a feminist perspective on the literary tradition, in itself of necessity largely masculine. The other is in the focus of female intelligence on female authors. It is the latter which is held to offer the more radical of the two and which seeks to free itself 'from the linear absolutes of male literary history', although it is difficult to see exactly in what moves such a freedom would consist. (Showalter herself writes reasonably straightforward and sequential academic prose.)

The open-endedness of this freedom poses again the question of what alternative mode of writing is proposed. And beyond this there is the question of what necessary conditions would be fulfilled to establish a poetics. We can see what a 'structuralist poetics' would be in terms of its conception of language, an analytic method based on that conception of language, the descriptive and explanatory effects of that method, and some idea of how those effects add up to another order of understanding. And one can find other models of poetics that proceed from other hypotheses. Here the implication that there is another, altogether different, critical model which will look at literature in a quite different way is not linked to specifiable conditions which such a poetics would have to fulfil. The result is not a describable change in mode of thought, but a pointing to certain sympathies and attitudes linked to selection of subject matter. These may be of great interest in themselves, but it is in this directing of attention that such critical discourse has its strength. As the strength of Kristeva lies in forms of argument which are not fractured by the concepts it employs. If we were to attempt to evolve a poetics from the 'chora' or the 'Imaginary' might a characteristic mode of reading arise from the very sort of concept that challenges its systematic use? Does the changed awareness of Mallarmé's language come about in a way that lies through difference, or does it join the repertoire of concepts and perspectives that are accessible to and operable by all? And if one begins to believe that there are 'female sentences' are they only readable by women? The consequences of thinking so would imply an interpretative mystique and a form of confrontational politics. That such a politics is a necessary condition of a feminist criticism pervades the work of Toril Moi.[11]

For one thing she is highly aware of the danger constituted by the very serendipity of the critical institution. And of course that institution has a material presence in other institutions – universities, journals, literary groups, publishers, etc. – which control the working conditions of those who read, reflect on literature and write about it. Partly perhaps as resistance to the absorption of feminist criticism into the academic tradition, certain writers have wished to distance themselves from institutional power and assert the particular force of feminist criticism as accepting its otherness and alienation. Hence the ambiguity of a stance which would find a falsification in success, unless that success were attached to a transformation of the social order. The implementation of any such programme is not entirely spelled out in terms of all of its social consequences, those precise features of a new social order which would recentre the possibility of women's literature and feminist reading.

What Moi identifies as a post-structural approach, derived largely from Derrida, is claimed to make possible a form of theorising which is not the linear chain of a traditional process. We have seen in Derrida a form of reasoning that is hostile to the very possibility of a critical language. One found difficulties in this account, but even if one accepted something approximate to Moi's adaptation one would have to go further than she does in giving the paradoxical task a working form. Her extended application of Derrida's method is essentially analogic. We can read Virginia Woolf's 'playful shifts and changes of perspective' in the light of a Derridean 'free play of signifiers'. And the use of the 'sportive, sensual nature of language' rejects the 'metaphysical essentialism underlying patriarchal ideology, which hails God, the Father or the phallus as its transcendental signified'.[12]

Woolf might not have put it like that, but the 'changes of perspective', the shifts and discontinuities, do suggest some similarity to what one could call a 'post-structuralist' analysis, as does the vague pointer to the questioning of the stability of personal identity. Of course such perspective shifts and problems of stable identity have other versions, not necessarily post-structural, but that will do. The effect of choosing by way of Derrida is precisely to put the possibility of theory in question. Here again the force is analogic, and the analogy is more suggested than applied. There is no close textual consideration of Woolf, but a reflection on the ways in which a number of feminist critics have failed to read adequately the gender conflict in *To The Lighthouse*. The point lies not in the understanding of Woolf but in construction of female identity and in the use of Woolf as a touchstone to the further elaboration of a feminist ideology, one in which the duality of masculine and feminine, its possible fusion or deconstruction, can be considered.

Yet the directions pointed through Derrida and Kristeva as working hypotheses contain a troubling uncertainty about the relation of critical and political dimensions such an analysis of Virginia Woolf would provide. If one works out some far-reaching consequences for the connections between awareness, features of language, sexual roles and social order there must be some form of extrapolation, and surely necessarily of reduction, for any version of an ideological formulation to be possible. But if hypothetically possible – *pace* the Derridean qualification – nothing like this is attempted. There is rather a reversal of focus which is directed from models of ideology that critics have used to the possibilities of reading operative through them. These meta-critical stances, rather than literary texts, provide our point of departure. It is the nature of 'the androgynous' that is primary rather than Woolf's ambiguities, or rather the nature of the conceptual schemes which would articulate 'the androgynous'. And the efficacy of such schemes depends in the end on their political character. It is perhaps the bottom line of this politics that is urgently present yet innately obscure. One may criticise Kristeva's lack of 'an account of other conflicting ideological and material structures that must be part of any radical social transformation'. Again, Kristeva 'seems essentially to argue that the disruption of the subject, the *sujet en procès* displayed in these texts, prefigures or parallels revolutionary disruptions in society. But her only argument in support of this contention is the rather lame one of comparison or homology. Nowhere are we given a specific analysis of the actual social or political structures that would produce such a homologous relationship between the subjective and the causal.'[13]

Yet the structure of such a relationship is not clearly established by Moi, and we have seen her own use of analogy. The intention is clearly there to move beyond the kind of comparison characteristic of critical argument, to a causal connection which would ground the changes in poetic language in the material circumstances of social and political structures. And it is hard to see how this project is consonant with the post-structural Derridean play of signifiers. The causal relation suggests instead the historical determinism of an old-fashioned positivist kind. One seems to be working with two sets of incompatible presuppositions.

That such causality implies a political explanation leads us to another aspect of the serendipity of the critical institution. For the conflicts which these issues contain have been channelled through critical contexts but seek their significant explanations in social and political terms. This would not of course be an approach to political issues by way of literature. It is rather the placing of the appropriate language of critical theory, and ultimately of whatever critical explanations there are, in terms of an account of material conditions. Beyond the morass of critical thought of any kind is the study of underlying cultural factors which can be expressed as a form of 'cultural materialism'. Yet that has been reached by way of the need for critical explanation and has often been represented as a version of critical theory. Eagleton embodies this paradox when he argues energetically that 'Methodologically speaking, literary criticism is a non-subject ... . If literary theory is a kind of metacriticism, a critical reflection on criticism, then it follows that it too is a non-subject.'[14] But if – as he has argued – the identity of literature itself and with it, criticism, the commentary on it, and the further reflection on both of them, are all dissolved, what then has Eagleton's book been about? The futile shuffling of words about words about words has only pointed us to the threshold of solid and committed social and political undertakings which are substantially absent.

Yet the whole rationale of these undertakings has arisen from the reflection on literature which it would condemn, is posed through the concepts such reflections has employed and is wholly naturalised in the critical institution. One of the problems would seem to be the ghost of the 'essentialism' which he would normally deride. To fail to find the distinguishing mark of literature, the essential method of criticism, the totalising critical theory is to employ the essentialism one denies. But the critical institution will even swallow its denial, indeed has already done so. The shifting and contingent family of discourses with a nominalist mode of description has merely added another fragmentary aspect. Aristotle noted that there was no word for what we now call 'literature'. The vast plurality of terms, methods, sources, modes of attention that have filled that space do not indicate its exhaustibility. Work in the field of 'cultural practices' which offers a vision of literature in terms of its human conditionality rather than 'piously swathed in eternal verities' is hardly a break with the plural tradition. At moments the pious platitudes seem almost artificially invoked as a foil to a robust reality that of course despises realism.

Neither Moi nor Eagleton tells us much about the politics which would embody a deeper perspective on our critical discourses. It becomes the indication of a point of reference which needs no explanation and which takes on a symbolic aura, a figurative dimension of our cultural world. There is a break certainly from its conventional uses that tends towards metaphor. Politics becomes the undiscovered country whose existence is posited, to which our theorising, our critical commentary, our literary production, are subordinate, and in which they will find some speculative consummation. However, my purpose is not to judge of such a project, but only to observe that such a realisation is to be reached through the very reflection on literature which is to be subsumed into it and that such reflection is the present and accessible discourse, the embodiment of a political aim in the institution of criticism.

For we have been observing a process of displacement by which one frame of reference substitutes for another. In the case of Ellman an investigation of feminine consciousness by way of the literary tradition had the double effect of a critical and a psychological or social form of explanation, as with Kristeva the multiple referential frames created – even if analogically – their own order of substitutions. Part of the effectiveness of the strange serendipity is an openness to such a process which resembles metaphorisation and continually expands and transforms the institution in this way. And while metaphorisation need not mean the dissolution of substantive issues into figurative language, it does imply that different orders of explanation may stand in for each other. And the analogies between them become the vehicles of imaginative connection which itself extends the possibilities of comparison. The procedures for examining into similarity and difference are neither systematic nor conclusive but part of a movement of mind which the process of metaphorisation never allows us to close.

Part of this openness is what our cases have shown us of the continuous presence of the valuing process in this play of substitution. It is precisely because the scene of the conflicting values of one's culture is transposable that such representation of conflict takes place through critical mediation, with criticism the language of crisis as de Man has said. That now traditional term 'revaluation' is consonant with the range of cultural substitutions. The entire force of canon revision, in whatever idiom its rationale may be proposed, reflects such a mediation on precisely such a ground of choice and placement among texts with the full sense of their implications. And the presupposition of feminist criticism, as with multiculturalism, is to effect those changes in thought and feeling which are changes in the order of values. The critical matrix has become the 'receptacle', a space of transformation where the conflicts of a social or psychological or political character may be played out. Not the only space of course, for the textual ground has both a density of reference and a capacity to represent and rerepresent which makes the critical family of discourses a powerful if elusive instrument for both radical revision and the renewal of the tradition. The radical proposals of the 'new historicism' or of 'cultural materialism' are only secondarily concerned with method. They are directed at a focal point of attention, at what is worth knowing, and worth our singling out as of cultural importance. And it is a similar form of cultural evaluation that animates Habermas, Kramer, Jameson and others on the character of the 'postmodern'.

That literature and its interest are ultimately inseparable from other aspects of a culture and its values should not conflict with an acceptance of its distinctive character. And those who worry about its 'privileged' status are again caught up in a version of 'essentialism'. The interplay of literary features with other cultural aspects, of the critical skills of close reading with other intellectual skills is part of a continuum. Certainly Richards saw the experiment of practical criticism as an attempt 'to introduce a new kind of documentation to those who are interested in the contemporary state of culture whether as critics, as philosophers, as teachers, as psychologists, or merely as curious persons'.[15] The speculative instruments were brought to bear on the inadequacy of intellectual discipline and reading powers. Here too, evaluation is part of the process of cultural analysis. And this process of evaluation has been extended by what I have called the myth of theory. For the activity of theorising has been part of the creation of that space of reflection in which, for our culture and our moment, as Rorty has observed, cultural conflict is enacted, understanding sought and commitments undertaken.

## 3    The Tao

If criticism is immersed in value it remains to give some further account of the 'transit point' to a prescriptivism which is neither that of doctrine nor of the reductivism which would elevate one language game above all others. I have already mentioned Barthes's remark about the difference between the commitment to value and the process of valuing. And there is a further suggestion in the 'exploration of the possible'. For if there is anything which is prescriptively necessary to critical procedures it is the inevitability of the exploration. At the 'case-by-case' level out of which any larger account must be shaped, there is no way in which one can refuse to consider the next case. There may be, as we have seen, a point of diminishing returns in the taking of possible meanings beyond the point where they can really be said to matter – 'one has honestly to consider what seems important'. But there is a profound sense in which the exploration cannot be refused. (The deconstructive move as much as any other.) The next case may be the relevant and illuminating move, the turn which gives a sense of further connections and consequences. One may say 'no' to the next comparison, but it is difficult to justify the refusal to consider it. Large classes of comparisons and possible moves may seem in accumulated experience to be useless, or even pervasively foolish; but one has also learned to distrust accumulated experience.

Then if there is no way around the obligation to at least consider the next move, even a negative decision shapes what is subsequent. Having taken thought one has embarked on the exploration. One effect is of course that pluralism is built into one's procedures. And criticism is therefore necessarily the enactment of liberalism. Whether as triumph or as offence it is built into its nature. No form of intellectual closure, doctrinal or otherwise, can be imposed where the next case may turn an unexpected corner, create a devastating reversal or force an unwelcome reappraisal. This of course is not a doctrinal liberalism, although I suppose you could work the rough contours of some sort of doctrine out of it. It is simply a necessary condition of its practice. And when strong doctrine or rigorous theory are engaged in such a practice, one has seen the abyss into which they can fall. In this sense, criticism is the liberal practice *par excellence*. The most committed theorist, the most severe ideologue, is transmuted into a liberal by the moment of engagement in it.

Such liberalism may easily be parodied in its comforting form, with the accommodations of 'a place for everything and everything in its place'; but this sense of a world where everything relates with gratifying smoothness of fit is wholly alien to the practical necessity I have described. Nor is it attached to something called 'humanism'. The claims of the latter, as a general stance or attitude, however rationally or arbitrarily derived, is no more attached to this liberalism than is the nihilism which is sometimes thought to oppose it. For these further coordinates, like other importations of grander and grander narratives, whether they would push us to the edge of ontology or not, involve us with commitments that are inevitably different.

However, if the necessary prescription, the critical imperative, lies in the inability to refuse the next move, the next turn of what becomes exploration, the intelligibility of that move depends on the assumption of a point of departure. The game is launched, but from somewhere. The point of departure with each succeeding small narrative is like a step in a Foucauldian genealogy where each generation, so to speak, gives the game a new shift, puts it on a new basis. A new ground is established at each move, although it draws all of its past in its train. Hence the steps of each small narrative however exploratory or radical are yet rich in immediate contexts and filiations. The genealogy unfolds step by step bearing its tangled past. Concepts like that of 'appropriateness' link the steps inexorably to the previous term. However we describe the excellence of the move or its hopeless inadequacy, it is impossible to avoid the notion that it either works or does not, or at least that its operation satisfies or does not, or mixes those two according to all of the uneven, piquant, disturbing, irritating possibilities with which the particular observation may be charged. Such a response, whether it represents a clear decision or a tangle of cross-purposes, nevertheless finds its effect in the relationship with its origins, with this impalpable but distinctive sense of the value of the relation attached.

Therefore the necessary other face of exploration is a notion which constitutes the heart of classicism, the notion of the appropriate, which has often been attached to a world of fixed standards, laws of proportion and precise criteria. But it is essentially relational. It simply evaluates the move. Of course no criteria can be given, for the relational depends upon that point of departure and the imperative of exploration. A knowledge of kinds and of expectations may have some use as a means of building up the case law which will provide the ground for deciding whether or not the notion of the appropriate is being 'appropriately' applied. It is the field through which the interpretation of the many cases is made possible – of course through each other. But the feature which is determinant in our sense of the appropriate is that point of departure for the given move. It contains both the vertigo of the possible and the fixed point within the field. That point is also subject to its own movement, in canon revision or shifts of historical perspective. It is only, in a sense, fixed for the moment. And that is what gives its force to historicism. For historicism is the recognition of that moment's contingency. The point of departure may be fixed for the move, but is changed by the very existence of what follows, and does not vanish into a time capsule like a fly into amber. The imperatives of classicism are not incompatible with the movement of time or of exploration.

Of course the notion of 'appropriateness' which is purely relational, answering to an operational need in a contingent world, may yet set an agenda for the history of criticism as a record of the continuous resituating of small narratives which are recognisably critical moves in those larger stories of cultural shapes and destinies. I have treated these latter largely as if they were theory-based, as my enquiry has been in the nature and uses of theory. But the same is the effect in use of those other larger stories that base themselves in the visionary or in tradition. And indeed aspects of the latter may be so deeply a part of a critic's identity that a weak sense of their presence is pervasive. But whether weak or strong versions in criticism they are used, given an interpretative role, found partial, a mixture of useful and inadequate, given a gestural role – a theory too becomes a touchstone – qualified, complemented, perhaps in the end reduced to a trace, both superceded and tangentially retained. The steps of critical argument, as one has seen most clearly in Bloom, may flutter these successive keys before the mind's eye as alternative fragments of their language games come in focus, dominate, retire, and seemingly vanish, or emerge resituated. In becoming so their meanings may alter. In this subversive way criticism is the grounding of theory – not of course in an ontological or epistemo-logical sense – but of giving it a situation in which it works, or rather perhaps, in which its force is mediated.

Such mediation is enmeshed in a double paradox. A form of practice is destructive of theory. Yet it is theory-mad, hungry, devouring, sucking in ideas which operate at many levels of generality. It is precisely this anti-conceptual 'black hole' that makes for a passionate intoxication, an intoxication which has slowly taken hold through a loss of faith in traditional mimeticism and authorial authority, with their transitive presuppositions about literary language. These grand narratives, faded, dismembered, put in question, but far from effectively dead, contained within themselves a complex discourse of controversy, but one which did not admit the possibility of denying certain connections between literature and the world.

One need not deny the existence of these connections, although one nevertheless accepts that they are not as straightforward as was once maintained, and recognises that the 'sense' of literature and the 'sense' of the world are not the same. And it is the very difference that creates the gap that 'theory' both widens in exploring its scope and bridges in seeking to elaborate explanation. Yes, of course, literature is part of the historical process, the economic order; the structure of the language it uses reveals through its figures the hidden features of psychic life. Yet oddly, one of the seductions of literature is to create a confusion. It was no doubt a flight from the corrupt and banal charms of mimesis that led Lévi-Strauss to turn away from the false and wearying 'neighbours' of the theatre. Yet Empson's invention of persons to explicate figure shows a curious reciprocity. Even Freud can talk of the characters of Sophocles as if they were real persons and not verbal structures, while Paul de Man can sometimes talk of Rousseau's Julie as if he were Dr. Leavis talking about Gwendolyn Harlech, as if a solid realisation drew one in beyond the close analysis of the status of fictions with which his essay is partly concerned, to endow Julie herself with a reflexive consciousness equivalent to his own.

The paradox is the same with respect to the representational powers of critical language itself. For we live in the world and recognise that the sense we make of literature, or find it impossible to make, does not bring us closer to saying that critical mediation is a proper representation of its subject. (The fallacy of translatability at one extreme, or paraphrase at the other.) The sober note of believing, *à la* Hirsch, that a substantial and definitive version of a literary text can be ultimately given, involves an absurdity of its own. And as a project it has the unintended effect of placing the dead hand on critical imagination in the course of controlling its irresponsibilities. Yet it perfectly expresses the moment when the music has to stop.

This is not to invite the cultivation of another absurdity by suggesting that the move, the pagan single step, from the point of departure to the next observation, comparison, etc., may abandon the sense of appropriateness altogether. It is only that the criteria any generality would require cannot be stated. But to accept such appropriateness as a condition of practice is not to believe that whatever picture criticism constructs is a true picture. For these representations, involving as they do the fragments of many language games, are charged with the energies and traces of whatever theories cannot transcend the separateness of commentary – that is, create out of interesting substitutions either identity or truth. Yet, if the Tao says – 'Go beyond what you can reasonably do', the notion of reason is still with us to mark the path.

And the substitution of new theories for old, theories based upon difference rather than continuity, may articulate the way in which the value of literature in part derives from this difference. The chimera that Mallarmé saw in the failure of literal intelligibility valorises the intense, remarkable and elusive thing that never gives its totality to our exploration. The otherness of literature is its power – which is why Derrida and de Man are so deeply in love with it. 'Impossibility' perversely plays out the most difficult game. The intellectual impasse becomes their homage to the grandeurs of the object. No doubt the cultural philosopher could pursue the ontological implications of this otherness. But this would not be the way of criticism, or reachable by its pagan methods. Rather the complex working of exemplarity suggests that the Tao of criticism is neither contained in theory nor can elude it. The sinuous path is like the genealogy, where the process of seeing through the relations of choice gives us that sense of having worked out our way so that 'the contradictions and depths that lie under your feet' are apparent enough.[16]

# Notes

I FROM CHAOS TO CASE

1 I. A. Richards, *The Principles of Literary Criticism* (London: Routledge & Kegan Paul, 1924), p. 6.
2 Paul de Man, *Blindness and Insight* (New York: Oxford University Press, 1971), pp. 3–5.
3 Paul de Man, *The Rhetoric of Romanticism* (New York: Columbia University Press, 1984), p. viii.
4 F. R. Leavis, 'Literary Criticism and Philosophy', *Scrutiny*, 5, 5 (1937), pp. 59–70. Hereafter cited in the text as *S*.
5 Geoffrey Strickland, *Structuralism or Criticism* (Cambridge University Press, 1981), p. 195.
6 Ludwig Wittgenstein, *Zettel*, ed. G. E. M. Anscombe and G. H. von Wright (Oxford: Basil Blackwell, 1967), p. 79e.
7 Renford Bambrough, 'Literature and Philosophy', in *Wisdom: Twelve Essays*, ed. R. Bambrough (Oxford: Basil Blackwell, 1974), p. 291.
8 Strickland, *Structuralism*, p. 162.

II THE BIZARRE TERRITORY

1 Raymond Picard, *Nouvelle critique ou nouvelle imposture* (Paris: Pauvert, 1965), p. 148. Hereafter cited in the text as *NC*.
2 Roland Barthes, *Criticism and Truth* (London: The Athlone Press, 1987). Hereafter cited in the text as *CT*.
3 Roland Barthes, *Sur Racine* (Paris: Seuil, 1963), p. 93.
4 Barthes, *Racine*, p. 32.
5 Strickland, *Structuralism*, p. 76.
6 Roland Barthes, *The Grain of the Voice* (Berkeley and Los Angeles: University of California Press, 1985), p. 227.
7 Terry Eagleton, *Literary Theory* (Oxford: Blackwell, 1983), p. 199.

III THE CURVE OF THE MIRROR

1 E. R. Curtius, *European Literature and the Latin Middle Ages*, quoted in Harold Bloom, 'The Breaking of Form', in *Deconstruction and Criticism*, ed. H. Bloom (London: Routledge & Kegan Paul, 1979), pp. 2–3. Further references to this essay are cited in the text as *DC*.

2 Stéphane Mallarmé, 'Hérodiade', in *Oeuvres Complètes*, ed. Henri Mondor and G. Jean-Aubry (Paris: Gallimard, 1945), p. 45. The translation is by Antony Hartley.

IV FROM 'SO COMPLEX AN IRONY' TO 'SUCH A TEXTUAL LOGIC'

1 William Empson, *Some Versions of Pastoral* (London: Chatto & Windus, 1935), p. 89. Hereafter cited in the text as *VP*.
2 Christopher Norris, *William Empson and the Philosophy of Literary Criticism* (London: The Athlone Press, 1978), pp. 46–7.
3 Julia Kristeva, *La révolution du langage poétique* (Paris: Seuil, 1974), pp. 473–4. Hereafter cited in the text as *RLP*.
4 De Man, *Blindness and Insight*, p. 8.

V FROM 'WIT' TO 'ASTONISHMENT'

1 T. S. Eliot, 'Andrew Marvell', in *Selected Prose of T. S. Eliot*, ed. by Frank Kermode (London: Faber and Faber, 1975), p. 162. Hereafter cited in the text as *SP*.
2 Georges Poulet, *The Interior Distance*, trans. Elliot Coleman. (Baltimore: Johns Hopkins University Press, 1959), pp. 15–16. Hereafter cited in the text as *ID*.
3 Georges Poulet, *La Conscience Critique* (Paris: Jose Corti, 1971), p. 286.
4 Wittgenstein remarks on this in several contexts. See the discussion in Cyril Barrett, *Wittgenstein on Ethics and Religious Belief* (Oxford: Basil Blackwell, 1991), esp. pp. 72–3 and 165–6.
5 Clifford Geertz, 'Thick Description: Towards an Interpretative Theory of Culture', in *The Interpretation of Cultures* (London: Hutchinson, 1975), pp. 7–10.
6 Ibid., pp. 28–9.
7 Poulet, *Le Point de Départ, Etudes sur le Temps Humain*, vol. III (Paris: Plon, 1964), p. 12.
8 Poulet, *Studies in Human Time*, trans. by Elliot Coleman (Baltimore: Johns Hopkins University Press, 1956), p. 15.
9 Ibid., p. 315.

VI 'FOOL' AND '*PHARMAKON*'

1 William Empson, *The Structure of Complex Words* (London: Chatto & Windus, 1951), p. 74. Hereafter cited in the text as *CW*.
2 Jacques Derrida, 'Plato's Pharmacy', in *Disseminations*, trans. Barbara Johnson (London: The Athlone Press, 1981), pp. 71–2. Hereafter cited in the text as *D*.
3 J. Hillis Miller, 'The Critic as Host', in *Deconstruction and Criticism*, ed. Harold Bloom (London: Routledge & Kegan Paul, 1979), p. 230.
4 Richard Rorty, 'Philosophy as a Kind of Writing', in *Consequences of Pragmatism* (Brighton: The Harvester Press, 1982), pp. 94–5.

VII 'THE MONSTROUS CLARITY'

1 Stéphane Mallarmé, *Igitur*, in *Oeuvres Complètes*, p. 436. Hereafter cited in the text. as *M*.
2 Poulet, *La Conscience Critique* p. 277.
3 Jacques Derrida, 'The Double Session', in *Dissemination*, trans. by Barbara Johnson (London: The Athlone Press, 1981), p. 231n. Hereafter cited in the text as *D*.
4 Paul de Man, *Allegories of Reading* (New Haven and London: Yale University Press, 1979), p. 205. Hereafter cited in the text as AR.
5 De Man, *Blindness and Insight*, p. 35. Hereafter cited in the text as *BI*.
6 'Such is the nothingness of everything human, that other than the Being who exists in himself, there is nothing beautiful except that which is not.'
7 This evocation of the action of critical finesse goes back to a seminar on Pascal shared with my colleague Martin Warner. This is only a fragment of 'complement' to his substantial work, *Philosophical Finesse* (Oxford: The Clarendon Press, 1989).
8 Leo Bersani, *The Death of Stéphane Mallarmé* (Cambridge University Press, 1981), p. ix.


VIII FROM 'ENSEMBLE' TO 'EXCEPTION'

1 Bersani, *Death of Stéphane Mallarmé*, p. viii.
2 Roland Barthes, in *S/Z* (New York: Hill and Wang, 1974), p. 13.
3 Hayden White, 'The Absurdist Movement in Contemporary Literary Theory', in *Tropics of Discourse* (Baltimore and London: Johns Hopkins University Press, 1978), pp. 261–82.
4 Jonathan Culler, *Structuralist Poetics* (London: Routledge & Kegan Paul, 1975), p. 96.
5 Tzvetan Todorov, 'The Structural Analysis of Literature: the Tales of Henry James', in *Structuralism an Introduction*, ed. David Robey (Oxford: Basil Blackwell, 1973), p. 73.
6 Ann Jefferson, *Modern Literary Theory*, ed. A. Jefferson and D. Robey (London: Batsford, 1982), p. 99.
7 Philippe Sollers, 'Programme', in *Logiques* (Paris: Seuil, 1968), pp. 9–14.
8 Murray Krieger, *Theory of Criticism* (Baltimore and London: Johns Hopkins University Press, 1976), p. 57.
9 Christopher Butler, *Interpretation, Deconstruction and Ideology* (Oxford: The Clarendon Press, 1984), pp. 89 ff.
10 John Bayley, *The Uses of Division* (London: Chatto & Windus, 1976). Hereafter cited in the text as *UD*.
11 Quoted by Nicholas Spice in *The London Review of Books*, 7 May 1987.
12 Cf. Wittgenstein, *Philosophical Investigations* (Oxford: Basil Blackwell, 1953), pp. 26–7.
13 Thomas S. Kuhn, *The Structure of Scientific Revolutions*, 2nd ed. (The University of Chicago Press, 1970), pp. 181 ff.

IX PAGAN PERSPECTIVES

1 Jean-François Lyotard, *Just Gaming*, trans. Vlad Godzich (Manchester University Press, 1985), p. 56. Hereafter cited as *JG* in the text. The word 'récit' has such variable effect in different contexts that I have sometimes translated it as 'narrative', sometimes kept the original when the text makes the implications clear. And I have sometimes paraphrased to bring out the theoretical or explanatory force of 'grand récit'.
2 Rodolph Gasché, *The Tain of the Mirror* (Cambridge, Mass., and London: Harvard University Press, 1986), p. 136.
3 Jacques Derrida, *Positions*, trans. Alan Bass (London: The Athlone Press, 1987), p. 69.
4 Richard Rorty, Paper and discussion at the Italian Institute, London, March 1988.
5 Richard Rorty, 'Idealism and Textualism', in *Consequences of Pragmatism*, p. 158.
6 Roger Scruton, 'Modern Philosophy and the Neglect of Aesthetics', *TLS*, 5 June 1987.
7 Martha Nussbaum, 'Perceptive Equilibrium: Literary Theory and Ethical Theory', in *Love's Knowledge* (New York and Oxford: Oxford University Press, 1990), pp. 192–3.
8 Jurgen Habermas, *The Philosophical Discourse of Modernity* (Cambridge: Polity Press, 1987), p. 210.
9 Michael Wood, 'Montaigne and the Example', *Philosophy and Literature*, 13, 1 (1989), pp. 1–15.
10 Paul de Man, *The Resistance to Theory* (Manchester University Press, 1986), p. 96.
11 Habermas, *Modernity*, p. 208.


X THE TAO OF CRITICISM

1 M. H. Abrams, 'Rationality and Imagination in Cultural History', in *Doing Things with Texts* (New York and London: Norton, 1989), p. 118.
2 T. S. Eliot, *The Use of Poetry and the Use of Criticism* (London: Faber and Faber, 1933), pp. 108–9.
3 Wayne Booth, *Critical Understanding* (Chicago and London: The University of Chicago Press, 1979). Hereafter cited in the text as *CU*.
4 Isaiah Berlin, *The Crooked Timber of Humanity* (London: John Murray, 1990), p. 11.
5 Stuart Hampshire, 'Logic and Appreciation', in *Aesthetics and Language*, ed. William Elton (Oxford: Basil Blackwell, 1954), pp. 168–9.
6 Richard Rorty, *Contingency, Irony, and Solidarity* (Cambridge University Press, 1989), p. 46. His reference is to Isaiah Berlin's *Five Essays on Liberty*.
7 Stanley Fish, *Is There a Text in This Class?* (Cambridge, Mass., and London: Harvard University Press, 1980), pp. 148–73.
8 Neville Coghill, 'Sweeney Agonistes' in Tambimuttu and Richard Mach, eds, *T. S. Eliot: A Symposium* (London: Frank and Cass, 1965), p. 85.

I owe this to the unpublished dissertation of Dr Ole Skilleas, University of Warwick, 1992.

9 Mary Ellman, *Thinking about Women* (London: Virago, 1979).
10 Elaine Showalter, 'Towards a Feminist Poetics', in *Women Writing and Writing about Women*, ed. M. Jacobus (London: Croome Helm, 1979), pp. 25ff.
11 Toril Moi, *Sexual/Textual Politics: Feminist Literary Theory* (London and New York: Routledge & Kegan Paul, 1988).
12 *Ibid.*, p. 9.
13 *Ibid.*, p. 171.
14 Terry Eagleton, *Literary Theory* (Oxford: Basil Blackwell, 1983), p. 197.
15 I. A. Richards, *Practical Criticism* (London: Routledge & Kegan Paul, 1929), p. 3.
16 Empson, *Complex Words*, p. 124.

# Index

Abrams, M. H., 81, 191
absurdist criticism, 149 ff.
anamorphism, 39–41, 63, 193–4
Aristotle, 160–1, 163, 210
Arnold, Matthew, 16, 59, 157, 161, 176–7, 194
Artaud, Antonin, 177–8
Ashbery, John, 45–6, 51, 52, 54–62
Auden, W. H., 58
Austen, Jane, 162

Bambrough, Renford, 18–19, 20
Barthes, Roland, 23–43, 53, 57, 99, 150, 158, 159, 170, 193, 200, 204, 206, 212
Bataille, Georges, 177
Bayley, John, 160–6
Beardsley, Monroe, 202
Benjamin, Walter, 48
Berlin, Isaiah, 198–200
Bersani, Leo, 146–7, 149
Blake, William, 12, 14
Bloom, Harold, 33, 44–67, 100, 147, 149, 153, 177, 179, 187, 190, 214
Bonniot, Edmond, 133
Booth, Wayne, 81, 197–8
Bowen, Elizabeth, 162
Bradley, A. C., 106
Bradley, F. H., 157
Bremond, Claude, 37
Burckhardt, Jacob, 15, 48
Burke, Kenneth, 47, 60
Butler, Christopher, 158–9

canons as forms of value, 176–80
Chomsky, Noam, 36
Cioff, Frank, 96
Cixous, Hélène, 206
Coghill, Neville, 203
Coleridge, S. T., 48, 62, 97
completeness as aim of critical account, 6–7, 75, 94–5
Crane, R. S., 37
Crews, F. C., 139

criticism as the destruction of theory, 156, 201–2, 214–15
criticism as a form of crisis, 161, 169
criticism as a language game, 163–9, 170
criticism as 'practical reason', 20, 151, 158–9
Culler, Jonathan, 36, 152
Curtius, Ernst Robert, 44–5, 47–8, 50

Dante Alighieri, 171
Derrida, Jacques, 10, 26, 77, 91, 99, 110–21, 125–34, 138, 140–4, 150–2, 156, 168–9, 172, 175, 177, 184, 187, 195, 208–9, 216
determinacy of meaning, 110–21
Dickens, Charles, 10, 162
Dickinson, Emily, 62
Dryden, John, 194

Eagleton, Terry, 16, 32, 36, 168, 210
Eliot, T. S., 53–4, 56–7, 58–9, 69, 86–9, 92–8, 157, 171, 187, 192–6, 202–5
Ellman, Mary, 204–6, 211
Emerson, Ralph Waldo, 48, 56
Empson, William, 10, 35, 68–76, 78–9, 82–5, 93, 97, 99–110, 115–16, 119–21, 132–3, 148, 165–6, 168, 212, 215–16

Fish, Stanley, 161, 202–3, 204
Fletcher, Angus, 60
Foucault, Michel, 179, 213
Freud, Anna, 50–1, 62
Freud, Sigmund, 47, 48, 50, 52, 64–5, 155, 182, 215
Frye, Northrop, 44, 174, 204

Gasché, Rodolph, 175
Geertz, Clifford, 92–6
Genette, Gérard, 37
Gide, André, 57, 88, 97–8
Guarini, Battista, 82, 163

Habermas, Jürgen, 185, 187

222

Hampshire, Stuart, 199–200
Hartman, Geoffrey, 145
Hegel, G. W. F., 116, 120, 183, 201
Hirsch, E. D., 196, 202, 215
historicism and relativism, 194, 196–200,
    213–14
Hölderlin, Friedrich, 46, 51
Hough, Graham, 175
Hume, David, 12, 41, 151
Hyman, Stanley, 204

impossibility and critical argument, 135 ff.,
    143–4, 216
irony as a critical instrument, 41–2, 66,
    68–75, 83, 165

Jakobson, Roman, 35, 152
James, Henry, 153–4, 175, 185–6, 189
Jefferson, Ann, 154
Johnson, Dr Sanuel, 161, 168, 194

Kabbala, the, 48
Keats, John, 162
Kermode, Frank, 170–1, 174, 176–9, 182
Kierkegaard, Søren, 183
Knight, G. Wilson, 106
Kott, Jan, 106
Krieger, Murray, 157–8
Kristeva, Julia, 26, 38, 75–85, 155, 158,
    168, 171, 190, 206–7, 209, 211
Kuhn, Thomas, 165–7

Lacan, Jacques, 35, 50
Larkin, Philip, 162
Leavis, F. R., 3–22, 23, 49, 52, 56, 70, 73,
    74, 86, 125, 146, 150–1, 157, 175–6,
    178, 180–1, 184, 190–1, 202, 215
Lévi-Strauss, Claude, 19, 36, 37, 78, 94,
    103, 215
Lyotard, Jean-François, 145, 165, 172, 178,
    180, 182, 192

Mallarmé, Stéphane, 41, 57–8, 76–82, 84–5,
    98, 122–34, 144–8, 150, 155, 168, 175,
    177, 206–7
Malraux, André, 40, 120
Man, Paul de, 2, 48, 125, 134–48, 149–50,
    152, 158, 161, 168, 172, 184, 186–7,
    193–4, 211, 215
Marivaux, Pierre de, 88–92, 98
Marvell, Andrew, 86–7, 93, 96, 187
Marx, Karl, 155, 170–1, 182
Mauron, Charles, 29
Miller, J. Hillis, 117–19
Moi, Toril, 208–10
Monet, Claude, 164

Murray, Gilbert, 31
myth as a principle of order, 36–7, 201

Nerval, Gérard de, 81
Norris, Christopher, 74, 83
Nussbaum, Martha, 184–8

Parmigianino, 66
Pascal, Blaise, 5, 143–4
Pater, Walter, 15
'philosophy' and 'criticism', 4 ff.
Picard, Raymond, 23–32, 40
Plato, 18, 110–21
Poulet, Georges, 26, 88–92, 96–8, 121–4,
    191
practical criticism and its presuppositions,
    24–5
Propp, Vladimir, 37
Proust, Marcel, 98

Racine, Jean, 26–30, 32, 40–1, 46
Ransom, John Crowe, 25
reception theory, 124, 202–4
relativism, 195–202, 214
rhetoric, figures and tropes, 51 ff., 60–3
Richard, Jean-Pierre, 26, 31–2, 41, 91,
    125–34, 144, 150, 168, 175
Richards, I. A., 1–2, 17, 24–5, 42, 80, 100,
    109, 127, 170, 202, 212
Rimbaud, Arthur, 81
Rivière, Jacques, 91
Rorty, Richard, 50, 120, 179–81, 182–5,
    187, 197, 199, 212
Rousseau, Jean-Jacques, 125, 136–42, 215
Royce, Josiah, 157
Runciman, W. G., 95
Ryle, Gilbert, 92–3

Sainte-Beuve, Charles-Augustin, 168
Schiller, Friedrich von, 51
Schopenhauer, Arthur, 48, 52
Schumpeter, Joseph, 201
Scruton, Roger, 180–3
Shakespeare, William, 68–74, 99, 101,
    103–10, 121, 161–3, 166–8, 171
Shelley, P. B., 12–14
Showalter, Elaine, 207
Sollers, Philippe, 34, 154–5, 157–8
Sontag, Susan, 95
Starobinski, Jean, 26, 91, 142
Stevens, Wallace, 55–6, 58
Strickland, Geoffrey, 10, 29

Taine, Hippolyte, 51
Todorov, Tzvetan, 37, 153–4, 156, 175
Trilling, Lionel, 187

Valéry, Paul, 57, 58, 129

Waissman, Friedrich, 160
Weber, Jean-Paul, 26
Wellek, René, 3–14, 17, 191
White, Hayden, 150
Whitman, Walt, 55–6, 58

Wilson, Edmund, 3
Wimsatt, W. K., 202
Wisdom, John, 18, 20–1, 112
Wittgenstein, Ludwig, 16, 91, 93, 161, 165
Woolf, Virginia, 208–9
Wordsworth, William, 14, 51